Truth Be Told

Life Lessons From Death Row

Correspondence of Agnes Vadas and Richard Nields

authorHOUSE™

1663 Liberty Drive, Suite 200
Bloomington, Indiana 47403
(800) 839-8640
www.AuthorHouse.com

AuthorHouse™
1663 Liberty Drive, Suite 200
Bloomington, IN 47403
www.authorhouse.com
Phone: 1-800-839-8640

AuthorHouse™ UK Ltd.
500 Avebury Boulevard
Central Milton Keynes, MK9 2BE
www.authorhouse.co.uk
Phone: 08001974150

First published by AuthorHouse 2/23/2006

ISBN: 1-4208-7592-2 (sc)

Printed in the United States of America
Bloomington, Indiana

This book is printed on acid-free paper.

A few letters, both Rich's and Agi's are missing and sometimes, especially durig the last two years the letters are more frequent and sometimes crossing, so the dialogue is not straight.

On copies of Agi's letters you can see Rich's numbering, highlighting, and here and there some comments and happy or sad faces.

The letters are not edited. There are misspellings on both sides and the punctuation is far from being perfect.

My heartfelt thanks to Janet Thomas for the many hours she spent organizing the letters and advising me.

Foreword

On a day in November, 2001, I was visiting my friend, Agi, when I noticed a letter on her coffee table.

"You've got mail," I said, half joking.

"Yes," she said. "It's a letter from my friend, Rich, on death row."

That was the first time I'd really paid attention to the correspondence between Agnes Vadas and Richard Neilds. On that day, I asked Agi to get Rich's permission to read his letters. A week or so later, in a letter to Agi, he granted permission and so I began to read this astonishing correspondence between two people brought together by the death penalty.

Agi met Rich through an Amnesty International program that links death-row prisoners with those who oppose the death penalty. It is a correspondence that began haltingly, the way relationships do. And then, through honesty, constancy, loyalty and humor, it became a relationship about love. Not the romantic love that comes and goes easily, but the transcendent love that transforms our lives. Over the years, Rich and Agi have grown to trust one another. They counsel and chide one another. They buck up one another's spirits, follow the details of one another's daily lives, and share a consuming passion for music.

They are both professional musicians. As a violinist, Agi brings her love of classical music to their correspondence. As a pianist, Rich brings his love of jazz. They riff back and forth in a melody of language and musical metaphor. It infuses their correspondence with that which only music can offer – transcendence over ordinary life and extraordinary suffering.

Like music, death, too, is a theme that transcends ordinary time. When we face our death, we become free to face our life. Through his letters, Rich faces both, even as he never loses sight of the daily blessings that slip by most of us unnoticed. As a Holocaust survivor, Agi writes of her own losses, but with relentless humor and acceptance.

There is something about these letters that illuminates all that it means to be human. When I began to read them, first of all I learned about my own prejudice. Rich is a death row inmate and my thoughts had gone no further. But when the letters revealed a man of insight, sensitivity, intelligence and a spiritual faith that was learned the hard way – through suffering and remorse – I began to know Rich as a human being. His life, and his death sentence, became real.

Nobody knows how long it will be before Rich is executed – if he is executed. For this, too, is a bewilderment. How he went from being assured by his attorney of manslaughter charges to being on death row is a story that comes to light in the letters, as do the details of a justice system that, once unjustly underway, cannot easily be restored. In November, 2004, when Agi and I sat in the office of Rich's public defender, he told us, "Rich does not belong on death row. And I have very little hope that he will not be executed." He said that publishing the letters might help Rich's cause.

As this book goes to press, Agi and Rich have six years of letters between them and no idea of how much time is left. By sharing their letters, they share their hope, most of all, for a future in which the death penalty will no longer exist.

Janet Thomas is the author of, *"The Battle in Seattle – The Story Behind and Beyond the WTO Demonstrations."*

May 4, 1999

Dear Mr. Nields,

I got your name and address from the Death Row Support Project. I wonder whether you would like to exchange letters with me.

First I will introduce myself: my name is Agnes Vadas. I was born in Budapest, Hungary. I am 70 years old. I live in this country since 1966. I am a musician, used to play concerts as a violinist, teach and play in orchestras. I was twice married and divorced and now I am retired and live with my cat and dog in a nice little house. My main occupation now is working for Amnesty International—maybe you know it is the foremost human rights organization. We are working against all kind of bad things happening in the world and one of our main projects is to abolish the death penalty. If you like to write me, please tell a little about yourself and let me know if I can help you a bit.

Do you need books, food, or anything else? If so, let me know how to send it since I don't know about prison regulations.

I hope to hear from you.

Cordially,
Agnes Vadas

May, 11 1999

Dear Ms. Vadas,

Thank you so much for writing to me, that's a very kind thing to do. Yes, I would enjoy exchanging letters with you. And, we have something in common…music. I've been a professional musician all of my life. I played the piano for 37 years, 27 years I made a living at it. I worked clubs, hotels, cruise ships, in jazz groups, pop groups, show bands etc.

I lived for 13 years in Southern California, in Orange County. In fact, I played in Washington a couple of times at the Spokane House in Spokane, and played a convention in downtown Seattle, in the early 70s.

Guess I should introduce myself a little bit. I'm 49 yrs. old, Caucasian, 5'7" in height, weigh 165, brown hair and brown eyes.

I grew up in a very small town in Indiana, Aurora Ind.; it's a river town right on the Ohio River, 36 miles down river from Cincinnati, Ohio. I like to read books. In here my favorite is good novels to vicariously escape into. Right now I'm reading some Wilbur Smith books, i.e.: "When the Lion Feeds" and "River God." Both excellent! Also, I enjoy history, biographies, and the Bible. I like movies and enjoy all kinds of music. Music I don't care for is: country music, rap, and a lot of today's pop music, I just don't like it at all.

I prefer the jazz station or classical station. I'm not classically trained in music; I grew up playing pop and blues and then more into the jazz standard tunes.

I would like to hear about your musical life—all musicians are special people to me - studying, teaching and playing music, in my opinion, makes a person more in tune to all aesthetics of life.

I really like Aaron Copland, esp. "Appalachian Spring" and "Rodeo" stuff like that, and I loved Leonard Bernstein.

I am an alcoholic and, not to justify, but my disease of alcoholism put me in here. No-no I really can't say that; I had a choice. I could have chosen not to drink and I should have done what they told me to do in AA. But, instead, I kept on drinking and here I sit isolated and lonely. In Ohio, death row inmates are locked in 23 hours a day. We get to come out of our cells for one hour each day for recreation. Needless to say, it's a true test of one's fortitude.

This is my first time in jail for a long period. Before this, the only trouble I was ever in was for D.U.I.'s (drunk driving) so I'm new to this prison life. It's a cold gray world where there isn't much culture and very few things matter and nothing matters very much.

OK, enough about me, how about you? I bet you have an interesting life story. I've never met anyone from Budapest, Hungary, or Hungary itself. Tell me about it sometime. What brought you to America? Where were you in World War II? Do you have relatives in Hungary now? You probably do and I bet you are watching the Kosovo situation closely.

War is terrible. Why can't people just live in peace; there's only one Race the Human Race.

Is it OK if I call you Agnes? Good. You can call me Rich.

Yes, let's be pen-friends and talk to each other. I'm a good listener and you being a musician, I know you listen closely, too.

Well, that's all for now and thanks for writing; it made my day brighter.

Take care and God bless.

Peace and love,

Rich

May 19, 1999

Dear Rich,

What a wonderful letter you wrote me! I am truly glad we became pen-friends. Thanks for all the information you wrote about yourself. I have a few more questions: are you, or were you ever married? Have children? Your parents alive? Have you siblings, friends? Anybody ever writes or visits you? Can you find any nice human contact there, in prison, or are you utterly lonely and miserable? I'm glad you can have books—tell me if I can send you some; how, and what kind? If you have a special request I will try to find it. Otherwise I will send you some novels, or history and biography. Just send it normally to your address?

Do you have TV? Can you listen to music on the radio?

To answer your questions about myself: yes, I have a rather interesting life story. I was a child prodigy, had my first public appearance at the age of 6. After the war I became pretty well-known in my country, was State Soloist—that is I got a salary for just playing a few concerts a year.

During the war I was persecuted as a Jew and a lot of members of my family were killed, including my only brother. My father was killed by a bomb. My family was very poor and not highly educated.

After the uprising of '56 - if you are interested in history, you might know about it - I left my country because I hated Communism. I left by walking, illegally. That's itself a story. I lived in Paris for 5 years, then in Germany for almost as long. Then I came to this country for a visit only but I stayed here, I got jobs at several universities: Indiana, Texas, Georgia and Ithaca NY. I also played concerts. Then I had a big trouble with my arm, couldn't play for almost 3 years. Meanwhile I got married to an American who lived in New York. I lived in NYC for 2 years free-lancing, then went to San Francisco and played in the Opera for 14 years, until my retirement. Now I live on this beautiful island - divorced, as I told you. I didn't play the violin for more than 5 years, but now I decided to play again.

This is the story in nutshell, but I can tell a lot more about. I wrote a few stories about my early life in Hungary. If you are interested I can send them.

Thanks again for your very nice letter. I hope to hear from you soon.

Peace and love,

Agnes

(My friends call me Agi, pronounced aaghi, you can call me so.)

P.S.   Do you prefer handwritten or typed letters?

May 23, 1999

Dear Agi,

It was lovely to receive your letter and thank you for agreeing to be my pen-friend. To quote the line, "This could be the start of something good."

I was so happy when I saw your letter coming under my cell door! (We don't have bars; we have solid steel doors with a small window on top.) And yes, I am very lonely and I'm hungry for good conversation. So, please, talk to me as often and as much as you wish. You can ask me any questions you want and as many as you want.

You asked me if I prefer handwritten or typed letters. Your hand is artistic and I can read it so hand would be fine, but if you prefer to type that's OK, too. Whatever is better for you, you pick.

Man, oh man what a life you've had. I can't wait to hear about it and yes, let's start with your early life in Hungary; I wish to read them so please send.

Here's some rules on mailing things in: Books, yes, I can receive books but you cannot send them in directly. They have to come directly from the bookstore. So, in other words, you buy a book from them and have them package it and send it. And, also "only paperback" are allowed. Plus, when I finished I can't send them back, it will be donated to the prison library. So, book rule: paperback only; direct from bookstore.

Music tape-cassette: has to be new unopened and, also same as book rule-direct from store, i.e.: they package it and send it.

Rules in prison, esp. death row, are very strict needless to say. Now, if you ever send something that I'm not allowed to have, no biggie, they'll just send it back, you wouldn't get in trouble. What the prison is watching for in the mail is contraband of course. Food – I wish you could but you are not allowed.

Have I ever married? You asked. Oh yes, twice but I wasn't good (faithful) at it. Remember, I was living in Southern Cal. during the sexual revolution of the 70s. And I was right in the middle of it – I love women! By the way, so you don't think I'm a pervert or something, I'm not in here for any kind of sex crime.

Do you have a good sense of humor? I hope so. I love to laugh, and I've been told I have a good sense of humor. And I also talk freely about anything - I don't embarrass easily and I'm very open-minded.

Truth be told, I lived a very wild, promiscuous lifestyle in my 20s and 30s; I was slowing down in my 40s. The drinking was catching up with me and by then I was a full-blown alcoholic.

Note: I'm not a very good speller; in fact, I'm not very good at writing a coherent letter. I'll jump all over the place and back again. I write real fast and just go where my train of thought takes me. So, my Lady, you have been fairly warned. Also, my punctuation, well I do the best I can. I've forgotten all of the basics i.e.: compound/ complex sentences, when to use a coma, yada, yada, yada…It's funny, before I came to jail in March of '97, I never wrote letters. Telephone, or maybe a postcard once in a while, but I don't remember writing too many letters in my travels. Hell, I was too busy. I was practicing, rehearsing, playing the gig and, then, afterwards, drinking, drugs and sex.

That was my life for many years. I wasn't a heavy drug user I enjoyed coke and smoke (marijuana.)

Anyway, back to the question of marriage. I married my high school sweetheart in 1969. Neither one of us wanted to be married, but she, Jackie, got pregnant and back then, especially in small town USA you got married you didn't even think of abortion. I have a daughter that is 29, but I left Aurora, Ind. when she (Allison) was 1 1/2 old, so I wasn't around to raise her. We don't know each other; she knows about me but we are not close. That's a long story which I'll share later in another letter down our road of discovery.

In '74 I got married again to Rosie, she was a Chicano, a very beautiful woman. But, at this time, I was traveling and I was not faithful. This was before 'aids' and being a musician, as you probably know, having many lovers comes with the territory.

Did you have lots of lovers? I would say living in the cities that you lived, the answer would be, oh my god, yes!

Well we can (if you want to) share our love/sex stories. Boy! I hope you have a light, fun, sense of humor. If ever I become too bold, just tell me to cool it, and I will. I just figure that you are a "hip" chick who has been around and has seen and heard a lot where you don't embarrass easily. Man, oh, man, you're probably already thinking damn this guy sure is a tad too bold. Well, I'm not shy and I've always found easier to talk to a woman than a man. I like women better than I do men. Most men bore me to tears. I find women much more interesting and they (not all) seem to enjoy the aesthetics of life more, don't you agree? OK, enough about women. Next question you asked. Parents: No, my father died in '84 and my mother in '94. My two brothers died in the '70s, and I have two estranged sisters. My younger sister, Debbie, I haven't talked to since my mother's funeral. My older sister, Rochelle, she does write and sends me some money about every 3 months. More on this later. But in short form: my alcoholism and being away from my home town burnt those bridges a long time ago. Truth be told: I have burnt many bridges - too many. The booze starts the fire.

No, I haven't had a visit since I've been in prison. Most of my so called friends are out west, where I should have stayed. I do get cards and sometimes letters, but you know how life can be, everybody today is into E-mail and letter writing is becoming obsolete. Heck, I'm becoming obsolete. Believe it or not, I'm also very old fashioned at heart. Truly, I am.

Yes, I have TV and a radio. My favorite TV station is P.B.S., the rest of the stations are pretty lame, in my opinion. I do enjoy magazine shows like 20/20, 60-min. Dateline, but silly sitcoms I don't watch. Confession: I do laugh at "The Simpsons."

On PBS I enjoy Nova, Frontline, Mystery and Masterpiece Theatre. We have an in-house cable system that allows the front office to show movie videos, so I do get to see the new rentals (movies) on videos when they come out. I do love movies, and for fun I keep a movie journal – I write a short movie review and rating of all movies I watch. Since I've been here I've watched 91 videos (movies) and probably have liked less than 20 of them. Hollywood just doesn't make too many good ones anymore for adults, in my humble opinion.

I don't care for all this special effects that's going on; I prefer the old movies best. I'm sure you do too. What are some of your favorite movies? "Gone with the Wind" "Casablanca?" I'm sure you like those; me too. I like any movie with Brando and Newman, but I like a lot of the actors from the '40s and '50s too.

So you were a child prodigy playing music at the age of 6, huh? That's wonderful. I don't understand how you do it except it's truly a gift you have, a gift from God.

I would love to see some pictures of you. Make copies, if you will, and send one every once in a while. I want to hear your life story. So, just go slow and share with me a little bit in each letter. I don't expect a complete autobiography, but bits and pieces a little at a time in your letters would be wonderful. Talk about whatever you want but please talk to me.

I enjoyed the movie "Amadeus," didn't you? Surely you love Mozart, eh? I know Mozart was a child prodigy, a great musician and one of the best composers ever. He wrote German Operas for the emperor in Vienna. Also, I know he wrote lots of string quartets. I have his Clarinet Concerto on my classical tape. I'm a jazz person and please excuse my ignorance, not only can I not spell well, but I'm not educated at all in the classical field. In fact, I'm not highly educated in any field. I have 14 years of school and 28 years of street education. I'm not smart but I am fun!

Anyway, back to you, my lady. If you were State Soloist, you must have been pretty damn good and, baby, I'm impressed! That's really something to be proud of in life time. Question: How many hours a day would you practice? On this level, you'd be a virtuoso, highly skilled, a master of technique, which would require hours of study of your scales, arpeggios and chords.

I was never a great player but a good player, I could cover the gig. At my best (early 70s) I would practice 6 days a week, 5 hours a day, and then go play the gig for 4 hours. So, I was playing 9 hours a day. The 5 hours a day for me, was enough. But I would always know that the great players were practicing 10 hours a day. I didn't have that much self-discipline; 5 hours practice was doing good enough for me. Then, later, mid-70s, the drinking and parties were more important, and I didn't practice at all; I'd just do the gigs.

On a sad note, I'm sorry about your family and what happened during the war. I'm sure for you these are sad and painful memories. If you want to talk about it, I'm here and I will listen and learn.

I don't know anything about the uprising of '56. I can't imagine the feeling of despair one must feel walking out of one's country. And, now, I'm watching it every night on the news. Unbelievable.

Where is your island? What part of Washington are you, east, west, where?

Well, it's time for me to end this too long letter I suppose. I just feel comfortable talking to you. Write back when you're in the mood to talk, I'll be here.

Happy vibes and friendly thoughts. And, Agi, remember: keep it "mellow as a cello."

Peace and love,
Rich

June 7, 1999
Dear Rich,

It is a great thing that you so obviously enjoy talking to me. I am grateful for this. I will send you books and music. And here are my first two stories – I will send the rest bit by bit. Well, let's see what to answer to your many questions. About TV shows: I don't have a TV! That is, I have a great big one, but living in a rural area I would need an antenna or satellite to have it work and I don't want that. I don't like TV, the commercials and all that stupid stuff. So I use my TV for videos only. I have a great collection of videos, mostly operas, but also a few rare old movies, "classics." Yes, I like "Gone with the Wind" and "Casablanca," but not enough to have them on my collection. I have 11 tapes of Charlie Chaplin whom I love and other stuff, like almost all the Shakespeare plays and I have lots of CDs—all classic—and many books.

About the uprising of '56: it was the first revolution against Communism and that time it was a very major event – you are too young to remember that. In one of my later stories I wrote about it.

My island is at the northwestern end of the country, at one point only about 3 miles from Canada. If you have a map, look at the San Juan Islands. It is beautiful and peaceful here.

Well, and no, I didn't have lots of lovers. I never was a very sexual type; the emotional side was always more important to me. And I didn't forget easily. I was suffering long after each unhappy involvement. And obviously they were unhappy, since I ended up alone in my old age. But I am contented - it is better to be alone – alone than alone with a man, you know what I mean?

Do I have a sense of humor? I most definitely do; I let you find it out in my stories. It might be a bit different from yours – there is many different kinds of that.

Oh, and I hate "Amadeus." They portray Mozart as a stupid clown, whose divine music came out of him like kind of in spite of him. Ridiculous! (By the way, he wrote 44 symphonies, over 600 works by the time he died at the age of 35!)

There is a lot about me and not much of you in this letter. But I took in everything you told me. It seems to me that you were a lonely, unhappy guy who went a bit astray with all that drinking and "sexing," because something was missing in your life. Sad.

Tell me what happened to your brothers? Why did they both die young? Continue talking to me, no matter how "bold" you are.

All my friendly thoughts to you,

Agi

P.S.   By the way I drink and smoke, too.

June 20, 1999

Dear Agi,

Thank you for your letter and your two stories. "Summer at the River Tisza" was fun to read; I like people's childhood memories. First loves are wonderful to remember. So it's my conjecture that Zoli was killed in the war? How sad. "Air-raid," well I guess you'd say cigarette smoking saved your life. If you had gone with your father, you probably would have been killed too.

I'm having a hard time finding words to say to you about what happened. It's just horrible-horrible, a sad, sad thing for anyone to have go through. I enjoyed reading about it, but I'm terribly sorry you had to live it. Never in my life have I had someone share firsthand with me about the war and the holocaust. Yes, I would enjoy reading more on your life.

I agree with you TV is terrible.

Maybe you could send me a postcard sometime of your island. I don't have a map but I watch to see it on TV or newspaper. But a picture postcard would be great.

Wow, I didn't realize Mozart wrote 600 pieces of music. Thanks for sharing that; I'd love to know more about classical composers, and their lives. So, anytime you want to put on a teacher's hat feel free to do so; I love to learn new things.

No, I wasn't lonely or unhappy during the 70s and 80s, and not my childhood either. It was just too much partying and finally the drinking caught up with me, and then I became sad inside, unhappy. My brothers died in the 70s. Doug, who was 2 years older than I, died in a car crash (1974) and Brian, who was the oldest boy (42 at that time), died of a cerebral hemorrhage (1977.) My dad died in '84 and mom in '94.

Well, next time I'll write a longer letter; been a little depressed lately. Take care and write back.

Peace and love,
Rich

July 7, 1999
Dear Rich,

I am sorry you are depressed, but, my God, no wonder! That's why I want to cheer you up, or at least give you a few moments of distraction and I want you to feel a human contact, because I have warm feelings for you.

Sorry to send you another sad story, but this is the next in sequence. Since you are interested in history, I give you the story of my country in the war: Hungary was the ally of Germany, but a reluctant one. The head of state went along half-heartedly, rather cleverly playing a double game: there were some restriction for Jews, for example they couldn't get to universities. (My brother!) But there were no killings or anything like the Nazis. Well, finally Hitler got tired of this and invaded the country, but as late as 1944.

They were obviously losing the war, but their most urgent business was to liquidate the Jews. They went to that with Teutonic thoroughness: they deported all the Jews in the country, except those in the capital. It was a hard nut to crack – there were about 200,000 there. So, what happened, they simply didn't have time to deal with us because the Russians were already there. They succeeded to kill about 600,000 though. They wanted to blow up the ghetto where I was, but apparently Raoul Wallenberg, a Swedish man, saved us. He was a hero, saved thousands of life – and when it was over, the Russians took him and this great man never came out of a Russian prison.

The most heartbreaking story. He gave everybody fake papers of Swedish nationality and they bought up apartment houses with Swedish flags.

This is to understand better this story. I also would like to tell you that I used a lot of "artistic freedom," things were not necessarily exactly the way I wrote it. I made up the dialogs. The only one is "Air Raid" which happened just about exactly as written. But the basic facts are true.

Well, the next story will be less depressing, although communism was awful too, but they didn't want to kill me, personally.

Right now I don't have a postcard of the island, but here are some pictures to give you an idea. On the one it's me with my dog who was killed on the road. Now I have another one - I need a dog. I love animals - do you?

Well, cheer up, friend. It's easy to say, I know. I wish I could help you.

Warmly,

Agi

P.S. I am going to play in a concert the 17ᵗʰ - the first after 5 years of not playing at all.

(There was no response from Rich for a long time.)

A Christmas card, 1999

Dear Rich,

I am very sad that you don't want to write to me any more. I really would like to know why? I am sure I didn't offend you in any way. Something must have mispleased you, but what?

Anyway I wish you have a better year at the beginning of the new millennium. We – Amnesty – are working hard for you!

Best wishes,

Agi

December 27, 1999

Dear Agi,

Thank you for sending me a holiday card. I was glad to hear from you, and I have been wondering how you are. How are you?

I got your last letter from July 7 with part 3 of your story and your beautiful pictures. No doubt Washington State is beautiful - I wish I was there.

Do you want to try again? I do. Truth be told, I've been meaning to write to you for months, but I kept procrastinating and, then after awhile, because I felt guilty of not writing, I'd talk myself out of writing again; by thinking to myself "ah hell, it's too late; she probably doesn't want to hear from you anyway."

You know how that goes, I'm sure.

Sorry about your dog in the picture getting killed. I do like dogs myself much better than I do cats. I'm glad you got yourself a new dog though. Same kind of German Sheperd? What's his or her name?

Are you getting lots of snow where you live? Back here it's cold and it is starting to snow off and on. My cell in winter is cold all the time. Last winter I had ¼' of ice on the inside of my rear cell window. All winter I live and sleep in sweat-pants with thermo underwear, with T-shirt and thermo top, and sweat shirt, two pair of socks and tennis shoes. I'm already looking forward to summer.

See, I'm on the bottom floor; whereas the second level cells, where the heat rises, are nice and comfortable now. But in summer the top level cells are really hot and my cell is nice and cool. So I'll take the cold of winter, which will be over in March anyway.

How did your concert go on the 17th? Tell me about it if you will. After not playing for 5 years, I'm sure you were a little apprehensive, eh? I know I would be after 5 years of not playing. I'm sure you spent a lot of hours beforehand going through scale and arpeggio studies, plus the music to be played also. Did it come back (your technique) pretty fast for you? Or do you practice still all the time even though you're not performing all the time?

Do you like Aaron Copland's music? I do. I love "Appalachian Spring" "Billy the Kid" "Our Town" and "Lincoln's Portrait." I really enjoy his music. It takes me away to the mountains or out west. I love music that's transcendental. Well, of course, all music should be transcendental, and art too I suppose. Yes, all art forms are transcendental to someone. Copland, well I travel with his music. There's others too. Remember I'm from the pop, blues, jazz field and classical music is something I enjoy more and more as I get older but I'm not educated in it. I didn't grow up listening to Mozart; I was listening to Harry James, Benny Goodman, stuff my parents played on the hi-fi. Then, when I got older, I was listening to rock n' roll, pop, etc...then later blues and jazz. But I like all of it...well not all, I'm selective.

Anyway, do you still have my first letters? Or should I reintroduce myself? I have all of yours letters, postcards, stories, pictures. I reread all of them last night.

I would like to talk some more with you. Let's go on and get to know each other. Share with me some past and some present. The last story was hard on me to read. I felt depressed afterwards and very sorry for you and your family and friends.

Please write me again, and we'll go on our road of discovery if you wish and I hope you do.

I promise to write one letter a month—depressed or not. I find after I write (talk) to you, I always feel better; like I do now.

Peace and love,

Rich

January 3, 2000

Dear Rich,

I was glad to receive your letter. Sure, let's try again. To answer your questions: winter is mild here due to some current. It usually snows once or twice but usually melts within a few hours – except once, 3 years ago when we got a huge snow-storm with 3 or 4 feet of snow for a week. I was snowed in – I have a long drive-way. Apparently last time something like this happened was in 1922. Winter is good so far this year, it didn't snow yet. It is raining a lot, but there are nice sunny days, too – temperature in the 40s.

Since we are at it – could I send you a small electric heater? Is it allowed? Answer this fast, before the winter is over!

My concert on 17 July went very well. I wasn't very nervous, the piece I played – Bach : Concerto for 2 violins – is technically easy and I played it many times. Since then I played two other concerts of mixed chamber music, no solo. But I will give a recital soon, February maybe.

I still have your letters, no need to reintroduce yourself.

If you want I could send you more stories. Don't be afraid, they are not so depressing, although they also deal with serious matters: life in Communist Hungary. But I personally didn't come to serious harm, only my career was kind of hampered. There are some amusing stuff in them, too.

Tell me what are you doing the whole day long? Reading? Do you have enough books? Playing solitary, or any kind of game? What do you need? I could send you books or cards or games. Can you talk to somebody sometimes, like at recreation? Tell me how can I help you.

All the best,

Agi

P.S. Do you play chess? I have a small computer chess which I play often. It is better than brooding.

January 12, 2000

Dear Agi,

I got your letter today that you wrote on Jan. 3 – thank you. I just want to remind you that the mail room here at Mansfield is pretty slow getting mail to the inmates' cells. There are 2400 inmates here, so that's a lot of mail coming in every day. But sooner or later I get it.

Thank you for the offer but, no, you are not allowed to send me an electric heater (that would be nice to have though). Luckily, the weather back here, like yours, so far, has been mild. Hardly any snow and the temp during the day in the high 30s or low 40s. Not near as bad as last year...yet.

Can you send books, you asked. Yes you can. Books <u>must</u> be sent by the bookstore directly; you can't send them yourself! Wherever you buy the book, <u>have them send it.</u> Most stores will do that for you. I would love two books (and I won't ask for any more until spring). I want a chess book to improve my game. I can't give you a title because I don't know one. Just pick one out on How to play better chess or whatever. Chess is popular here for play during rec. (recreation) I'm not very good and I want to get better. I'm not a beginner; I'd say an "intermediate level" player I am. So just pick one out "intermediate to advanced" level on playing chess.

Later, if you want, we could play a chess game in our letters. One move with each letter. I know how to read chess language. If you want, let me know, OK? I'll leave that up to you. Oh yes, I have a board and pieces in my cell. I bet that's fun to play on your computer, huh? What level do you play?

Since you're going to the bookstore – I know I'm being presumptuous but if you don't want to that's OK. But, if you will, and I'd appreciate it, I'd like the book (paperback) "The Testament" by John Grisham. Yes, we have a death row library, but most of the paperbacks are 10 -12 years old. So, I'll leave it up to you and like I said I won't ask for anything (another book) until spring. Books and music tapes are the only items you are allowed to send to me. Music tapes: same rule as books. (Cassettes only.)

If you are on-line with your computer? Amazon dot com is OK too. Or any on-line company that sells books and music.

Any time you send me a book I share it with the other men in my pod, and then I'll give it to the library. We are not allowed to have a bunch of books in our cells. The rules are very strict on DR.

Send me part 4 of your story. I still have the first 3 parts here and I'm ready to continue. You are the only person I've met in my life that knows firsthand what it was like to live under such horrible conditions in the war. I promise I won't get depressed this time.

Oh hell, don't think your story got me so depressed I couldn't write, because I have wide mood swings in here with or without outside influences. It's just a depressing place...period. I mean some days I just wake up in a funky mood and don't know why.

I'm glad to hear your concert went well – good for you Agi.

More later.

Peace & love,
Rich

February 1, 2000
Dear Agi,

You are so kind! Thank you very much for the wonderful books. I received all four of them yesterday from Griffin Bay book store.

Last night I started "Critical Mass" by Steve Martini. I've never read a book by him but he hooked me on the story real fast; halfway through the prologue I was hooked. And, to my surprise, chapter one starts on your island – Friday Harbor. I thought that was great. So there are 400 islands in the San Juan chain, eh? It, Friday Harbor, sounds wonderful; sometime down the road (no hurry) send me a picture postcard or map or whatever so I can see it. The picture of you standing on the boat dock – that must be Roche Harbor, huh?

Man, oh, man, this wonderful chess book will keep me busy for a few years at least! Thank you. I went through the first game this morning. Boy I have a lot to learn about this – I like it so I will practice. Can you read chess language? Are you serious about chess? Or is it more for hobby, fun, or whatever.

Myself, whatever I do in life, before I came to prison, and even now (but there isn't much to do in here) I always want to do it well. I'm not a fanatic over the game but if I'm going to play it I might as well learn to play well – I'm sure you agree. I didn't know they notated games – master games – and kept record now for 150-200 years. Like classical musicians they take this very seriously. I wonder if Franz Listz played chess? I've seen some of his piano music and heard it too. Talk about difficult music to play – unbelievable! I'll stick with my simple jazz pieces. (smile)

Even though, truth be told, Duke Ellington wrote some tough – difficult music to learn – if you play it as written. Some of his music has a different chord on every beat (not every measure – but every beat) A lot of piano players leave out some of those chords and justify it, by saying "Oh, they're just passing chords anyway" but Mr. Ellington didn't leave them out when he played them. These are "jazz chords" too, not simple diatonic chords. Anyway enough about music for now and chess too, but thank you for the wonderful chess book and the novels too – that is very kind of you – to spend your money and take time to help a man on death row. I really, really appreciate it and I know they will bring me many hours of enjoyment. May God bless you for your benevolent heart.

Speaking of God – are you religious? Do you practice your Jewish faith? Have you ever read any books by or about Josephus? I read the old testament last year and I like the history part the best. I've never read the whole old test. Before; I'm a Christian and so I spent my bible time in new test – when I spent time in the bible. Which wasn't much time at all truth be told. For years I didn't know if I believed in God or not. When you drink like I did for years (remember I'm an alcoholic) you give up everything – I did – even God. But God didn't leave me – I left him. I went looking for peace and serenity in a bottle but only found misery. I thought I was having fun but I knew (inside) I was deceiving myself or like they say in AA I was in denial.

Well, my friend, looking forward to getting a letter from you soon; and when I do I'll respond quickly.

Once again, thank you very much for the wonderful books. I'll be back soon – take care.

Peace & love,
Rich

February 1, 2000
Dear Rich,

Thanks for your nice letters. I am glad you enjoy those books. There was not much choice for chess-books; if it works for you, that's fine. I am not too serious abut chess but I play a lot with my computer. (By the way, could I send you one? Let me know.) It's fun, especially when I win – my little computer has 72 levels and I am at level 30; that shows you I am not exactly a champion. What is funny about it, the thing has no memory! It does moves that I can trick and it does the same thing again – still inferior of human mind. To play a game in correspondence? Sure, if you want, but it would be an awfully long business.

How strange you mentioned Franz Liszt (spelling!) I just gave a lecture about him last week – I am teaching music appreciation at the miniature college here, right now on Shaw Island which has 164 inhabitants. Liszt was of course the greatest pianist, something like Paganini for the violin.

Four hundred islands of San Juans? They probably count those tiny ones which would barely have a cottage on. But it is beautiful; I enjoy those ferry rides when I go to the mainland or to other islands.

Am I religious? No, and I never practiced my Jewish faith. I always felt about the Judeo-Christian religions that they picture God as a white-bearded man sitting on a cloud and judging us – this was always unsatisfactory to me. I approached Buddhism for a while, but finally came to the conclusion that all religions are <u>man-made</u>, you know what I mean? They all claim to have all the answers, they know exactly what it's all about and they alone know, all others are wrong. Not to mention intolerance! But I definitely believe that there is something out there and we are more than a piece of shit. And there is plenty of evidence for that, what the stupid materialists don't want to see: ESP, the near-death experiences, out-of-body experiences, etc. I am very interested in these things, are you? I could send you books about it.

Here is my next story. I hope you will enjoy it. The two main characters – Sandor and Gyuri – are really great guys. Gyuri is still alive and is a <u>major</u> composer, a big shot in Europe. We are still in touch; I have seen him a few years ago in Europe.

Well, enough for today. Take care.

My best,

Agi

February 20, 2000

Dear Agi,

How are you today, my friend? Hope all is well with you. I love the picture postcards you sent of your islands. What a wonderful place to live – I love the ferries too. Thank you for sending those; I do like to <u>see</u> what people, places look like; also, I'm a geography buff I like to know where places are. The postcards I put up on my cell wall with your picture on the boat dock.

I got your letter and part 4 of your story "The Castle." So you're a woman at 23 and you have friends that are bright and deep thinkers. Bartok, yes I like his music. I used to have an album of his String Quartets I enjoyed. I'd forgotten he was from Hungary. Well I'm happy you can play his music or any music today; Stalin was evil!

So you couldn't play any diminished chords? No diminish chords inside a very diminished and <u>demented</u> political structure; I suppose anyone playing jazz would go to jail or shot, eh? (That's a joke or my attempt at humor) I know they didn't have jazz music in Hungary in the 1950s – or did they?

Where was Stravinsky from? I've heard some of his music and it was dissonant and very intense. I didn't care for it. Just because (they) say this guy is great or he's a genius or whatever doesn't mean I will like it. I choose what I like, and enjoy, and what I don't. That goes for any genre or style of music. Just because it's jazz doesn't mean I'll like it. There's a lot of jazz I don't enjoy, too.

In the mid seventies I worked with a band that had a Sanskrit word for its name – SADHANA. (Sounds SA-DONNA – you don't pronounce the H). I always liked that name and I really enjoyed the band. We played the college circuit up and down the California coast. Played at Berkeley a few times; now there was/is a far out school. I liked it.

Sadhana means in 'search of God' or something like that – I've forgotten.

In the 70s I went through my search of God period. I read books like Dianetics by L. Ron Hubbard the founder of Scientology. Also books on/or about E.S.P. and Eastern Philosophy, all kinds of psychic phenomenons, etc. etc. numerology yes – my color is orange/red and my psychic note is D flat. Oh great that makes me feel better. (Smile – humor).

Southern California has a different religion or occult on just about every street. I ended up saying "screw them all" and practiced Hedonism, where pleasure was my goal. I became agnostic and also an alcoholic and just didn't care about God stuff.

Today I have my Lord and Savior Jesus Christ. I'm not one who preaches and try to convert people. No, I don't do that at all. To me religion is a private and personal matter. I'm happy with Jesus and whatever other people on earth want to believe that's A-OK with me; it's everyones own prerogative.

Have you ever read "The Prophet"? By Kahill (sic) Gibran? It's not religion but spirituality/poetry I suppose you can call it. I read all of Gibran's books back in the 70s and indeed I truely enjoyed them; in fact, I had a spiritual awakening during that period. It felt wonderful for a few months and then the feeling went away. I felt 'at-one' as they say with everything. No fear. I wasn't afraid to die or to live. Just felt inner peace, serenity, and it was beautiful. And no, I wasn't taking drugs; in fact, I was doing yoga every morning – deep breathing and stretching exercises and meditation.

Send me next part of your extraordinary life. I'm enjoying it now that the war and killing is over. Take care. And remember "keep it mellow as a cello."

Peace & love,

Rich

March14, 2000

Hi my friend,

I liked your last letter, thanks. I find it extraordinary that you enjoyed the Bartok String Quartets. How come you find Stravinsky dissonant and not those Quartets? They are dissonant all right, but great. Dissonance can be beautiful! The reason 20th century music is dissonant that it expresses the horrors of the epoch: the two world wars, the Holocaust, the atom bomb. How would you express these with a D major chord? It is expressed with not even a diminished one, but something like (chord written) don't you think? Being on death row can be expressed about the same way, don't you agree?

By the way, now that we are friends, I feel, I can ask you the question: what did bring you there? Answer me *only if you feel like it.* If not, that's all right.

I was going to send you my next story which you would have enjoyed because I am telling about my first lover :) but my computer went berserk – I think I need new batteries. Well, I am stupid for computers; that answers your question whether I am online.

Stravinsky was from Russia but lived most of his life in France, Switzerland and the US. Bartok came to the US in 1940, escaping the horrors. After the war he would have returned to Hungary but by then he was very ill with leukemia. He died in New York in '45.

You will get my books before this letter. Enjoy!

I feel so sad that you had a moment of inner peace and "at-oneness" and that went away and you turned to alcoholism and lost all that.

Oh hell, life is difficult. But it's good you have your religion.

My best thoughts to you.

Till next letter.

Cheers!

Agi

March 15, 2000

Dear Agi,

How are you? I hope all is well with you. I'm doing OK myself under the circumstances. Lately the weather has been pretty nice, for March, warm and sunny. I got to go outside last week for a couple of hours and it felt wonderful. I haven't been out since last November.

I want to thank you for the two books: "The San Juan Islands" and "The Saxon Shore." I just finished "The Prodigal Spy" and I enjoyed it. That was a strange period back in the 50s and 60s. Well more so during the mid-fifties with the "Un-American Activities" trials going on. Washington sure was paranoid, huh? I know a lot of lives – innocent lives, families, jobs and careers were lost because of overzealous politicians and police.

Prague, in the 60s, sure was a cold and gray world, huh? Have you been to Prague? Have you played there?

I got a kick out of Benny Goodman playing there. I'm not a fan of big band music per se, but I do appreciate Benny's talent as a clarinet player. He was a fine player him and Artie Shaw both, and there's others, too. Before Nick left Prague, I figured Larry was the bad guy (Silver). Too bad Nick had to shoot him; he lost both of his fathers (real) and (step) to the world of espionage. Good story. I enjoyed t; in fact, indeed, I enjoyed all three books. I'll be starting "The Saxon Shore" today – more on that later.

Also I'm working on my chess book slowly, very slowly. That's something I can and will work on for years. I enjoy it a lot but man, oh, man, I'm not very good compared to the great games in the book.

It's the melodies of Bartok that I remember, I especially enjoyed. Stravinsky, it was the intensity of the piece I was hearing I didn't particularly care for. I'm not hip to classical music at all to make an objective opinion. I see your chord D7+9(E) +11(G). What kind of chord would I play to express death row? I would play a suspended chord: D7sus. Everything is just hanging – waiting to be resolved.

The mail just came and I got your letter where you ask me why I am here. Well, yes, I will tell you but I'll wait and do that when I'm just starting a letter and not closing one.

I will tell you this – I killed my best friend. Not to justify – but if alcohol and drugs were not in my life, it wouldn't have happened. In other words I didn't plan it, it happened in a black out – an alcoholic black out. Sounds like I'm making excuses now, huh? Well maybe I am; I don't know. I do know it is hard for me to talk about, but I will, I promise. Believe me, I think about it every night when I lay in bed. My conscience is not going to let me forget. It's a horrible thing to live with, knowing you have taken a person's life.

I never thought in a million years that I would someday kill a friend in a drunken rage – never! They told me in AA that one of three things would happen to me if I kept drinking: 1: Insanity. 2: Death. 3: Prison. Hell, all three happened. Patty is dead from my insanity, and now I'm in prison and will die here.

Patty was my girlfriend. We lived together for about ten years down in Cincinnati, Ohio. Needless to say it was a very intense, dysfunctional, sick relationship. We fought all the time especially the last three-four years we were together. She was Italian and had a temper and liked to throw things. I was a drunk and I would throw things back. It was a love/hate relationship. When things were good, it was real good, but when things were bad it was scary, intense – just horrible!

Anyway, it all came to an end Mach 27, 1997. We were having a bad argument in the house and we started to get physical. Throwing things like dishes, telephone, TV remote etc. and then pushing and then I just blew. I don't know what happened inside my head but I'd had it! I threw her down on the kitchen floor and strangled her to death. It was rage, insanity, I can't explain it. I just hated her so much at the moment I wanted her dead. I killed my best friend that I lived with.

Needless to say, I will never be the same nor will life be good. I just exist now. Not much matters now, and what does matter doesn't matter much. I'm just sitting here waiting to die. Oh yeah, I'm scared to die. People who say they're not are lying or are insane. It's normal to be scared of death. But I do believe in an afterlife, heaven or whatever you want to call it. I believe in Jesus and I do believe I am forgiven for all my sins of the past. I don't know all of the answers but I try to keep the faith. I believe in salvation by grace, by faith.

Well that's what I did to end up here. I was over-indicted in Cincinnati. My first lawyer told me I'd get 8 years for manslaughter. I'll have to explain in a future letter why my charge was raised up to murder one. "The first thing we do, let's kill all the lawyers." Shakespeare (Henry VI)

Peace & Love,

Rich

last three-four years we were together.
She was Italian and had a temper
and liked to throw things. I was
a drunk and I would ~~through~~ throw
things back. It was a love/hate
relationship. When things were good
it was real good, but when things
were bad it was scary, intense -
just horrible.

Anyway it all came to an end
March 27, 1997. We were having
a bad argument in the house and we
started to get physical. Throwing
things - like dishes, telephone, TV remote
etc. and then pushing and then I just
blew. I don't know what happened
inside my head, but I'd had it!

I threw her down on the kitchen
floor and strangled her to death. It
was rage, insanity I can't explain
it I just hated her so much at the
moment I wanted her dead. So Patty
died. That's what I did. I killed
my best friend that I lived with.

Needless to say I will never be.

March 27, 2000 (God, I just realized it's the anniversary of…)

Dear Rich,

I am eagerly awaiting your explanation: Why did you get on death row? Your case is definitely not first degree murder. Did you have a stupid lawyer? Well, I can't say much till I hear from you.

Yes, alcohol and drugs ruined your life, my poor friend. I can see you lying awake and thinking of Patty – how awful.

To answer your questions: yes, I went to Prague several times but always very shortly. I played there a bit: in a competition, where I won 3rd prize; that time no other than a Russian could win. And another time an amusing thing happened: I played at a kind of "popular" concert in a huge stadium, or whatever it was. I played two small, "easy" pieces: Bartok: Romanian Dances and De Falla: Spanish Dance. I played all right, I thought, and was rather dismayed by a very cool response from the audience. Then I was told that the microphone didn't function during the whole time! Hell, I was sweating for nothing – poor audience didn't hear a goddamn thing. It must have been funny to see a pantomime of playing the violin.

And yes, I am a great fan of Shakespeare – at one time I read all his plays. Now I have almost all of them on video. Only those I don't like I don't have. Some of them I don't like, I even hate one or two of them.

I also have 143 operas on video, many of them doubled or tripled. Friends often come to see videos. I also have some great old movies. Do you like Chaplin? I adore him; I have eleven tapes of his. Also I have some scientific ones, about Einstein and others; some spiritual things, the Dalai Lama, etc. And some tapes about the so-called "near-death experiences," which I find enlightening.

I am doing all right, practicing, preparing for a recital on the 29th of April in Victoria, Canada, which is just a few miles away from here.

Please, write soon, I am very curious of your explanation.

All the best,

Agi

P.S. Next time I send you another story.

April 14, 2000

Dear Agi,

I got your (3/27) letter; always good to hear from you. Oh, yeah, that's an anniversary I'll never forget-that's for sure. You know, you see and hear these guys on newsmagazine TV shows, like 60-Minutes; Dateline, 20/20; etc…inmates/murderers that are being interviewed for whatever reason?! And, a lot of times, they are asked, "do you think about what you did?" And they mostly say "every day" well…I believe them now, because I know I do. The guilt is so profound it's hard to find words to explain the feeling of remorse I feel every day. If I could trade places with Patty, I would. Without a doubt!

Why was my charge raised up to murder one? You asked. Well at first I was charged with murder, and my first lawyer told me he'd get it down to a manslaughter charge (make a deal) and I'd get around 6 to 8 years. Well that didn't happen.

Because I drove her car away from the scene of the crime and I took money out of her purse, they added a robbery charge. So robbery and murder – two felonies together equal murder one. Even though I drove her car all the time, they called that a robbery. Now, the money from purse? Well, when I went to get the car keys, I dumped her purse and inadvertently I took the money. Hell, when I was arrested about two hours later around the corner of the bar, I even told the police I drove Patty's car and took money from her purse, but they didn't charged me with robbery. <u>One</u>: we lived together and they knew robbery was not a motive. There was no motive; there was provocation on both parts and it just got out of hand. I didn't need to rob Patty. I had money and I had my own car. After you do something like that, you are not thinking straight. I mean, really, at that point in time right before, and during, and after, I was insane – hell, I was nuts! I was distraught; lots of mental conflict and I couldn't think. I remember thinking about running, I thought of suicide, and I thought of turning myself in. But me, being an alcoholic who's already drunk and in a blackout what do I do? Hell! I need a drink, of course! So I go to a bar around the corner, and order a screwdriver. Figure I'll have a few drinks and decide on running, suicide, or turning myself in later.

After the bartender brought me a drink, I told the stranger I just killed my girlfriend. Well, the police were there in a few minutes, and I was taken to jail. I confessed right there.

I've been through six different lawyers. One was fired for drinking; one quit because of his nerves, he said; but I think he had a drinking problem too. Because I'm poor, indigent, I cannot afford a paid lawyer; I have to use public defenders. Believe me they are not worth a damn. A murder trial especially a capital murder trial is very complex indeed. That's a big argument of one of my appeals is the incompetence of my original trial lawyers. It is a fact, that the majority of inmates on death row are people who could not afford competent lawyers. It's a big sham. People with money make <u>deals</u> and end up in general population; people like myself, who cannot pay $ 50 or 100 thousand for a lawyer, come to death row. You never see any wealthy people being executed – do you?

My trial was so long and involved I'll have to share a little at a time or I'd be writing for a week to explain it all. I'll share or tell you anything you want to know. You can ask any questions you wish and I'll try to answer all of them the best I can.

I was so tired after and during the trial I couldn't wait for it to be over. I was going into – in and out – of the courtroom for nine months. On days I had to go to court, and I didn't keep count, but probably around 75 to 100 different days, the cops (people who run the jail), would get me up at 4.30 AM and keep me up until 10.00 PM, and man that wears a man down after a few days like that.

You don't see all that goes on behind the scenes on TV or read about it. The police really work on breaking you down, physically, mentally and emotionally. It's like brain washing.

Hell, I couldn't wait to get to prison and away from Cincinnati. For nine months all I heard was how bad a person I was. I did a bad thing but I'm not a bad person. I'm not a lifetime criminal; in fact, I've never been in trouble my whole life except for traffic tickets which did include drunken driving. Truth: 7 DUIs from different states. But the D.A. made me out to be a "cold blooded killer." That's what they called me to the news media. My wimp lawyers would just sit there and not object to these kind of derogatory, malicious, statements, and so the DAs ate my weak, stupid, lame lawyers for lunch. Hell, they even made it sound horrible that I played music for a living. You know, "Peter Pan" syndrome, "never grew up," never had a real job, etc., etc. All you hear is how bad I am and how good she was; nothing good about me, and nothing bad about her. If I was so bad and Patty so good, why would we stay together for ten years? We were <u>both</u> good and bad. All I know is, by the end of the trial I was just ready to have them take me out back and shoot me. Well more on this later.

I saw a mini-documentary on Isaac Stern and, my gosh, that man is incredible, huh? What key is a violin in? I'm thinking "G" but not sure. What are the four strings? I used to know it but I have forgotten. He had a violin made in 1793.

Have fun April 29th.

Peace and love,

Rich

Coda: Cards, small letters a little but often, you don't have to always write long letters. I just like and look forward to hearing from you. Thanks for being my friend. I'll be back soon.

April 25, 2000

Dear Agi,

Hello friend. I hope so still? I'm a little worried that maybe now that I've told you what I did you might not want to write any more. I'm not one of those innocent people on death row. I'm guilty but I'm not a cold hearted murderer. But, also, on the other hand, I can't justify what I did, or why I did. It's hard to explain alcoholism except to another alcoholic. It's a cunning, baffling, and powerful disease which tells you 'you don't have a disease and everything will be better tomorrow, so it's okay to drunk today' et cetera.

I'm thinking that someday before I die I'll write my story down. I'm not good at writing and in here I have a hard time staying focus; my mind just wanders around. That's why I like to read.

Well I hope I hear from you soon and you send part five of your story. Don't worry about thinking you have to write ten page letters or nothing. I enjoy one page or cards or anything; I just like to hear from you once or twice a month. To receive mail on death row from the frontier of real life is a wonderful feeling. It's like having sunshine come under my cell door.

If you can't or don't want to, that's okay. But I wanted to ask you if you could/would get me a magazine subscription? I'm sending you a coupon with a big discount. It'd be great to read about other news besides what you see and hear every night on TV. I'd like to keep up with what's going on in the world of music, arts, theatre, science, et cetera, and Newsweek would have that each week for me. If you can – great – if not I'll understand. I asked both of my sisters but no reply from them. Maybe for my birthday in May 19th I will be 50 but I feel a lot older.

Well that's all for this time. Have fun on the 29th at your gig, and I do hope I hear from you again.

Peace & Love

Rich

P.S. Joke: Do you know what kind of lights Noah had on the ark?? Flood lights.

April 25, 2000

Dear Rich,

It is heartbreaking. You shouldn't be on death row. If you would be rich (yes, pun intended) you wouldn't be there. I know about all that shit going on, I am working on the death penalty with Amnesty International; that's how I got in touch with you. But maybe, maybe, something can be done. I don't want to give you false hopes, but I will try.

I don't have a TV (so I don't see all that what you talked about.) That is, I have a great big one, but it's used only for video. Living in a rural area I would need an antenna or satellite for TV programs and I don't want it.

What do you mean by what key the violin is? We use the g-clef (picture) and the strings are: GDAE. Isaac Stern is of course damned good; but some things I don't like too much – musically I mean. Technically he is wonderful. He probably has a Strad (Stradivarius) which is now about 2-3 millions worth. I used to have a wonderful violin, not nearly as expensive, but it was made in 1673. I sold it when I retired; I thought I will never play again. But it seems I can't live without that piece of wood.

Rich, I *enjoy* writing to you. Don't think it's like charity.

Cheers,

Agi

P.S. What do you know about Amnesty?

May 5, 2000

Dear Agi,

"My life was a strange mixture of glamour and squalor between the heat and applause of concert-halls and the chill of the depressing home and my mother's hysteria…" great writing (page 3 part 5 "Escape") In my opinion this chapter was your best as far as the writing. It read easy, it kept my attention going and hungry for more – I didn't want it to end. Very good indeed. Something to consider: Dates! If I didn't have your earlier letters, I would not know the year this all took place. I'm guessing 1956. Your 2nd letter told me you left after the uprising, but if I hadn't had your letter I'd had no idea what year this took place. Most younger people wouldn't. Your life story is not only interesting to read (most Americans not suffered and seen the things you did) but your life story is a living history. Therefore it should and can be a discerning story. To see and understand the history dates are required – not specific days or even months, but at least the year or years. Stories need a place and time in my opinion. Just a friendly suggestion I truely hope you don't mind because believe me you're doing a wonderful job at this, and I'm proud of you knowing the little I know about you and persevering like you have. Hell not too many young girls get shot at trying to leave their country! Man oh man what a childhood you had. I'm impressed that you could stay focus on practicing your violin with all of this going on around you! Such discipline you have. Do you have a picture of yourself as a young girl in Hungary? If so, make a copy and send me one if you will; I'd like that. I have a couple of pictures of me: one picture and one business card with picture, if you want to see them. I'll send them to you. Just let me know, but you do have to send them back 'cause they're the only pictures I have of myself. (My sisters whom I am estranged with won't send me my photo albums). Long story, but they – my sisters – don't and won't do anything for me. I burnt that bridge years ago when I went to California. Families sometimes just grow apart. Someday I'll write on my childhood maybe a little at a time. Did you know I have a daughter? Yes I do, in fact, she, Allison, will be thirty years old this month May 20th the day after my birthday, and I'll be 50.

The violin isn't like a guitar. Open string guitar plays a E chord of some kind, violin I see tunes to 5th's (G on the bottom I suppose?)

The song "The Man I Love" is one of my favorite Cole Porter tunes; in the key of C.

Peace & Love

Rich

May 11, 2000

Dear Rich,

Thank you for your two letters. Don't worry, I am your friend.

I want to give you a little sunshine in your dark life. Did you get my letter with the story? You don't react on it at all. I would like to know, it's kind of important. It's possible that somebody from AI will interview you, I don't know when. If that happens, tell them your story the way you told me.

The "Man I Love" is by Gershwin – maybe Cole Porter wrote one, too. I don't know what key it is in, I wrote it by ear. Is it the one you think of?

My "gig" in Victoria can be considered a success, although I wasn't in my best form. I am invited back; I got a good review, standing ovation, etc.

Yes, you told me you have a daughter – you don't hear from her at all? How sad.

I did the subscription to the Newsweek. Let me know if you get it.

Here is the story of how I got an apartment – a half one – in communist Hungary. No "artistic liberties" there, that's exactly how it happened. I hope you get a good laugh.

Cheers,

Agi

P.S. Yes, send your picture(s)! And send back mine!

May 15, 2000

Dear Agi,

Yes, you are right; 'The Man I Love' in E flat by George Gershwin. My mistake; my memory esp. of tunes and keys is diminishing a little bit.

I enjoyed seeing your lovely pictures. Can you make me a copy? You were sexy with a tiny waist. You can be in my band any day!

If you can, make copies of all three pictures so I can have them too.

Yes, I got your letter with your #5 story 'ESCAPE'! Also your apartment story. (That's a funny story).

I will write more latter a longer letter. I just wanted to get these pictures to you.

Thanks for being my friend.

Peace & Love

Rich

May 29, 2000

Dear Agi,

Hello my friend, and how are you today? Well it's Memorial Day and truth be told summer holidays like today and July 4 and Labor Day make me a little depressed. These holidays are harder on me emotionally than winter holidays. Why? Well because I know that everybody is outside doing things and I'm stock locked in a cell.

I have a lot of fond memories of summer holidays of being on the beach, or in the mountains of Big Bear, or on the River (OHIO) or playing tennis, or just jogging around the park.

I'll tell ya, being on death row is really hard to deal with. If I can get to general population someday, that would be a lot easier to deal with. At least I could get outside more often than I do here. Here I get to go outside for 2 hours every fourth day, which is better than nothing; I guess I shouldn't complain.

You asked me what do I know about Amnesty? I don't know anything about them. Maybe you can enlighten me of this organization? I've heard of them, of course, but I don't know what it is they do.

So you had a violin that was made in 1673, eh? Wow! That's amazing. I know you had to take a special care to maintain such an old and delicate instrument. It must had been hard for you the day you sold it when you thought you wasn't going to play anymore.

Nice to read you got a good review, standing ovation, in Victoria. What piece did you play? What size groups did you perform with?

Question: on the average, about how many pieces (instruments) would be in a full symphony orchestra?

A couple of days ago my first "Newsweek" magazine arrived. Thank you again for getting me a subscription. After I finish reading it I'll put it in the rec pod so the other men can read it too. It's nice to see what else is going on out in the world besides all the bad stuff you see on the nightly news cast.

Sometime down the road , I want to read some Ernest Hemingway. Also: "The Sound and the Fury" by William Faulkner. I'd like to read some of the great American writers; the stories that are considered classics by the literary critics, e.g. "For Whom the Bell Tolls", 'A Farewell to Arms" etc. etc. Culture is what I'm hungry for.

The books in our D.R. library are mostly crime novels, which I enjoy a little bit, but mostly they are "B" novels – second class stories of nuts and sluts by unknown writers.

So you like operas I see. Sorry to say I have never seen or heard an opera. Of course I know about them; but never had the pleasure of experiencing one in the theatre.

You asked me if I like Chaplin? I don't know. I haven't seen enough of his work to know. I've seen documentaries on the man and bits and pieces of his films. I know he was a genius. Question: who would you consider a genius today?

I'll be back soon. Take care of yourself and enjoy your beautiful island.

Peace & Love

Rich

June 2, 2000

Dear Rich,

I had a nice visit last week: my step-daughter came with her 7 months old baby. She is my ex-husband's daughter. The whole week was busy riding her around, having parties and card-games, etc.

Amnesty International is a world-wide human rights organization; its goals are: freeing prisoners of conscience (those imprisoned for political or other reasons,) insuring fair trials for them. Ending torture, abolish the death penalty; working for refugees so that they are not sent back to their country where they might face torture or execution, etc. AI is completely independent of any governments, parties or religions. I am an activist of AI; since I am here on the island I founded a group and we are doing all kind of things: public lectures, a yearly Christmas sale, etc. In August we have a booth in the San Juan County Fair, where we advocate our goals and selling things; the money we send to AI. I talked to the death penalty coordinator of Ohio on your behalf; he was very nice and said it was possible to help you. We will see. My personal focus in AI is the death penalty. I am writing many letters to governors, heads of state, etc.

In Victoria I played a recital with a pianist; played sonatas by Brahms and Debussy and pieces by Tartini, Szymanowski, Bloch and Bartok. An average symphony orchestra has approximately 14-16 first violins, 12-14 second violins, 10 violas, 8 cellos, 6 double basses, flutes (1, 2 and maybe 3), oboes (same as flutes), English horn (a deeper kind of oboe), clarinets, bassoons, French horns (4) trombones, sometimes tuba, harp. The orchestra of San Francisco Opera where I worked for 14 years was slightly smaller: 12 violins, etc., but whenever we played operas demanding a large orchestra (Wagner, Strauss, etc.) they used extras.

Opera is the most expensive form of art: it needs an orchestra, chorus, sets, often ballet, costumes, soloists, conductor, stage director, and so on. Big names like Placido Domingo get something like $15,000 per performance. No opera company can exist without subsidies, because the costs are enormous. Ticket sales – although they are very expensive, a good seat about $100 – don't cover but maybe a fourth of the cost. San Francisco Opera is a good one, second only to the Met (Metropolitan) which is now probably the best in the world. So we worked with all the big stars – productions were lavish. The Opera was the cherished child of the city, always sold out.

Too bad you have never seen an opera. A lot of them are great music, too. I wish I could send you some, but not even CDs are allowed, what?

Well, enough for today.

Cheers,

Agi

June 16, 2000

Dear Agi,

How you doing today, my Lady? I do hope all is well.

I received your June 2nd letter with pictures – thank you. Also I got all the Amnesty International pamphlets. I didn't realize that you have an A.I. group right there on your island that you meet with monthly. Looking at the address, you can walk to your meetings, eh?

Yes, I'd love to see them get rid of the death penalty. No doubt about it there are innocent people on death row, and in prison in general population too. Lots of 'em!

With this new D.N.A. testing you are hearing so much about lately, lawyers and investigaters are finding innocent people by the dozens in prison that shouldn't be there. The problem, as I understand it, are the laws that are written which do not allow new evidence to be enter into the case after so many days after conviction.

Hell, if a person is proven innocent by D.N.A., or any reason, it shouldn't matter how many days, months, or even years after conviction: he or she should be allowed a new trial to get out if D.N.A. testing, or incompetent lawyers, or whatever new evidence has exonerated them. Yet the old, archaic laws do not allow that – yet – hopefully these laws will be changed.

Anyway, I'm proud of you and I think it's admirable of you to be involved in Amnesty International. There's no doubt in my mind that you, Agi, with the experience you suffered as a child i.e. lost of Father and a brother and friends in the war; having to sneak out of your own country to find freedom – artistic freedom in your case – and being shot at doing it! My God, yes, you make an ideal advocate for human rights.

Well it was nice to read you got to see your step-daughter and her baby. A whole week visit, huh? That's wonderful. Where do they live? I would guess down around San Francisco, maybe?

Thanks for info how many players in a symphony. Also, you really opened my eyes to what's all involved in putting together an opera – man, what a production to pull off. I'd never given a thought before until you wrote it in your letter. Here's another question I have sometimes wondered: why are all (or most) operas in Italian or German? Do they not write them in English? I always thought, if they would translate them into English, more people would understand what it's all about – the story I mean. I listen to opera when it's on my classical (N.P.R.) radio and enjoy the melodies. And I know how hard it is to sing those notes, so I appreciate the talent but I have no idea what is being said.

Truth be told because I don't sing I never really paid a whole lot of attention to words in English songs either. I always focused on the chord changes and the melody. By playing with singers, of course, I'd hear the words, especially the chorus, but I never paid attention to <u>all</u> the words on every verse.

<u>No</u>, I'm not allowed C.D.s. Inmates would be breaking them up for weapons. Only books and magazine subscriptions can you send.

Agi, let me know your birth date – please? I'll be back soon – take care and enjoy your beautiful island.

Peace & Love
Rich

June 24, 2000
Dear Agi,

Well, I get to go outside today for a few hours for exercise and fresh air.

They put us (5 men only) in a chained-linked fenced cage. Inside there is a basketball and goal, so we shoot around and play 2 on 2 sometimes. Also they give us a jump rope. It's a small area (about ½ the size of a tennis court.)

Anyway it just feels good to get outside to feel the sun's rays and breath fresh-air for a while.

I'll mail this on the way out (now) and I'll write you a letter in a few days.

Peace and love,
Rich

June 26, 2000

Dear Agi,

Hello my friend and how are you today? I hope you're feeling good and that the weather is beautiful on your pretty island.

So what are your plans for this summer? Are you going somewhere to visit or sightsee or tour? Of course, when I think about it you're already there – you live in paradise – no doubt about that. Thousands of people come to where you are especially in the summer to get away from the rat race. Yeah, you're there already.

When tourists come, do you enjoy seeing all the people, or does it make the island too hectic for you?

So you have a County Fair on your island in August, eh? I love fairs of any kind. Yeah that struck a chord with me when you wrote that. I haven't thought of fairs in years. And now when I think back, I played a lot of fairs in my lifetime. Not just on the fair's stage but also in booths and on flat bed trucks moving slowly in a parade somewhere. Yeah, those were always fun jobs usually – not serious – but light and something silly gigs; I'm talking about the music sometimes was "corny" and silly in content. You know dumb songs that I'd be hired to play – over and over again – whilst moving through the parade route. (Hey man, a gig is a gig, it helps to pay the rent, or in my case, the bar tab.)

Yeah to survive, I had to take any gig I could find. I had to play music I didn't like sometimes, but it's better than not working and not making any money that week or whatever. You understand – I know.

(I guess?)

You are a higher class (a lot higher) than I was. I'm just a club, bar musician. I mean I've had some nice gigs in real nice hotels around the country and a few cruise ships, but also, I've had to work a lot of dumps too. And, like I said before, sometimes I would have to play music I didn't care for at all. But to me, it was better to play and make money than not work and not be able to pay the bills at the end of the month. I did a lot of freelancing because…well, hell, I had to; it comes with the territory of being a club musician.

Now I did have a few hotel gigs that lasted 1 to 3 years, which was real nice, but most of my gigs you're usually talking weeks or months. But I loved it! I'm proud to say I did make a living playing music. Even though I never made a lot of money, I had a wonderful journal. I went into music because I enjoyed playing, and bringing joy and good times to people felt good to me. If I would have made the big time, yeah, definitely that would have been cool, but I have no regrets about my music career.

Well…of course I regret the drinking, drugs and promiscuous lifestyle I ended up in but I'm not talking about that now; I'm just talking about the gigs. Actually, I was going to talk about fairs, but I digressed a bit, didn't I?

I would guess the best gig you had was the 14 years in San Francisco with the Opera? Man, what a beautiful job that was, I'm sure! First class all the way with big, full productions and music – serious music – that 's close to your heart. What beautiful memories you must have of those years I'm sure.

I'm proud of you Agi. I know your story because I've read it a couple of times. Yeah, you did really well – well, more than well – you did great with your talent. I'm proud to be your friend. I have your pretty picture on my wall and the guards and other inmates (porters) ask about you, and it makes me feel special knowing a special person like you. And you are special and very kind and worldly.

You <u>see</u> and <u>care</u> with your heart - I love you for that.

Peace and love,

Rich

July 3, 2000

Dear Rich,

Two extra letters from you, with the nice thank-you-card! How nice. Thanks pal. I am well; the ear problem is apparently solved. Still frustrated, not having a computer - I am waiting to get one - and not being able to send my Amnesty letters and work on my stories. But it will be OK in a few days.

I don't have any plans for the summer, no trips. I had too much expenses lately - new car, computer, surgery of my dog, etc.- so I better have no extravagancies now.

About my "gig" of San Francisco Opera: I have heard many times what you said, how wonderful must that have been. Well, I am sorry to disappoint you, friend. Although it was certainly interesting and there were good moments, it was not all roses. For one thing, it was an awful lot of work. When season was on, I worked very hard: most days, rehearsal and performance, which meant 7 hours of playing, two roundtrips - we lived 16 miles from the city – and between the two I walked the dog, cooked, cleaned, shopped. My husband didn't help at all. I went home around midnight, but you can't go to sleep right away. I had my gin and tonic and sat up for at least an hour before going to bed.

Besides, there was a lot of frustration of bad conductors, stupid colleagues and so on. For 14 years I was suffering about people sitting behind me – you hear them the most – who were a lot of time just a split second ahead of beat, who couldn't play syncopations right, and the like. It might sound strange that things like this happen in a good orchestra. I am convinced it happens in the best ones. But it drove me to the wall. And my stand partner – violinists and all strings sit by two at a stand – got nervous and overstrained, like everybody, toward mid-season and he regularly started to bitch at me. It was of course a hard job – operas are difficult, I mean many of them, and the slightest mistake can be disastrous. It is a very high concentration – it is illegal to play more than seven and a half hours – regulation of the union – because one simply can't do more, not well, I mean. And the conductors! It is amazing how many bad ones conduct in the best places, because nobody but the musicians can judge that and the administration doesn't ask our opinion.

There was one, the boy-friend of the director, for example. He was so incompetent that the whole orchestra protested and went to the director. He said yes, yes; and the guy came back to conduct again. Sure, there were some good ones and then you could enjoy the music. I was suffering particularly about the bad ones, because I know how it should be done. It may sound conceited, but that's the truth. So I became famous about my "goddamshit" I was bitching. I made a copy of the card I got at my retirement party; you will get a good laugh I hope.

Besides, I was never really an orchestra player; I was and am a soloist. The two things are very different. For example my stand partner was a good orchestra player, better than I, but came nowhere near me as a soloist or chamber musician.

And I didn't do well or great with my talent. I was supposed to make it big, an international career as a soloist. I didn't, for many reasons; maybe I will tell you about another time.

Well, cheers, enjoy the cross-words.

Agi

July 9, 2000

Dear Agi,

And how are you today, my friend? I hope all is well with you and you're feeling good and all is serene on your beautiful island.

Yes, I got your card/letter of 6-26 thank you for writing; it's always good to hear from you like sunshine after rain when I see one of your letters coming in under my cell door-it just feels good all over.

Definitely your story has a lot of potential - it really does, and you should keep writing. If you can't fix the computer problem, heck, just get a typewriter to write it. The premise is there, you lived it, you need to tell it. Only you know the story but probably down the road you'll need a "professional" writer to help you to put it all together. Everybody today is writing a book it seems. We all have stories and our egos tell us "yeah this is worthy of a book and people are going to want to read this" we say to ourselves. I've said it to myself but it's all bullcrap and I know it too. But...and now listen to me...are you listening? Your story is worthy of being published into a book. Hand on heart I truely mean it!! If I didn't, I wouldn't write on this subject, I would have just ignored it altogether, so I am sharing my honest opinion.

Here's some more of my honest opinion or maybe I should call it unsolicited opinion/advice, eh? Oh well, we're friends and lovers of music, and besides, I feel comfortable talking to you. So my thoughts are: continue the story what happened in Paris for 5 years, Germany for 5 years and New York City that's a lot of chapters right there. For example (I wonder) in Budapest you are known, respected and loved as a great violinist – a State Musician a child prodigy et cetera…good stuff and you need to write more on this too. You need to 'add' more chapters to your "childhood" part of the story. Maybe show more of the contrast i.e. bombs exploding around you; you live in constant fear but yet you keep your love alive – your love of music – you play and study melodies of the heart, harmony of consciousness, whilst living in discord of humanity.

OK – I'll cool it with my childlike attempt at creative writing, but that's how I see your early life story. Remember I asked you (I think?) how could you <u>focus</u> on music (your love) in time of fear and war? That's what I wanted to hear more of – your inner battle to play through this. More stories of music – lessons, the early concerts (maybe while bombs are dropping?) take some artistic freedom – Hollywood does etc. etc…Then after your escape – what happens in Paris, Germany, and New York City. If you can make it there you can make it anywhere, right? But now, as a young woman, you have to compete with hundreds of great violin players trying to get the best jobs in the world's best symphonies. A whole bunch of chapters here, not only the big cities of Paris and NY but Indiana, Texas, Georgia too. Then the finale (in the most beautiful city in America-my opinion) and you made it! Yes you did!! Playing 14 years with the San Francisco Opera is making the big time – believe me – I know. Hell, I thought I made it playing Vegas. That's a joke. I had fun though. Anyway, yes, truly, indeed, hand on heart, please keep writing your story – you <u>do</u> have one people would want to read. I didn't want it to end, I want more and that's good because you have "meat and not milk"(metaphor). You get your computer fixed or get a typewriter. But, please, keep writing. While I'm thinking about it what happened to your mother? Did she understand that her daughter was a <u>"world"</u> class musician? Yes, you have a good book there in the making and you might have doubts on some days yourself, but that's common in creative people. Keep writing, my dear friend, and I'll be back real soon.

Peace and love,

Rich

P.S. I think you're a wonderful woman.

July 17, 2000

Dear Rich,

It was a very nice letter about my writing. I started to work on my stories, extending them. The last story I broke in four, I write more details, account of my first marriage, etc. (My computer is fixed, hallelujah, after several months of frustration.) And I just started a new story which was missing in the chain of events: from the German invasion till the protected house (Transitions.) This would be a book entitled "Tales from Hungary." My later life in Paris, Germany and the US might be a later project. Actually I started writing because I wanted to write a novel about my marriage; but I realized you don't just sit down and write a novel, so I wrote those stories.

By the way your picture of my giving a concert while bombs are exploding is somewhat naive my friend. For one thing, when "enemy" planes were nearing the city, alarm was sounding: loud sirens wailing through the whole city and everybody went to the air-shelters. Also, Hungary was relatively lucky: until the Germans were invading the country in March '44, we didn't feel the war too much. The head of state was playing a double game, half-heartedly going with Hitler, giving some troops, but not involving the country too much. The same he did about Jews. There was trouble but not nearly as bad as in Germany. You could see this in my first story: in '42 we were still living a human life, having vacation and no life-threatening troubles. So the nightmare was "only" about 10 months in Budapest and a little more for the western part of the country. During those months I didn't practice or have lessons either; for one thing it was risky to keep the violin, so a friend – non-Jewish – kept it. There was a short period when things looked better, then I practiced for a few weeks, but essentially I stopped for 10 months. Bombings were mostly in that period.

I have a lot of interesting stuff in my later life, maybe I will get to that after this book is finished. If I wanted to write a whole autobiography, it would be awfully long. I could write a novel about my marriage, a satire about "Academe," my teaching jobs, an amusing account about SF Opera, and so on. Well, it wasn't the peak of my career. As you say, my colleagues from Hungary regarded as my downfall: playing in an orchestra, not even being the concertmaster, instead of being a famous soloist.

Well, we talk about me an awful lot. I wanted to ask you: do you have a friend or friends among the inmates? Or somebody you can talk to a little bit? You see them only at recreation, right? Tell me about it.

You must have gotten the crosswords and book meanwhile. Hope you enjoy it.

Cheers,

Agi

July 24, 2000

Dear Agi,

And how are you today? I hope you are feeling better and the flu has left. I hope your ears are back to normal too and the medicine took care and dried up the fluid on them.

I worry about that, too, getting sick here on death row, because believe me going to the infirmary is a real pain in the butt. I went last summer when I hit my head playing basketball and spent 3 days there. They put me in a cold cell with one blanket, no pillow, no books, no smokes, no radio, no TV, no nothing. A real drag and the doctor gave me aspirin and that was it. I couldn't wait to get back to my cell. Hell, I could have taken aspirin here in my cell; I didn't need to be there for 3 days.

Thank you for the book on Opera. In fact, I read the chapter on the history last night. Very interesting. It's a good book, well written, and any information I'll want to know is in there.

Also, I just finished reading "A Farewell to Arms." I really, really enjoyed that. I don't know if you have read it or not so I don't want to ruin it for you in case you haven't read it and might some day by giving the story away. It wasn't like I thought it would be and at first I didn't like it but I kept reading and it grew on me. And by the end I didn't want it to end and I was surprised at how the story ended.

There sure is a big difference between literature and pop novels, eh? It's not so much the story itself that's great but how he tells the story that makes it a wonderful book. His sense of pace, his timing, his word choice, his rhythm and his descriptive powers, that's the beauty of his writing. Yeah, Hemingway is one cool and hip guy. Have you read this book? You would like this I'm sure.

Well how is the computer situation going? Did you get it fixed? I hope so you can continue writing your story.

I'm hungry for more and that's good. That means you do have an interesting story to tell. It's a lot of work doing that though, but hopefully you enjoy it. Maybe like learning a musical instrument, if you love music and playing music then practicing the scales and all the other technical stuff isn't work at all, it's more like manifested love, and I hope writing your book is like that for you.

So, I guess you're probably starting to get things ready for the County Fair, eh? When is it in August? When I was a boy I loved cotton candy and those apples on a stick, (the red ones) hell, I forget what you call them – candy apples, I guess? I can smell that now, the smell of a fair and the sounds, lots of different sounds, counterpoint sounds coming and going, some up and some down like a John Cage or Charles Yves' music. I sure do miss things, simple things, like that.

I don't mean to sound like an old geezer who spends my days muttering I remember when, but I do remember.

Peace and love,
Rich

July 30, 2000
Dear Agi,

How are you my friend? I'm glad to hear that you're well again and no problem with your ears, either. I got two letters this week: Monday, 7/24, I got your July 17 letter and Friday, 7/27, I got your July 3 letter. Yes! July 3 letter with the extra sheet of your friends signatures but NO crossword book.

No they wouldn't let me have them – they 're contraband. It's my fault and I do hope you don't get upset with my stupidity. I should have checked out the rules myself clearly before I told you that it would be OK for you to send them in yourself and not use the bookstore. Well (now) I know that you cannot send any books in yourself, they all have to come from the book store – Griffin Bay directly like you've been doing. It's really stupid and it pisses me off: one, that they wouldn't give'em to me this time – hell I didn't even get to see them – and two, that it took so long to get the letter! You sent it July 3 and it took until July 27!! Bullshit!!

Well, anyway, that's death row and the bullshit rules of prison which I nor anyone can do anything about; I am a ward to the state. I do what they say and keep my mouth shut, because it does not pay to argue with the authorities in here – inmates never, never win an argument, or I should say a disagreement of any kind. But it is my fault – yes it is – I should have checked the rules first. So I apologize to you my friend for the loss. Next time go through Griffin Bay bookstore.

I'm real happy that you got your computer fixed, that's great. Questions: Are you on-line, on the internet? Two; do you have an encyclopedia in your computer or hardware? We had Windows 95 in our computer and we had an extra (rom-rom, whatever they are called?) disk that was an encyclopedia and I used that more than anything. I'm a curious guy and I enjoyed looking things of who, what, why, when, where and what happened, up.

Remember, I'm not an educated man, and now I truely regret I didn't go to college and study. I have two years of junior college I took music theory and played tennis. Oh hell, I regret all kinds of crap; hindsight is 20/20, eh? You struck a chord when you talked about incompetent players in the orchestra and the boy friend conductor situation…yes I can relate to that. I've played accompaniment to many - mostly female – singers who were downright horrible, but got the gig because she was going to bed with someone, usually an agent, with the ultimatum do the gig with her or don't do the gig at all type of thing. We could talk on this for days, huh? Now just I wanted to let you know because I didn't mention it in my last letter that: yes, I finally got July 3 letter but not until the 27th. And NO I didn't get the crossword books – my fault – and I am sorry about that and I hope you don't get mad at me for being stupid or "goddamshit" I messed up. I'll be back next week and finish responding to your nice, talkative letter of July 3rd and 17th.

Peace and love,
Rich

August 6, 2000
Dear Agi,

How are you my friend? Are you at the fair this week or when?

I saw and read this article on Charlie Chaplin and I know you are a big fan of his so I thought you might enjoy reading it. I was amazed when I read "700 takes of the tightrope sequence" man, oh, man that's a lot, eh?

I heard a beautiful piece of music the other night called "Adagio for Strings" by S. Barber. Man, I love that piece. Have you ever played that one? Oh yeah, this was Isaac Stern too playing the lead part if that's what you call it. Have you heard of Mark O'Connor? I'm sure you don't like his music but he is a good player.

Re "Job at San Fran. Opera – not all roses" (letter of 7-3). Yes, I must admit I always assumed that any musician who was playing in a professional orchestra would not have a problem with basic things such as timing, tuning, syncopation but I guess I assumed wrong.

Are you on the internet? The reason I ask is because there are a couple of places I might like to write and I'll need their addresses. One is Alcoholic Anonymous' main office in New York City. I'm thinking about (and you are my inspirer) of writing my A.A. story for one of their monthly magazines. You know one of those "what it was like, what happened, and what it is like today" kind of story. Anyway, I'm thinking about it.

Well, my dear music lover friend, time to go but I'll be back real soon.

I just finished reading a book from the library on Lewis and Clark – great book. I love history on the American frontier. Next week I'm starting William Faulkner.

Take care, my friend. Keep it mellow as a cello.

Peace & Love

Rich

August 11, 2000

Dear Rich,

Thanks for your letter. The best thing in it was your intention to write your story for AA. Go for it, pal! I think it's great! Use your time in that hell creatively and doing some good, don't just wither away.

Unfortunately I couldn't get the address. I don't know if it's my computer or my stupidity. I am no good for computers, I hate them! But just do it, write first, I promise you I will get the address, it shouldn't be too difficult. Thanks for the Chaplin clipping, too. I know how he worked. I have 3 videos of interviews and stuff, in addition of his greatest movies. I haven't played the Adagio by Barber but I know the piece.

You have great taste. One more thing about SF Opera: those players were good, they could play the violin – the trouble is they are judged by auditions, playing alone, and, as I said, paying solo and playing in orchestra are different matters. That's why this kind of thing can happen in good orchestras.

Fair is next week. I am already working on it. For 4 days I will be at my booth from 10 am to 10 pm – with some help to be sure, but I do most of it. And the preparation – I am going around in stores begging for donations for raffle prizes. We make quite a bit of money for Amnesty by selling raffle tickets, T-shirts and jewelry, mostly made by myself. That's one of our 2 major fundraising events, the other is a Christmas sale called "Holiday Art Bizarre" in December. I am proud to say that my group is one of the best in fundraising in the country. And there are hundreds of AI groups. So next week will be my busiest of the year.

I also will give a recital here the 13th of September. I will play with the pianist from Victoria and the same program we played there.

Well, enough for today, cheers my friend and start to write! You will feel better, I promise you! To do something useful, something good, even in hell, that's greatness!! I just received a book "Prison Writings" by Leonard Peltier, the Native American imprisoned for 25 years for a crime he didn't commit.

Well, you know, life is hell sometimes, but it should be used for something.

Cheers,

Agi

P.S. Meanwhile you should have gotten the crossword book.

August 27, 2000

Dear Agi,

How are you my lady? Probably a little tired from working the fair so many hours; 10am to 10pm is a very long day indeed. But, I hope you took a little time off to enjoy the fair, and I hope were successful in your objective for AI.

Thank you very much for the wonderful crossword book. That should keep me busy for a few years, I would say. I find crossword puzzles to be a fun way to learn new words. I never did them before I came to jail, thinking I wasn't any good at it and I wasn't. But now I do enjoy doing them. I like doing them in the early evening after dinner while I'm watching the national/world news on TV. I'll say one thing about you, I know you don't skimp. You always send me the best of whatever it is and, my friend, I appreciate everything you have done for me out of your compassionate and benevolent heart. From my heart I thank you.

By the way, that chess book you sent me (wow!) it's the best; my game already has improved tremendously. I play everyday by myself for a couple of hours just playing the games of masters. It's fun and very enlightening; there are games in there from the 1800s. I'm starting to understand and discern the difference between an open game as opposed to a closed game. But I have a whole lot to learn about all the varieties of different defenses and other things too. As you know, chess is like music, in the way that it's infinite in play and a profound subject of study.

If I wouldn't have been an alkie all my life, I think I would have enjoyed doing other endeavors, too – besides just the music thing. I really messed up a potentially good life that I could have had. So many things interest me now that I am sober and can think somewhat straight for the first time in years. Too bad I'm on death row and my freedom is gone; before I got here I was free but my mind was gone. Because of booze I'd been living in a fog of self-delusion since 1976. I was completely lost and maybe I knew it but just didn't want to admit it. I had a disease that told me I didn't have a disease; in other words, <u>denial.</u> We alkies will live in denial until death, jail or insanity if we don't get help. I'm not on the pity-pot, no, I'm just sharing with you my thoughts and there is no need for you to reply because you probably don't know what to say which is OK because really only drunks understand drunks. If you want to say something, that's fine too, but no pressure from me - I'm just talking out loud to my friend on her beautiful island.

Peace and love to you – you're a wonderful friend,
Rich

September 9, 2000

Dear Agi,

How are you my friend? Probably busy getting ready for your recital this Wednesday. Have fun and enjoy your gift of playing music. It is a gift you know. Not everyone can play music especially on your level.

Sometimes I dream I'm back at the Six Mile House or the Briarwood Restaurants playing my dinner gigs. I really enjoyed doing those. Yes I imagine it sounds corny to you me enjoying playing for dinner but I truely did enjoy playing and learning at the same time all those tunes from the 20s up through the 40s.

I did my share of playing in bands in bars, in hotel lounges, playing rock and pop and blues and country (ugh! my least favorite) music. So, when I turned 40, I decided no more bands for me. Solo, or duo, at most, from then on.

My parents were big band fans, esp. music from the 40s, so I had heard a lot of these tunes back in the 60s but I didn't sit down to learn them on the piano.

I was learning rock and pop, country and blues; music I could make money playing in bars with. So, anyway, when I started doing the restaurant jobs, I knew about 75 jazz standards – enough to get started and so I did. At the same time, for the first few years, I practiced more than I had in years learning new tunes (for me new tunes) and I would write down every request I'd get for songs and there were a lot of them I'd never heard of or I didn't know the title anyway.

At last count my book went from 75 to almost 500 songs I can play at request. Yeah, I liked it a lot, it was fun and non-group hassle free. But boy was I drinking a lot! Man oh man, the drinks just kept coming. Up to a point, I can play pretty hot whilst drunk – to a point.

One of my favorite, of many, piano tunes "It Had To Be You" in D maj. I like the sound of key of D but I love playing in B flat best.

You're smart moving to an island and not watching TV because it's horrible! The networks stink except for a few magazine news shows like 20/20, Dateline, etc the rest is pathetic; only PBS is cool in my book. We do have a video channel where the office has a VCR and they show us two movies a week and a lot of them are crap too. Hollywood doesn't make a whole lot of good movies these days. Mostly films for young people: bang-bang shoot'em up with special effects lots of skin – the skin part I like but usually I don't watch the movies unless the story line is halfway decent.

Speaking of a good story, I love this "For Whom the Bell Tolls." I think Hemingway is a hip writer. No one writes like that except him; in my reading experience which is somewhat limited. Question: Have you read Hemingway and opinion please. Thanks again for the books; it truely is a reprieve from the real-life nightmare here. Through reading I can travel anywhere, and right now I'm in Spain for a couple of weeks.

Take care my friend and play a few notes for me.

Peace and love,

Rich

September 12, 2000

Dear Rich,

Sorry I didn't answer your letter right away. I was preoccupied with my recital which is tomorrow. I have a quiet evening now.

The Fair went very well, we made almost $ 700 and filled many sheets of petitions and talked to a lot of people. I could enjoy it sometimes too, when there was help for the booth. I bought a few things, ordered a pair of shoes made for measure, quarreled with a few people - about voting for a third candidate in the election. There was a booth of the Green Party and people wore buttons of Nader. I think voting for a third candidate would just help Bush. I am quite concerned about this; it would be terrible if that fascist bastard would win.

So my recital is tomorrow and I am appropriately nervous. I play a very difficult program.

This is all for today but I will write soon longer.

Cheers,

Agi

September 16, 2000

Dear Rich,

How nice and understanding you are! Thanks for your 9/9 letter. Well, my recital was a big success, standing ovation and all that. People were literally raving abut it. It was a good program, very varied, each piece different style. And goddamned difficult, especially two of them. It was not perfect but there was certainly intense musical feeling I was able to give. Friday Harbor audience doesn't hear much of this kind of music and playing and they were very enthusiastic. Too bad I didn't like very much my partner, he was rather hindering than helping me. A very nice man but not my ideal partner.

Yes, I read Hemingway "For whom the Bell Tolls" and other things – I recently bought all his short stories. I do like him; I wouldn't call him my favorite writer though. One of his books I like especially: "The Old Man and the Sea." That's a masterpiece in my opinion. Do you want me to get it for you?

I wish I could play for you – how stupid I can't send you a tape. They taped my recital and I have a few past concerts recorded.

Well, cheers my friend,

Agi

September 19, 2000

Dear Agi,

How are you today? I hope all is well and you're feelin' good and you're happy.

I got your letter. Glad to hear your recital went well and that the people on your island enjoyed it.

The weather in Ohio is changing into autumn now which used to be my favorite time of year. It's really beautiful down in the river valley (Ohio River) by my hometown. Thousands of trees all changing color at once. Here from my cell window I can't see one tree, and I miss seeing trees. There isn't any trees on the prison ground at all, none I can see anyway.

Nature? Yeah I miss it. The ocean, the river, trees, the moon and stars things I can't get to or look up and see in the sky. I sound like I'm swimming in self-pity, huh? Really I'm not; just sharing my thoughts with you.

George W. Bush? Like you, I can't stand that guy. The only reason he's the Republican candidate is because of his dad. I loathe politics and I don't listen to it too much because to me it's all rhetoric, anyway. Really George W., in my opinion, doesn't seem smart; when asked a specific question, sometimes he just stumbles on and usually ends up saying some superficial soundbite and never really does give a clear answer.

Truth be told, I don't know all the issues, but a few that I agree with Gore on is abortion – I do think it's a woman's choice – a hard choice, for sure, but the government shouldn't make it illegal again because they are going to take place anyway, if a woman wants one, and usually then, if they are illegal they happen in a back alley by a quack doctor or whatever.

I like Gore, too, because he seems more environmentally conscience than Bush. We, all people, need to take care of the planet; earth will cease to exist without a healthy environment.

I remember days when the Santa Ana winds would blow out all the smog from Orange County. God it was beautiful! I actually could stand on the beach in Huntington and look east and see the mountains with snow on top. It only happened a few times a year for just a day or two and it always made me realize what a shame we live in all that smog the rest of the year. Without the smog Orange County is beautiful but too crowded for me, now. When I was young I could deal with it , but not anymore. I'd like to live where you live on a island in the Northwest. Quiet and peaceful, I'm sure

Books: Yes, I'd like a few please. "Old Man and the Sea" (always wanted to read that). A book by John Updike (you pick one for me). "A Man in Full" by Tom Wolfe. I remember the reviews in the paper last year were good. How about "Moby Dick? " Is that really good or over-hyped? You choose for me – you're smart and hip and well-read so you <u>teach me.</u>

I like to read and I'm open to anything. I just want to experience and read the good stories, books by renowned writers and this a good place to do that.

Take care my delightful friend.

Peace & Love

Rich

October 11, 2000

Dear Rich,

You always ask me how am I today – well, today I am <u>mad</u>. First my computer drove me to the wall: the damned thing just froze when I was looking for an important e-mail (Amnesty matters) and I couldn't shut it off. It is still on, blinking, goddamshit! Then I went to the monthly Amnesty group meeting: one member was there, then 15 minutes later 2 others showed up, one leaving in ten minutes. The whole group doesn't give a damn; I am the one keeping it going. And it would have been important, we are launching a new campaign to stop torture. It is amazing, torture is well and alive at the very end of the 20th century. In <u>150</u> countries they practice torture, in 70 widespread and systematic. It is the basest, most detestable thing man can do. Sometimes I think mankind is hopelessly stupid and cruel – but I think everybody who thinks the same way as I do should do something against it. That's why I am doing Amnesty.

I talked to the man who can help you – right now they are working on those who are in imminent danger of execution, but they will get to you in time.

What about writing your story? I know it's difficult to start, but just sit down and do it! Start any old way; you can always rewrite it later. I have a writer friend here who could help you. When you have a version you are halfway satisfied with, send it to me, OK?

I am working on my stories, too. I have more now and they might be published. If that happens I will let them send you a copy.

I will look for the books you asked for.

I hope you will be able to enjoy nature some day. Don't give up hope my friend.

My best to you,

Agi

October10, 2000

Dear Agi,

Well how are you today, my friend? In your last letter of 10-2 you are mad or I should just say you are having a bad day, eh? Your computer is down and no one is caring or showing up for the A.I. meeting. Well things will get better I'm sure. The computer problem can be solved that I know. But getting people interested about A.I. issues…now that is tough; especially living on a small island with a small population. And I would guess that the majority of the people living there are retired professionals and are more focused and concerned with fun things to do. I'm sure issues like death penalty, torture, don't carry much weight on their consciences, and truth be told I can understand that. Just do what you can (and I know you are) but don't become resentful over other people not caring. You are rare and probably somewhat solitary on your island for two reasons that I surmise: your first-hand experience with the Nazis as a young girl which left an indelible image of the inhumanities to men, and two you are a musician of very high caliber which not only fills your heart with passion but also add the two together (your experiences and your violin) and you, my lady, are full of compassion towards humankind, especially the downtrodden people who are suffering oppression and so on. That's how I see you in my mind's eye. I admire you. Not just your musical talent which I know is good because you would not be working with the country's best operas if you weren't and, also, I admire your tenacity to come through all of that discouragement of the war years. So, my friend, be happy and enjoy the sunset of your life, and I do imagine you are doing that too.

Well, I finished Hemingway's "For Whom the Bell Tolls". Excellent! I like Hemingway. He sure can tell a story, eh?

I do hope you do keep adding to your life's story. You have a story that's interesting. You keep writing – you are good at it.

Lots of news this week: terrible fighting in the Middle East, terrorist bombing our navy ship in Yemen, and our presidential election debates going on, and I really don't give a crap about any of it – except I don't like to see the killing going on in the M.E. That's a big dilemma to say the least. What's your opinion?

I'll be back soon – be happy and have a drink on me
Rich

October 26, 2000.

Dear Rich,

You asked me to have a drink on you – well, I'm just finishing my gin and tonic and am mad again. There is no end to my computer troubles: my printer doesn't work now that I am trying to send off my stories, and I can't connect my internet which is important for my Amnesty work. Hell!

These are minor troubles to be sure, compared to yours – and mine in my life – but very irritating.

I read "For whom…" long time ago, I don't remember details, so I can't comment on it. I hope you got my two packages meanwhile, hope you enjoy it.

You are right, there are many retired people on this island, but there are quite a few younger ones who have the right mind to do Amnesty. In my group there is only one retired person and several much younger ones and in spite of this they don't care enough. Without me the group wouldn't exist.

My three best friends are all younger than I; the oldest one is in her sixties, an artist. Very poor, but still very active. Until recently she made her living by cleaning houses – now she starts selling her pottery and teaches how to make them.

The second and third are in their fifties, one an actress – a good one – the other a writer. All rather poor. There are many wealthy people here, too. There are an amazing amount of private planes. Once I was picking up somebody at the airport – there is an airport in Friday Harbor! A tiny one – I had to wait a bit and I couldn't believe: every 3 minutes a small airplane took off or arrived. Too bad I don't know any of those wealthy people and it's probably not a coincidence that none of them are my friends.

I heard about "Dead Man Walking" the opera, from my colleagues in San Francisco. They said the same thing, the music is not good. That's a pity, but Sister Helen Prejean, the author of the book, is considered for the Nobel Peace Prize. Would she get it, it would help us a lot in our effort to abolish the death penalty.

Well, that's for today my friend.

My best,

Agi

October 30, 2000

Dear Agi,

Wow! What can I say? Thank you my loyal and benevolent friend for the wonderful books. I received 5 of them, and I will take my time and savor each one. Thank you Agi. I do, and the other men in my pod, appreciate your kindness.

Oh boy, for what I'm seeing on the TV news and reading in the paper the polls say it's very close for Bush and Gore. Even in your state, Washington, right now is too close to call, and Nader they say is strong up there, which is a vote for Bush, especially in the undecided states. I really don't want Bush to be elected our next president. But it is going to be very close indeed.

Well the other day we had a surprise, impromptu shakedown. This impromptu inspections , which we've only had 2 since I've been here, are the most humiliating . They come running in our pod yelling everybody up and strip down and wait! So I get naked and stand there in my cell and wait for a guard to come over and look at me. They look you up and down, open your mouth and raise my tongue, look at my ass and penis... God I hate that!

Then you put your underwear back on and bock up against the cell door where they open the food slot and handcuff you behind your back. Then they open the door and tell you to step out and face the wall and don't move, whilst two guards go in your cell and look for contraband of any kind.

Hell, truth be told, prison makes me nervous even without the shakedowns. I'm not a tough guy at all, and don't pretend to be. Well, I'm not a sissy either, but the thing about being in prison I don't like is you really can't be a nice guy; niceness is looked upon as weakness. Prison is weird that way. I'm learning to just be stoic. In here, I think that's best. Prison is changing me, and I can see that already, and I've only been here three years. My physical environment is somewhat acting upon my psyche, I feel. I see some guys in here little by little going nuts dealing with the daily isolation. That's why I do so much enjoy your good books you send me, because I can escape daily into the story and vicariously travel anywhere and into any time.

My cell has radio, TV, books and mags to escape. It's really not that bad – lonely yes – but nothing compared to what the Jews went through at Auschwitz that's for sure.

Keep writing, be happy. I'll be back soon.

Peace & Love
Rich

November 17, 2000
Dear Rich,

Well, what do you think of this incredible election? It will go down in history and maybe there will be changes in the system because of it. Those stupid electoral votes! Nobody understands them, and why complicate the matter? Why not going by the number of votes simply?

Whatever the outcome will be, I am thoroughly disgusted with the American people. Because it is a goddam shame that that fascist bastard can get half of the votes. The media and the commentators are corrupt, paid or dependant of the big corporations – they gave the edge to W. at the debates for no reason at all. He couldn't answer any charges, just bubbled away. When Gore said Texas ranks no. 46 on education and no. 50 on women's issues, W. said something like "Oh, we are for good education and respect women's right." And no commentator said anything about this.

But at one point I got furious with Gore. Somebody finally mentioned the death penalty and that idiot suddenly agreed with W. in all points, saying even that it is a deterrent. It is proven by many studies that it is not. Furthermore he didn't mention the killing of juveniles, the mentally retarded people, the innocents killed by fucking W. (and others.) Juveniles – who committed the crime before they were 18 – are universally spared, for obvious reasons: they can be reeducated. Only five countries in the world execute juveniles: Pakistan, Nigeria, Iran, Saudi Arabia – and the United States. The US is the last country of the civilized world to retain the death penalty. The whole of Europe, except the former Soviet Union, Canada, Australia, and some third world countries, abolished it.

I don't know if you know of the case of Gary Graham, a black man in Texas. He was sentenced to death on the basis of <u>one</u> eyewitness who saw a black man running from the distance of about 30-40 feet – several others stated he was with them at the time of the crime, miles away. He was 17 at the time. He spent 18 or 19 years on death row and was executed in June. The law states that one can be sentenced to death only "if the guilt is established beyond reasonable doubt."

That idiot of Gore could have crushed W. on that issue. I was so mad, I wrote him a letter – big deal! But somebody would read it. I told him I would vote for him but only because of W. And I said it is sad enough that you can't vote _for_ somebody in this most glorious of countries.

So, you see, I am mad again. Hell, there is something thoroughly wrong with this world, with the human brain.

Well, thanks for your letter. How awfully humiliating is that inspection! I am glad I can help you in a small way – read your books, play chess, do crossword puzzles – escape!

Cheers friend,

Agi

November 19, 2000

Dear Agi,

Happy Thanksgiving to you, my friend. I do hope you have a nice meal and delightful friends around for the holiday.

Do you cook? Do you enjoy cooking or do you prefer to eat out? Being a musician and working at night all your life I would guess you probably enjoy eating out in a nice restaurant. I know I do.

I got your letter and I'll respond to "up" things only today. It's a holiday; I want to stay happy thoughts and friendly vibes – no death row talk but I do know the Gary Graham case.

The election? I still feel and hope Gore will win at the end of the day. But! But the courts, as you know, I'm sure, will have to allow _all_ the votes to be counted. If they do that, this election is Gore's, I really believe that.

I stayed up the whole night Tues. Nov 7 and I was happy and sad, and then mad, and then worried; I'll tell ya it drained me emotionally – it really did.

No doubt after this there will be big changes in the way we vote. I do think we should get rid of the electoral college vote and elect our president by our national popular vote only.

By the way Nader, as you predicted messed it up for Gore: I do believe even in Florida. Oh well.

I loved it! "The Old Man and the Sea." I was right there in that small boat with him. Yes, he should have taken mandolin, the young boy with him, eh? Hemingway is so hip, isn't he? I really relate to him.

You know I wish the U.S. would open up friendly relationship with Cuba again. I especially enjoy (for awhile – like a night out) the music of Cuba – Latin music. It just feels good. Man, I miss playing my gigs. Somedays I wonder why I keep on livin'. OK Nields, you said no down stuff – oh, yeah, that's right.

You have a good time this weekend, and have a big ol' drink for me and a piece of pumpkin pie, too. My favorite.

Love

Rich

November 29, 2000

Dear Rich,

I had a nice Thanksgiving, thank you. I was invited to a friend's house, there were children around. It is a funny thing though: I don't eat turkey – I am vegetarian, except for sea-food – I hate pumpkin pie (sorry, pal!) and I am off sugar again (I will tell you the story, why) so I can eat nothing but mashed potato. Well, that's a joke, there were plenty of other stuff to eat and I made a vegetarian dish, too. That brings me to your question: I am a good cook! I have dinner guests quite often and I enjoy cooking. I always make up new dishes. Vegetarian cooking can have much more variety and imagination than meat and potato, say. I don't go out eating very often, I prefer the quiet of my house. I have a nice little house and 4 acres of tall trees. It is way off the road and I don't see any neighbors. It's very quiet and I love it. And I can watch an opera in the middle of the night when I feel like it.

The election! I don't even follow it anymore, I am so disgusted. I don't know if there's any hope, may you be right!

Right now the excitement of my life is the upcoming Christmas bazaar which my Amnesty group puts up every year. It is called "Holiday Art Bizarre" and it's next Saturday, the 2nd. A lot of work for me: I go around town "begging" for donations, making up flyers and putting up in shops in town, mailing it, etc. My study is now a holy mess with stuff piling up. We make this way good money for Amnesty – I'm proud to say my group is one of the best fund-raisers in the country. We also combine it with a lecture – this year it will be about the torture campaign and a speaker will come from Oregon. We also offer food: a local restaurant always gives us some goodies and I make a cake. Let's hope it will be a good one this year. We got lots of donations – we sell artworks, toys, jewelry – among them my own "masterpieces" of beads – books, household items, clothes, anything we can get. We also have an Amnesty table with flyers, information, booklets, posters, etc.

Well, till next time my friend.

My best,

Agi

December 3, 2000

Dear Agi,

Well how are you today? I hope all is well on your island. Do you get snow there? Back here in Ohio we are starting to get some snow. How about in Hungary? Does it snow much there?

We still don't have a president-elect, yet. Isn't that something? I still believe Gore won it but it's up to the courts, lawyers, and judges now to what the outcome is going to be. I don't care for lawyers at all, needless to say. I quit watching it on TV because all it is now is partisan politics.

The only thing I kind of worried about is that the media esp. the political pundits are starting to suggest that maybe Gore should concede. I say no way, bullcrap!! See that's one thing (of many things akin to what you said too) about the media I hate.

They get this idea going on the air, at every interview they bring it up until finally the gullible American public starts thinking maybe they're right and Gore should concede.

Yeah, I followed the Gary Graham case as much I could from TV, and newspapers. I agree with you that there <u>was doubt if</u> Graham did that killing. He was convicted on the testimony of a single eyewitness who claimed that she saw him from a distance in a dark parking lot while she was sitting in her car. I don't think that was beyond reasonable doubt especially when there was two other people who saw Graham in the store and said (I don't think they got to testify) but told the police Graham was <u>not</u> the killer. "He was too tall" they said. There you go – that's doubt right there.

Even though Graham was a bad man with a long and violent record, I do believe Texas has killed an innocent man. And I do believe that Texas has killed a lot of innocent people. The justice system in Texas is just horrible.

I've seen it a lot on PBS "Frontline", a legitimate news show. That investigates and documents social issues, and also on 60 Minutes, Dateline, and shows like that. Living in death row you have big interest in following any execution no matter what state it's in.

I'll tell you a case – an execution – that bother me was when Texas executed Karla Fay Tucker. Oh yes, she was guilty and she said so. But when she did her crime she was so messed up on drugs I would say that was temporary insanity. But while in prison I truely believe that she changed; she wasn't faking it she was reborn again of the spirit. Don't kill her, use her for goodness. Put her in general population for the rest of her life and let her teach the inmates that are going back to society someday about the dangers of using drugs and alcohol. She was very capable of doing that. She was articulate, and intelligent, and most importantly, in my book, she was sincere! Needless to say there are a lot of cons in here but some people have a change of heart and I believe she did.

This might sound weird to you but Karla Fay touched me. I know that's strange, even to me. But when I heard her interview I greatly admired her courage at facing her execution which at the time of the last interview was just a day before her date with death. Man! She was so strong. If my day comes, I hope I too can be brave and strong.

I remember the day when the judge sentenced me my legs were literally shaking from fear. I thought that was only in the movies. Yeah, that was the scariest day of my life. I'll never forget it.

I saw two old movies on PBS I enjoyed. 'Raintree County' with the young and beautiful Elizabeth Taylor and the cool Montgomery Clift. And also I really liked: 'The Cat on the Hot Tin Roof' with the delicious E. Taylor and my favorite of all time (well him and Brando) the sublime Paul Newman. I loved the dialogue of Tennessee Williams. That man could write!

Take care Agi – you are a wonderful friend.

Peace & Love

Rich

December 9, 2000

Dear Rich,

Tonight for the first time there's rain mixed with ice. There's not much snow here usually, maybe twice during the winter and it doesn't last long. Except three or four years ago when there was a tremendous snow-storm, about 4 feet of snow – when I opened the door the snow was up to my chest. I was snowed in for a week. They cleared the roads but I have a long drive-way, impossible to get out. But I managed to have a New Year's Eve party anyway. Friends took me to the grocery store and they were parking somewhere nearby. They said the last time this happened was in 1922.

In Hungary there was a lot of snow, winters cold, summers hot, quite regular four seasons. By March spring was there. Here on the island what bothers people is the darkness – being so far north it is dark by 5 pm and just starts to be light at 7am. But then in June it's light till 10pm.

My dear fellow, you are not the only one who was bothered by the execution of Karla Fay Tucker, and it's not strange at all. That beast of W.! See the enclosed letter – now you know better why I hate him so much. The Gary Graham case was also outrageous. He was a bad guy, but obviously innocent of the crime he died for. And he was 17 at the time. Double crime of Texas justice – it's an accepted international law not to kill juveniles. It's absolutely shameful for the US. And that guy spent more than half of his life in the death row. No matter how bad he was, he was punished terribly.

But let's talk about more cheerful things: I have a dog and a cat, both rescued by me from a bad life: the cat I found here on the island before I moved here. I was staying in the bed-and-breakfast place of my real estate agent (I bought the property and let build the house 1 ½ years before I could retire and of course had to come a few times.) I had to step out to smoke – it was winter time and there was that cat who came to me and wanted to get into the house, but was not allowed. One day I picked her up and she started to lick my ears – this seduced me. I took her back to San Francisco and I have her ever since. She is a Siamese-Burmese mix. Her name is Zizi.

My dog, Kali, is also a mix, black and tan. She adopted me – I took her from a neighbor. She was abused and neglected. Now she has a good life. Right now she is lying next to me on her blanket on the couch and is utterly contented. Do you like animals? I love them. Living alone they are my companions, my babies.

This is all for today. Cheers and forget the damned election. Take my motto: Fuck'm all!

Agi

December 27, 2000

Dear Agi,

Happy New Year Agi. Welcome to the 21st century, eh. And a new millennium, too.

Thank you for my Christmas card. The line you wrote..."this is a Christmas card, I shouldn't be goddamshitting" made me laugh. (happy face) I like a woman with a sense of humor. I like to laugh too.

Yes, I like animals, all animals except snakes. I'm scared of those.

I enjoyed your story on how you found Zizi and Kali. And I'm sure they both love you tremendously and are grateful to live in such a warm and friendly house with music in the air. It sounds so cosy. Do you have a fireplace and do you use it, or is it too much of a hassle?

What do you think of Andrea Bocelli's singing? He was on PBS during Christmas week singing, and I thought he sounded pretty good; but is he a legitimate opera singer or is it hype trying to sell it as so?

OK Agi, just a short one this time. Just wanted to thank you for my x-mas card and say Happy New Year!

Love

Rich

January 8, 2001

Dear Rich,

First I try to answer your questions: I don't have a regular fireplace, only a wood-burning stove which I use to heat the house. Only rarely do I put on the electric heat, when it is very cold. So far it's great, very mild weather.

Andrea Bocelli is a perfect example for what publicity can achieve. He is a very mediocre singer, but the poor guy is blind and some agent saw business in him. And he was right.

Did they let you have a little fun during the holidays? I am sad when thinking of you sitting in your cell. Do you get along with other inmates or guards, do you talk with them?

You didn't comment at all about that copy of W's letter and I sense that something you didn't like about it. If so, why? I wrote hundreds of letters trying to save people and sometimes I get answers. That's what Amnesty is about.

Well, cheers my friend,

Agi

February 6, 2001

Dear Rich,

About my arm: that's a long story. 30 years ago I had a mastectomy and there is not enough lymph in my right arm. Three years after the surgery I got a bursitis in that arm, went to a doctor – it was a few weeks before my New York debut recital. The doctor gave me cortisone shots, which enabled me to play the concert. But a few months later I started to feel again the pain. During a concert – I played the Brahms Concerto – something dramatic happened. Starting the third movement:

at this very chord something clicked in my arm and I could hardly raise it. You can't stop in a performance: I clenched my teeth and finished it. A few days later I had another concert, so I ran back to the doctor and got two more shots. Then my calvary started: a few weeks later I woke up with my arm double sized, horribly swollen. I went to one famous New York doctor to the other – every one of them made it worse, so that after a few months I could not raise my arm at all. I lost my job – I was teaching that time but there was also a faculty string quartet which had to stop because of me. I was unemployed for two years. For more than two years I couldn't play at all, but finally a chiropractor cured me. Ever since it was all right, maybe here and there I felt something, but during all my years in SF Opera I worked hard and also played a lot of solo stuff, and my arm was OK. And now I started to feel the same old spot in my arm, who knows why. So naturally I got alarmed and stopped practicing. I will wait for a while and if it doesn't get better I will go to the east coast to see my "pope," the chiropractor who did the job twenty some years ago. That's my sad story in nutshells.

I just got back from town. I bought the dictionary and a novel for you. Enjoy!

My best,

Agi

P.S. I just read about abominations our shithead of President is already doing. Hell, the best is just not to listen or read, to keep our tension down.

January 22, 2001

Dear Agi,

How are you this week? If you are like me (and you are a little bit) you're depressed knowing George W. Bush is sitting in the Oval Office. Damn! Unreal!

Sorry I didn't comment on your letter from George W. Bush. It's just the whole thing makes me tired and depressed and sick inside talking about the mendacity of most politicians.

I guess, in my heart , I've given up on <u>fair</u> justice. Like Bush said in his letter "I concluded that judgments of heart and soul of an individual on death row are best left to a higher authority." And you marked it nauseating hypocrisy! ☺☻ I agree with you, my friend.

But in my heart I don't sing Amazing Justice; I sing Amazing Grace.

I admire you and all peoples of groups like A.I. and others who are trying to make a difference and changes in the justice system and to abolish the death penalty. I salute you. At least you are trying and taking action and not just talking about it. I've never had a friend who is or was a political activist.

In my life I've been self-centered and selfish. I just wanted and did play music, hang with other musicians, and party-women, and drink and smoke pot. And that's what I did for 25 years. Wasted days and wasted nights brings about a wasted life; that should be my epitaph – sad but true.

You asked if I get along with the other inmates. Yeah, I do, OK. I kinda wish there were some older guys in here (my pod) with me. Most of'em are in their mid-thirties and sadly most are lifelong criminals and I don't have much in common with'em. A lot of them like to share, and/or brag about their past crimes i.e. cars they have stolen, houses they have broken into, stores they have robbed and so on, and needless to say I don't care to hear about that.

When in Rome, eh? So I try to be congenial so not to be ostracize because then I would not have anyone to talk to or play chess with. The guards here do not talk to, hang with, befriend anyone. They change all the time, too so that doesn't happen.

Take care, my friend.

Peace & Love

Rich

March 2, 2001

Dear Rich,

As usual you have a few questions – it's good, a clever way to let me talk. Well, I hate New York City – I was there only two years and had bad experiences: in these two years we were twice burglarized in our miserable apartment. My husband's car was stolen and mine wrecked on the street where it was parked. In profession I also had bad experiences: everywhere I worked they intrigued against me when they found out I was any good, afraid for their position. A few people who could have helped me were very nice with words but didn't do anything. It is nice to live in NY if you have money and nice to visit great museums, good concerts, etc.

But if I have to see my "pope" it's not in NY City, it's in Ithaca NY, where I taught for 6 years and yes, I have a few good friends there still. So it won't be unpleasant to go there.

I don't know the book you were talking about, I don't know "Catcher in the Rye" and I don't know Wilbur Smith. But I can tell you about Kafka: he was one of the most influential writers in the 20th century. Czech origin, lived in Austria and wrote in German. One of the so-called "German expressionists," painting everything in the blackest black. One good example is his famous novel "Metamorphosis," where a guy wakes up one morning being "metamorphosed" into a huge insect. I don't advise you to read this stuff, you don't need to be more depressed or have nightmares.

I don't like this kind of art – German expressionism got into all, music, painting, everything. This blackest black is simply not true, just as the blushing virgin of the 19th century wasn't. You know what I mean?

After a very nice winter we had a surprise on 16 Feb.: there was a real snow! Lasted only one day and I think we are heading for spring now. The days are getting longer which is nice.

Well, cheers my friend,

Agi

March 25, 2001

Dear Agi'

Well, how are you doin'? I hope all is well on your island and things are back to normal since the earthquake. I haven't heard from you though so I'll think positive and assume everything is A-OK.

I just finished reading "The Razor's Edge" by Somerset Maugham that you sent me. Fantastic!! One of the best books I've ever read – I really liked the story and loved the characters, all of them. Have you read this book? If not, you should. You'd like it too. Chapter 6 is profound; where Maugham invented the conversation to build up the climax of Larry's guest. (Larry went to an ashram in southern India.)

It got me thinking again about Eastern philosophy – i.e. Karma, reincarnation, enlightenment and so on. I believe in some way these things are true.

Back in the 70s I read some books by Ram Dass that I saw the light so to speak and I never forgot that. I think the name of the books were: 'Be Here Now' and 'The Only Dance There Is.' Yeah, I agreed with a lot of it in theory.

It's easy to talk of these things in words, but to live it, implement the teachings of Buddha and/or Jesus Christ is the hard part. Letting go of my ego, that's the difficult part I'm talking about. In my opinion, I think Jesus and Buddha, and others too, reached the state of enlightenment because they had no ego and created no karma. I think maybe our life's purpose is to become enlighten (sic) and maybe we do keep coming back until we get it right. And maybe we do pay for bad karma from previous lives – it's a possibility. I feel and can see with my mind's eye. The law of karma is "what comes around goes around" and in the Bible it's "as you sow, so shall you reap" – same thing, eh?

Some news on my case: My direct appeal has been scheduled for oral argument on Wednesday, April 25th. I'm moving on through the system quickly under the new law. I'm passing up guys who have been here 8-9 years. Anyway, I will not be returned to court for the hearing, only my lawyers will go.

It's been a long, cold winter up here in Ohio, and I'm really lookin' forward to getting outside hopefully later this month if it warms up and doesn't snow anymore. I haven't been outside since last October and believe me I could use some fresh air and sunbeams.

I am one white guy in a grey world trying to keep my disposition sunny which ain't easy needless to say.

Hard to believe it's been four years this Tuesday March 27. And, truth be told, not many days go by where I don't think about what took place that night in the kitchen on March 27, 1997.

The sharp edge of a razor is difficult to pass over; thus the wise say the path to salvation is hard.

Touche. Peace & Love

Rich

April 3, 2001

Dear Rich,

Meanwhile you must have gotten my short note, thanks for your letter. Eastern philosophy and Buddhism interested me very much, I think I told you. It's very good what you are saying about it. I came to the conclusion that you don't have to choose between Buddha and Jesus Christ or Mohamed and Moses. They were all great men and all wanted the same, but I don't believe any of them has the absolute truth. So meditate, find out the truth about yourself and have faith. I don't think the path to salvation is hard, actually there is some <u>evidence</u> that it isn't. I'm thinking o the so-called near-death experience, do you know about it? If you are interested I can send you some books. Anyhow, people who <u>actually died</u> and were revived tell amazingly the same story – it looks like we all go to heaven. It's beautiful, utter peace and love and all that.

Right now I am sick as a dog, have an awful cold, congestion and coughing terribly. I can't smoke! That's not fair. Well, I went to the doctor and got some medication, it supposed to get better by tomorrow.

I did read "The Razor's Edge" and have seen the movie recently. Yes, it's good and interesting.

You weren't outside since October! That's terrible! Those guys shouldn't treat you like that, that's criminal.

Well, that's all for now.

Cheers,

Agi

P.S. You might be interested to know that I met Ram Dass.

April 1, 2001

Dear Rich,

Just a quick note now: I contacted Amnesty about your upcoming hearing. I just talked to the person and they might be able to help you, but they need to know your lawyer and more detail about your case. A year ago I sent a copy of your letter to the man – I hope you don't mind – where you described what happened on that fateful day, so they know something about your case.

So, if they contact you, trust him and tell everything you told me. His name is Michael K. I hope to God they can help you.

More soon. (I got your letter, will answer.)

Cheers,

Agi

April 8, 2001

Dear Agi,

How are you feeling today? Hopefully happy, joyous, and free.

Yes I got your note and your letter of (no date) first week of April.

"Catcher in the Rye" by J.D. Salinger is considered an American classic. I always wanted to read it because I've always heard it was good and, yes, it was very good. Not a great book like Razor's Edge but nonetheless a good and entertaining story.

So you met Ram Dass, eh? Tell me about it when you're in the mood.

You asked me if I'd be interested in reading a book on near death experiences. Yes I would but only one book on this subject, for now. I don't want to dwell on death too much. I still wish and think life, culture, music, good stories, art, chess – things that make me feel good. I know death is coming but I'm in no hurry…hell who is, huh?

Death will be coming here next week in Ohio's death row. A man who I don't know, Jay Scott, is going to be executed.

I've been going to the dentist and having all of my top teeth pulled out so I can get dentures up there, He, the dentist, is good. No pain; just a little scary when I hear the snaps, crackle, and pop of bone breaking off. Two more visits and he should be done pulling teeth, thank God.

You are a special person, a gifted musician, a loyal friend, indeed.

Peace & Love

Rich

April 23, 2001

Dear Rich,

Why the hell are they pulling out your teeth? That's pretty awful. Do you have a gum disease? Well, hopefully you get soon your denture and will be all right.

My book came out; I will send you a copy soon. It's quite a proud feeling to be a published author, at my age for the first time, especially because it's not my profession. Talking about books, the encyclopedia you were asking for is available only in hardback, so... About the near-death experience: I am sorry if you felt like I am talking about it because you are on death row – hell, I sincerely hope you won't end your life there. But we are all going to die and I think the near-death experience is the best news that could be at all. Those who experienced it – and there are many! More than you think – have no fear of death whatsoever. They all describe it in a way that's almost too good to believe. I am very interested in this, have many books about it and I wanted to share it with you. I will send one along with my book.

How I met Ram Dass? I met him just shortly in a Sufi camp. Sufis are a spiritual sect, derived from Muslims. I had a guru, a Sufi master. There was nothing like a religion, nothing like anything Muslim, just meditations. I went several times to summer camps with him, back in my San Francisco years.

I am holding my fingers crossed for your hearing. I hope Mr. K contacted you and they would assist you. Please, let me know right away how it went.

Cheers,

Agi

May 5, 2001

How are you, my friend? I hope all is well on the home-front and you're feeling better.

I thought I'd drop a line and let you know what's going on with my case. Well actually I'm meeting with my lawyer next week so I'll know more after that, of course. But, I did get a letter from him, Mr. L, my lawyer, who is doing my direct appeal; and he said that things went pretty well. He feels, and knows, that my case never should have been charged as a capital offense. He got some ammunition for the argument in an article in the Cleveland Plain Dealer (local paper) in which Ohio Supreme Court Justice Paul Pfeifer (who assisted in writing Ohio's current death penalty law) berated the court for its failure to provide oversight in death penalty cases. He used that information as the basis for our argument that my death sentence should be found invalid under the court's "statutorily mandated proportionality review." In other words, he argued that the facts of my case did not merit a death sentence. He went on to say that our argument created quite a bit of controversy among the Justices. He said that Justice Pfeifer asked a number of pointed questions of the Hamilton County Prosecutor, which seemed to indicate that he was favoring our argument. Man, let's hope so, huh?

Anyway, I'll be seeing him next week; I'll let you know what happens.

Peace & Love

Rich

May 20, 2001

Dear Agi,

How are you my friend? You know the first thing I want to say to you is – wow, I am really proud of you and congratulations on getting your book published! That is truely something to be proud of for anyone to write a book and get it published. I am anxiously looking forward to reading it.

Yeah, the dentist pulled out all of my upper teeth because they were getting loose and a few of'em were painful because they were bad.

I saw my lawyer last week and, truth be told, I really don't have much faith in him. These public defenders are more like public pretenders; they do, at best, a perfunctory job and it leaves me feeling hopeless. But I laugh and I'm not worried about it anymore Whatever happens…well, shit happens, right?

Mr. L, my lawyer, didn't say much more than what I've told you in my last letter. We are just hoping that Justice Paul Pfeifer writes a dissension, which can be helpful down the road when we get to the Federal Courts.

I'll write more when I get up again; lately I'm down and when I'm down I go quiet. Send me your book; I want to read it

Peace & Love – God bless, your friend

Rich

May 28, 2001

Dear Rich,

So, you are "down," friend. Depressed? Sick? It is awful you have no upper teeth; you must not be able to chew at all. How are you eating? Would they give you special food? I hope you get it done soon.

I will send my book soon, but you know it already pretty well. I worked on it a bit before it got published but most of it you know. I am getting nice comments, here many people know me and buy it. The library has 3 copies and apparently it's in much demand.

I am glad your hearing went rather well (so why are you down?) I find interesting that you don't comment at all about my trying to help you. Something you don't like about it, that's clear. But why? What? Out with it if you are my friend! I won't be offended, whatever it is, I promise.

Mr. K told me also that they are working on a moratorium in Ohio and they hope it will happen next year. They did get in touch with your lawyer and keep in mind your case.

So cheer up! Do you have good books to read? Playing chess, doing crossword puzzles? Do you want me to send some good novels?

Write soon.

All my best,

Agi

June 20, 2001

Dear Rich,

Of course you get depressed, it's more than natural, you are absolutely right. Yes, of course, we in AI are working to abolish the death penalty. I am writing hundreds of letters to governors, attorney generals, and so on. And it looks like our efforts bear some fruits now. The execution of Timothy McVeigh was one of those which caused international and national bad feelings. One of the papers in Oklahoma, which was favoring the death penalty, wrote that the abolition is a question of time. But we don't only work for the big picture, it's possible that they can help you. Well, enough of that, I don't want to give you false hopes.

I ordered a book for you, which I like very much and I hope you will enjoy it. It is very sexy and a great novel. I will pick it up tomorrow and send it along with my book.

Weather is funny here, May and June was mostly cold. Here and there we had beautiful days, but then it went back to cold. Today it's great, warm and real summery. Days are very long now – it's way up in north – at 10pm is not quite dark yet.

I'm planning a recital here and maybe on the neighbor island for early September. I got this time a pianist I like very much. She was my steady partner in San Francisco and she agreed to come to play with me. On my last recital I wasn't happy with my pianist.

Write soon, I always enjoy your letters.

Love,

Agi

July 2, 2001

Dear Agi,

Hello my friend. I hope this letter finds you well and feeling good. I bet it's real pretty there on your island in July,eh? I'm sure it is.

The weather back here feels good, hot and sunny – on the days I get to go out. During the summer, they let me go outside every fourth day to the outside rec cage. I'm always in a cage of some kind; just like an animal at the zoo, except the animals are treated with loving care and here apathy is the best I get from my keepers. Oh well.

So you are going to give another recital this fall, I see. But this time with a pianist you know from San Francisco which I'm sure will make the music a lot smoother. What pieces are you going to play?

Well , there's some whispers going around that Mansfield is going to open a new unit for 40 men. In this new unit, it will be more open for the inmates – i.e. not locked in our cells all day. The cell doors will be open for the 'honor' inmates to come and go in and out of the pod. I don't know all the particulars, and Man.C.I. moves slowly on these kind of things.

God bless Jack Lemmon. He did A-OK with his talent. Truth: sometimes his nervous act got on my nerves. And, then, some of his movies/characters I enjoyed. One to rent (if you haven't) "The Days of Wine and Roses." A story of an alcoholic.

By the way, I loved "Daughter of Fortune." I enjoyed reading about how it was (pretty crazy) in San Francisco in 1849. Back in 1972 I went to China town, up by Broadway, I remember, and this book brought back the sights and sounds of that area I had a wonderful time there.

Enjoy your life, my friend.

Peace & Love

Rich

July 5, 2001

Hi Agi,

I wanted to drop a line and thank you for the two books I got this morning from you. "Dona Flor and Her Two Husbands" and your book. ☺ Thanks for signing your book; that made me feel special and good. Also, I'm very proud of you for writing and following through and completing your story. The picture of you on the front cover is darling. And still today , you are that and more.

You are talented, compassionate, and very kind-hearted. I'm truely honored to be in your life and that you call me friend.

Love,

Rich

July 11, 2001

Hello, my friend,

I just watched a wonderful movie with such beautiful violin music played all the way through; it really touched me – gave me cold chills – you have to hear this! The name of the movie, that is at your video store now is: "The Red Violin." I really want you to see this film I'm sure you will truely enjoy it. I think the solo violin parts in the filmscore was played by a musician name Joshua Bell (I think?) I tried to catch the name but the credits went by pretty fast.

The story is about a violin built in the 1600s and worth millions today and what happened to people who owned it through the years.

Writing fast so I can mail this tonight.

Please rent this –"The Red Violin."

Your fan and loyal friend,

Rich

July 14, 2001

Dear Rich,

Thanks for your two letters, the second was especially nice, friend. I hope you will enjoy "Dona Flor," I love that author. It is funny and sexy. Amado is a Brazilian, a Nobel prize winner. You will find a few new things in my book, but a lot of it you know already. People seem to like it. The library has three copies of it and it's never there – I think it's great.

My pianist in San Francisco can't come after all, so I had some trouble finding one I know and like. Finally, today, an old partner of mine agreed to come – from the East Coast! But I will have to reschedule the concert because he can't come that time. What will I play, you ask. The so-called Kreutzer Sonata by Beethoven – he dedicated it to Rudolph Kreutzer a famous violinist that time. It's a big, wonderful piece. Then I will play the famous "Chaconne" by Bach. It's for violin solo, a great masterpiece. The second half will be two French pieces: Chausson: Poeme and Ravel: Tzigane, both very beautiful, the Ravel is a fire-work of virtuosity. It's a good program. There will be two concerts, one on a neighbor island, and maybe even a third one, on another island.

The weather is finally summery here – May and June was mostly cold and rainy. I like warmth and sunshine, love to swim. There is a lake nearby and I will start going there pretty soon.

In August there will be the annual San Juan County Fair where we – the Amnesty group – always have a booth.

Well, till next time my friend.

Love,

Agi

P.S. I hope you got your denture by now.

August 12, 2001

Dear Rich,

My house is a mess, packing for the Fair. Tomorrow morning guys are coming to take the big wooden board, pick up a big table at a church – they are lending it – and Tuesday I will have to arrange all. Here is a picture, that's what it looks like, except now we have a big colorful centerpiece, which looks nicer. On the left you can see my masterpieces of necklaces.

To answer your last letter: I have seen "The Red Violin" two years ago in New York. It is very interesting, good violin playing by Joshua Bell. But to be honest with you, a few things irritated me a lot: blood in the varnish? Bull. The "great teacher" whose "method" is to take a metronome and get faster and faster? Terrible. And playing the violin while f…making love?? Come on! I guess no violinist should see it, because these things ruin the overall value of the movie. Sorry pal, if I cooled your enthusiasm.

Talking about violin, I had to re-schedule my recital to January, I couldn't get the right pianist for September. Maybe I told you this already. In January this nice guy, with whom I played before, will come from Ithaca NY.

It is finally summer weather here and I went swimming in the nearby lake. I love that.

Well, till next time.

Greetings,

Agi

August 21, 2001

Dear Agi,

Hello my friend. I got your letter and picture of 8/12; always good to hear from you.

Well, I hope the fair was a huge success for your Amnesty International group, where you raised awareness of the issues to the people on your island, and made some money too, to support your diligent effort.

So, you saw the movie, "The Red Violin," eh? No, you didn't cool my enthusiasm at all – it's just a movie. Our friendship is on the level, at least, where we can agree or disagree without any bad or hurt feelings. I prefer to keep it honest – my opinion – and I know you do too.

Besides, on the subject of films, books, and music all opinions are subjective at best. Which is better an apple or an orange? Beethoven or Haydn? The Beatles or Rolling Stones?

Speaking of subjective opinions, this book "Dona Flor"…well I don't like it – I can't read it – it's redundant! Believe me I'm trying to get through it but man, oh man, come on enough about Vadinho, already, he's dead and buried let's go on now, and why is everybody named Dona? (I'm on page 200 and I'll try to finish but it's an arduous read.) I think he, Jorge, <u>is too wordy.</u>

So you went swimming in a lake, eh? Yeah, now that sounds great, refreshing, I'm sure.

Nothing new here happening lately. No news on my case, which is okay with me, because usually I get only bad news when I hear from my lawyers.

I think there is an execution here sometime next month, and I heard that the inmate is asking to be executed by the electric chair instead of the needle which is weird, I think. Why he's doing that, I don't know. Why go through all that pain with the chair?

Sorry this is not an 'up' letter but I'm down again and I'm sure I sound redundant too a lot of times. I'll get back up and be back soon.

God bless.

Love,

Rich

September 4, 2001

Dear Agi,

Well, hello my friend and how are you today? Are you keeping up your swimming in the lake? How rejuvenating that must feel to swim in lake water of the Northwest instead of a pool with chemicals. I bet it's a tad cold at first, eh?

Nothing new here going on, nothing that's interesting anyway, to me.

I just wanted to say hi and to apologize for my last letter, which I'm thinking might have been a tad sharp or biting or harsh because that is what my mood has been lately, so please forgive me for being uncouth if I was. (I don't remember verbatim what I wrote, but I recall the mood.)

I have stopped on the Dona Flor book for now but I promise I'm keeping it to finish when my mood brightens up. Also I still have The Saxon Shore book to finish that too after I finish the one I'm reading now, Shogun. Shogun is fantastic. It grabbed me at the very beginning and hasn't let go yet. Have you read it? Did you like it? You definitely don't want to piss off a Japanese samurai, ha?

Have you been to Asia? If given a chance, would you want to visit Japan or China or Vietnam or any Asia country? Do you like oriental food? How about Japanese music, have you ever studied oriental scales with their quarter tones? (You could play quarter tones on violin but not on a piano.)

We should talk more on films. Don't you rent movies? What's the last good movie you watched? Enjoy your summer.

Your friend, peace and love,

Rich

September 7, 2001

Dear Rich,

Well, we are even now: I didn't like the "Red Violin" and you "Dona Flor." Yes of course, I prefer to be honest, that's fine. In case you didn't finish the book: the joke is that she marries a man exactly the opposite of Vadinho, he is very proper and boring, the kind who does it Wednesdays and Saturdays. So one day while they are at it, Vadinho appears, laughing his head off on the way it goes and he and Dona Flor are back making love. And from then on he is always at her side, invisible to all but her. In the movie they made of it, Dona Flor goes out with her proper husband and at her other side there is Vadinho, naked. I find it very funny and psychologically very clear.

We did make a huge success at the Fair: made 965 dollars, more than ever. And it was because of my book which sold like hot cake. We didn't have enough of it, there is a waiting list of 21. I am a best-selling author in Friday Harbor, hey that's something. I also got the first royalty check, I was very proud. We also filled 23 sheets of petitions, 9 of it for a moratorium on the death penalty. And there was a vendor just a few feet from us who turned out to be a Russian who was a political prisoner in the Soviet Union and Amnesty helped him. It was the best advertisement for us.

It is already like fall here – I just put on the heat, I was so cold, a shame in early September. And there was very little summer, here and there a few warm days.

Cheer up, my friend.

Love

Agi

September 17, 2001

Dear Agi,

Praise the Lord and pass the ammunition, eh? Being facetious but with some sad honesty too. There's going to be more blood, that's for sure.

I imagine you have probably walked by the towers of the World Trade Center, whilst living in New York City? So beautiful, those towers. I was completely shocked when I saw "live" on TV the towers fall – I couldn't believe it.

I thought after the towers withstood the two plane crashes that the firemen would go up (which they did) and just get the fire out. But now I know, like everyone else, that a jet fuel fire gets so hot – 1500 to 2000 degrees

– that the skin of the building and the steel itself began to buckle and finally fall in on itself and pancake down very fast. Horrible, so horrible!

Airport security that day was lax, needless to say. How these terrorists could hijack four planes and use them as flying bombs just really, really pisses me off. Unreal! Those stories of people calling from their cell phones from the flames of the towers and the planes, too, saying goodbye to their loved ones really tear me up sometimes.

I had and have so many different emotions this past week: sorrow, pride and probably most anger. This week I'm going to spend more time in my Bible. I find comfort there in God's word. Truth be told: I'm not real good at praying for a long period of time anyway- but I do enjoy reading and studying the word in both the New Test and the Old Test.

King David was a great man of war. He was fighting God's special people-Israel's enemies three thousand years ago. Question: have you ever read your history? The reason I asked is that you don't speak of God much and I wonder if you are agnostic or some "new-age" something.

Even though I live on death row, I'm a patriotic man – I love America. God bless America, God bless the Earth, God bless you Agi.

I'll be back soon. Oh yeah, I got your 9/7 letter. Glad to hear your fair was a success and your book is selling. You're a wonderful person and a cherished friend.

Peace & Love,
Rich

October 1, 2001

Dear Rich,

I have two letters from you before me. One written after the catastrophe, conveying your feelings – I can't add anything to that, I guess you expressed well everybody's thoughts and feelings. In a way this, what happened, will do some good, too, security and anti-terrorist action will probably increase in the whole world. They won't be able to do anything easily from now on.

In your earlier letter you ask me questions: I was in Asia very shortly, in India and Nepal. I would like to know more and see other countries, and I love oriental food, especially Indonesian and Thai. About movies: I do rent some here and there, but very often shut it off after a few minutes – I can't stand violence, it gives me nightmares, and raw sex disgusts me. I like old classical movies, I have some. I love Chaplin, have 11 videos of his. Also some French classics and, of course, some Hungarian ones.

I am not an agnostic. I believe there is something out there, call it God or whatever. But I don't believe in any religion, they are all <u>man-made</u> in my opinion. In other words I am spiritual but not religious.

Well, cheers my friend,

Agi

October 10, 2001

Dear Agi,

Well how are you doing? Are you enjoying the autumnal season? Fall back here in Ohio is pretty. You can see the trees with their leaves turning colors, but I don't have any trees in the view from my window. I wish I did though - I love trees.

I was wondering if you would do me a favor and this won't cost you anything.

Look on your computer either on the internet or if you have 'Windows' on your hardware and look in your encyclopedia and find the "RULES OF CHESS" and if you can the "HISTORY OF CHESS." I would like to read and know both.

My game is getting better because of the wonderful book you got me. But there are no rules in there – no explanation of "En Passant" that I'm interested in. There's some other ones too.

So, if you will, and can, get me any information on rules of chess. The history of chess is just for my own curiosity; I love the game and I want to know some of its history. There have been a few heated arguments over what is a <u>set rule</u> and what is an arbitrary rule, and so on.

Also, while you're on your computer can you get me a small article on the war of 1812?

If you can't find these things on your computer maybe a small book that college kids use for a quick study – you know what cliff-notes are – I'm sure.

So, that's my request: rules of chess and history of chess, and the war of 1812.

Truth be told: I'm having a small disagreement with an inmate and I need to prove my point and if you can find these things it will.

Thanks Agi. More later.

Peace and love,

Rich

October 16, 2001

Dear Rich,

I'm so sorry, I couldn't get anything on my internet about your request. Well, I just got a new computer, I still have to learn about it. I am also stupid with computers. I got only books indicated when I looked up "Rules of chess." But ask me questions, I might know the answers. For example "en passant": when your pawn is in your original square and the "enemy" pawn is two spaces above next to yours; if you move your pawn two squares, he could take it <u>as if it would have moved only</u> <u>one square, but only if you do it right away</u>, next move. (picture) Is that any clear? If not, I will try to explain again. What other questions do you have? Any other rules (other than how pieces are moving, which you certainly know) are castling: the king moves two squares on either side and the rook comes next to it – but only if neither rook nor king moved before and not under check and <u>not if</u> <u>the king has to pass a square which is under check.</u> The only other rule I can think of is: when a pawn goes all the way through the other end you can change it for whatever you want – naturally one changes it to queen most of the time.

I will look for a "History of Chess" book. Any other book you would like? Do you have anything nice to read?

The war of 1812: hey my friend, you give me tough tasks. I tell you what I know about it: Napoleon invaded Russia that year, went as far as Moscow, but it was empty. Everybody fled and the few remaining ones set fire to the city, which practically burned down. Then they defeated him in Borodino – the French army retreated and the Russian winter, extremely cold, did the rest: they were driven out of the country. (By the way of human stupidity: Hitler fared the same way.) The thing to read about it would be Tolstoy's famous novel: "War and Peace" – but it is very long, I don't know if you would want to go through with it. If so, I would be glad to send it to you. It is one of the great masterpieces of literature and there is also a beautiful story of personal fates and love.

This is it for now, cheers my friend,

Agi

October 31, 2001

Dear Agi,

Thank you for the books, "Anne Frank" and "Plainsong." I just got'em yesterday and I'm looking forward to reading them.

Thanks for info on 'en passant' you're right on that and I understand.

The war of 1812, sorry I wasn't clear on that; I meant the war in America, where the British burnt down the White House in Wash. D.C. An inmate upstairs got a book on it and I'm going to read it after he's finished.

No new news here – just a drag. I can't even get through Shogun so I think I'll stop on it for awhile and read Plainsong. That looks like a feel-good book I can get into.

I do have something (news) I will write to you about later – once again lately I'm down – but I heard back from the Ohio Supreme Court and they affirmed my conviction and death sentence. I even got an execution date of Nov. 27, 2001. (Next month!) (No wonder I'm depressed.) Boy, that was a weird letter to receive, needless to say. We are filing a motion to stay and, of course, we'll get one. (I did get one dissent which might be of some help down the road; later I'll write on this subject.)

Also, I lost a nephew due to the plague to my family – alcoholism. I don't have much family left and those people never write, visit or anything. The only one who writes 2 or 3 times a year is Rochelle, my older sister it was her son who died from a fall whilst drunk. (More on this later – if you want to hear it.)

OK, my friend I'll write soon and share some new news on my case – in case you're wondering – corny pun, eh?

Thank you for the books. I needed that.

God bless, Agi.

Peace and love,

Rich

November 10, 2001

Dear Agi,

Hello, my friend. I hope all is well with you and your island.

I'm doing OK this week. I just got back from Holt, Colorado. I met a man named Guthrie and his two sons Ike and Bobby. A nice family. Ella, Guthrie's wife, has left for Denver to live with her sister. She (Ella) needs therapy to help her come out of her depression. It's hard on Ike and Bobby; they miss their mom. But Guthrie, yeah, he'll be alright, and I hope he and Maggie Jones get it together, which I think they will.

The McPhersons' brothers…man, I love those guys. What they did with Vicky was so beautiful I was rooting for all three- the brothers and her- that it would work out. That girl needed some love and real friendship, and Raymond and Harold came trough like two angels on earth; God bless'em.

Anyway, I know you know the story. It was so captivating I read the whole book in one day and I didn't want it to end. It was so <u>real</u> to me. I could relate to a lot of it. I also grew up in a very small town; the people and circumstances. As a kid, I had a paper route, a bike, stole cigarettes from dad, put coins on the railroad track, saw a little sex through a window, had a real old lady friend, my grandma, who made tea, cookies, milk potatoes and baloney sandwiches for us to eat. (A psychic once – a long time ago – told me that when I die my grandma will be there to help me through to the other side.) I kind of believe that; I see her a lot in my dreams.

Yeah, I love this book. So simple yet so real or surreal to me. To me a true picture of small town USA. When I tuned twenty, I couldn't wait to get out and go to the big city. But now, when I dream, I don't dream of the big city, I dream of Aurora, Indiana.

Life is a cycle. The man becomes a child. I just want to go home and ride my bike down Main Street and sit on the edge of the river and watch the boats and barges go by.

Till next time – Peace and love – your friend,
Rich

November 17, 2001
Dear Rich,

I have two of your letters to answer. When I got the second one I thought for a moment you were out of your mind: "I just got back from Holt, Colorado." You know I didn't read that book, just picked it randomly in the bookstore. I'm glad you enjoyed it so much. How is the other one, Anne Frank?

Here is something important: I have a good friend, a writer, with whom I will do a joint book-reading on Dec. 2, at our annual Christmas sale. She wrote a book about the WTO in Seattle.* She just came by and your latest letter was on my table – she knows about our correspondence and finds your letters very nice and touching. She would like to read one or two of your letters at that reading event – do you object? Also she would like to have my letters to you. Do you have them, or some of them? If so send it to me <u>right</u> <u>away</u>, so I get them before Dec. 2. Of course I would send them back if you want them.

My poor friend, I wish you could sit at the river to watch boats go by – it is my ardent wish that you could do that one day.

Till next time. Cheers,

Agi

She is of course Janet Thomas

November 26, 2001

Dear Rich,

I am right now very busy with organizing the "Bizarre," as we call it. It involves "begging," going around town asking for donations, printing and making flyers, making sure that everything is ready at the place, etc. It's fun but a lot of work.

A bad news: one of my dear friends – the husband of the lady who wanted to visit you; they live near Mansfield – has cancer, a bad kind. He is about your age. His father, also a friend, lives here, the violinist I mentioned before. That poor guy is struggling with his wife, also very sick, and now his son, a wonderful cellist…Very upsetting.

Till next time, best wishes,

Agi

November 26, 2001

Dear Agi,

Just a quick note before the C.O. comes to collect the mail.

I just got your letter a few minutes ago so I'm making to get your letter out.

Yes it is OK for you to read my letters, or your friend to read them.

In fact, I feel honored…well maybe not honored…can't think of a word – well I just feel good you'd want to read 'em out to people. Thanks. You make me feel special – you always have, my friend.

I have all your letters here. I just picked these at random. If I'd more time, I would have reread all of 'em to choose the finest ones. But heck, they're all fine.

More later.

Peace and love,

Rich

December 19, 2001

Dear Agi, my Angel

I'm going to order commission tomorrow and get me some sweets – yeah, I do have a sweet tooth – most alcoholics do, and I'll store up on tobacco, coffee, tea, rice and ramen noodles, and cereal.

In case you are wondering, yes, I have a hot-pot in my cell. That's how I fix my coffee and tea and prepare my rice and soups etc.

The food here, needless to say, I'm sure, is pretty bad. And we basically get the same dishes every week. They serve us a lot of pork for some reason and it's terrible in sight and taste. They don't cook it enough. I like those Ramen noodles with oriental rice added to the mix.

The best meal they fix here is breakfast. Usually we get eggs, either scrambled or hard-boiled. Sometimes the scrambled ones are green but they still taste okay, and I put ketchup on them anyway. (My second wife, who was Chicano, got me started on that-putting ketchup on eggs. Do you like a little ketchup on your fried or scrambled eggs? (I bet you don't.)

My favorite egg breakfast without a doubt, when I'm a free man, is eggs benedict – hum-hum good. I like that sauce they put on it. And, once in a while, we get French toast for breakfast. And that's not bad at all. So breakfast is the best meal; also we get cereal and peanut butter and jelly w/ bread, sometimes.

But lunch and dinner? You definitely have to add, embellish it, to give it some flavor – i.e. add spices like Cajun seasoning, minced onions, bacon bits, parmesan cheese, BBQ sauce etc., whatever it takes. Sometimes nothing can help, so I just give it back and make rice & noodles.

Anyway, Agi, with all my heart, thank you for making this sad situation I'm in better. Thank you for being in my life and for making me a part of your life on your island – I like that.

More news next time on my case; I have some stuff I want to share about what the Ohio Supreme Ct. had to say. Be happy (coda). If I was there, and I wish I was, I'd give you a big hug and kiss. SWAK

Love,

Rich

December 30, 2001

Dear Agi,

Thank you for my Christmas card and Happy New Year to you, my friend. Hard to believe it's the year 2002, eh? Man! Time sure does fly about $\int$ =220 even when you're not having fun.

Hell no we don't get anything extra for Xmas in here except for a turkey for dinner and a piece of apple pie for lunch Xmas day. You really wouldn't even know it's the holidays on death row except for the things you see and hear on the radio and TV.

In general population, I have heard, they have Xmas parties, and decorations for the inmates within reason. They have groups from the outside to come in and play music and sing; actually in general pop. They have concerts year round, I hear. Musical groups of all kinds volunteer to come in and play. Life is so ironic: I even played (volunteered) to play with a jazz band at a prison in Chino California back in 1977 or '78. Anyway, it was OK, and definitely a captive audience needless to say. But I never imagined in a million years that 20 years down the road of my life – which was at that time starting to get out of control – that I'd end up living in a prison in the winter of my life.

Man, it's cold! And I'm not talking about the temperature. It's a cold, cold world where men grow older but not necessarily wiser or kinder.

I've been here at Mansfield 4 years now; I got here Dec. 23, 1997. My first few years I was worried about all the guilt and pain I created along with having to live in a cold world where kindness is looked upon as weakness and know that my heart would harden so much I would never feel anything good again. But I was wrong. Through you I have seen the very best sides of the human spirit and human dignity and wisdom.

Truth be told: I'm honored to be in your life and that we are friends. I know your story – not all of it but some – and you have seen and experienced more than most by far. That's why you're a woman of compassion, i.e.: fear, pain, oppression, hate and other negative vibes, you know first-hand; you understand. OK, let's change the subject, shall we? I'm starting to babble and drivel.

News on my case: the Ohio Supreme Ct., as expected, affirmed my conviction & death sentence. I got one written dissent from Justice Paul Pfeifer. He said: "The type of crime that Nields did is not the type of crime the General Assembly did contemplate or should have contemplated as a death penalty offense. While Nields took some traveler's checks and drove off in the victim's car, thereby satisfying the requisite robbery element for a death penalty offense, this case is not about robbery. (Very true!) It is about alcoholism, rage, and rejection (true) and about Nields inability to cope with any of them. It is a crime of passion imbued with pathos and reeking of alcohol. It is a crime that is all too common, but in stealing some traveler's checks, Nields bought himself a death sentence." Pfeifer then goes on to criticize the Hamilton County Prosecutor's Office for failing to exercise its discretion "to look for reasons to spare persons from the death penalty rather than to look for ways to shoehorn cases into the death penalty scheme. I believe that Ohioans thirst for justice, not blood," unquote.

My case is headed to the US Supreme Ct. and it will be kicked back down to the state's Federal Court probably by next summer. If I'm going to get a lighter sentence, that is where it will happen – in the State's Fed. Ct. Because I'm under this new law (1996) no one knows how long it will take to get through the system – but I'm moving fast I 'll tell you that! I have passed inmates through the system that have been here over 10 years already.

My lawyer thinks about 4 to 5 years left before I'm completely finished with appeals. So we will just have to wait and see what's in God's plan.

I'm so sorry to read of your friends – the cellist, and the father's wife – being so ill. Life is fragile. You take care of yourself my friend. Have fun playing your concerts – music is joy.

Thanks for your friendship, love & support,
Rich

January 5, 2002
Dear Rich, my friend,

Your letter, which I got today, is really wonderful. If I help you keeping your human spirit in your terrible world, that's the best thing I've ever done.

Bless the heart of Judge Pfeifer! It is only sad that he was the only one seeing your case the right way. Everybody else is stupid and evil? Hell.

I don't like the fact that your case is going fast. Time is working for you! Tell your lawyer to slow it down if possible. Although 4 or 5 years is a lot of time and the tide is slowly but surely turning about the death penalty. It is already clear that it's an international shame and the whole civilized world is looking down on the US. There were already cases where other countries refused to extradite criminals because they would face the death penalty here. England declared that if they capture bin Osama they wouldn't turn him here because of that.

I have two concerts next week, Friday on a neighbor island and Saturday here. My pianist is coming Tuesday with his wife who used to be my pupil. I didn't see them for about 20 years. Last I played with him in New York in a centennial recital of Bela Bartok, the great Hungarian composer. It was in 1981. It will be nice to see him.

Till next, bless you,

Agi

January 22, 2002

Dear Agi,

How you doin', my friend? I hope this letter finds you well and happy.

I was just re-reading your Jan. 5 letter and wondering how your concerts went? Did you play well? Was it an enjoyable experience for ya?

When I was playing six nights a week, my 'chops' stayed sharp. It always felt good to play; i.e., my fingers, the agility, strength, you know, all those things were always there. But, in contrast, whenever I would have time between gigs, it sure didn't take long to feel out of it.

Note: I think because I usually drank so much, that my fingers would always tend to get fat on me real fast i.e. bloated.

Anyway, my short question became long (sorry) but how does it feel to play gigs with so much time between jobs? Do you keep your chops up by practicing scales etc. on a regular basis? Do you miss your job down in San Fran.? I'm sure that's a yes a little and a no, too, eh? Probably miss your friends and the camaraderie but, of course, not the headaches.

In truth, I sure miss playing. I miss playing music more than I miss sex.

Peace and love,

Rich

January 25, 2002

Dear Rich,

Sorry for the delay to send back these letters. I find it quite touching that you numbered and highlighted them. My friend is crazy about our correspondence and talking about publishing them. That's not to be taken too seriously, to be sure.

I didn't hear from you lately. Are you all right?

I had my concerts which were much acclaimed, but I wasn't happy about them. But I had a very good time with my pianist friend – who played wonderfully – and his wife, my former student. They stayed a week, two days after the concerts, when I drove them around the island and had a nice party for them. It was all really nice. He is a real good guy and a wonderful musician.

As ever,

Agi

February 3, 2002

Dear Agi,

Hello, my friend. I hope all is well on your island and in your life. I feel better lately.

I used to play this beautiful tune called "Laura" (not Laura's theme from Dr. Zhivago) but from a film made in 1945: "Laura", starring Gene Tierney, Dana Andrews, Vincent Price and Clifton Webb. I enjoyed the film; a neat little mystery, drama, whodunit type of movie.

In truth, this is the first time I have seen the actress Gene Tierney, and in my opinion, a fine actor and very beautiful indeed.

When I started playing by myself, doing yellow cocktail music dinner music, I was learning all these older songs from the '20s through the '40s, which I liked. But a lot of them I had no idea where they came from, or actually what they were about ("they" meaning the fictional character.)

It's a trip when I see one of these old black & white films – which I always enjoy, more and more, it seems lately – and I hear a tune or song I used to play and my talking to myself head goes, wow, I didn't know that tune was from that movie; well hell, just color me stupid.

On PBS on Saturday nights, they play old classics, without interruption. I love these old movies. The dialogue tells the story and not special effects like in today's films. I don't have to explain to you, I know you know.

Last month I saw 'The Maltese Falcon,' 'Treasure of Sierra Madre,' High Sierra,' and 'Key Largo.' Have you seen these, and what is your opinion of Humphrey Bogart? I have one (opinion) but I'll wait for yours first.

You're a woman with a heart of gold and a loyal friend.

God bless you.

Peace & Love forever,

Rich

February 21, 2002

Dear Rich,

Thanks for two letters and your lovely Valentine card which I just got today. One of your questions I partly answered already – about my concerts. And you are certainly right about my feelings regarding my SF Opera job.

I miss my friends but not the job itself and surely not the headaches. I sometimes talk to some friends and they tell me what they are doing and I am glad not to be there.

My poor friend, I wish with all my heart that you could play again one day. But I don't wish you would drink again! I know it's hard but listen to your heart or whatever tells you to run away from it like from a deadly snake. I have several friends who fought alcoholism successfully – I am thinking of two, they both were about ruining their lives – not to the extent of your trouble – and they are living happily now. One of them is my ex brother-in-law, a clergyman! He didn't touch a drink for about 20 years now. He is happily married and doing fine work helping people with AIDS and stuff like that. That's the hard price to pay for your happiness.

I am teaching a music appreciation course which I enjoy very much. It is so much better to do it in my house instead of the college.

Days are getting longer now which is nice – you know winter is very dark here being way up north. There is about seven hours of difference between June and December. I'm waiting for the spring.

Do you have something good to read? Do you get the Newsweek? I did renew the subscription. You want me to send you some books?

Well, till next. Love,

Agi

February 27, 2002

Dear Agi,

Well, how are you today, my Lady? I do hope you are feeling happy and free. A few more weeks and spring will be here, I know you are looking forward to that. Me too! Heck, I haven't been outside since October, and I could use some fresh-air, that's for sure. The air inside the building is very dry, dusty, and dirty. We have cell cleanings twice a week and you would not believe the dust and dirt that gathers under my bed in just a few days. It's unbelievable.

Last week the state of Ohio killed another man. They executed John Byrd. In truth, this execution bothers me more so than the last they did. I believe Byrd was innocent of murder and yet our Republican governor would not show some compassion and give Mr. Byrd a lighter sentence – i.e. life in prison without parole.

I think that once you're in the system, it's almost impossible to get out of it. Mercy is losing its place in our system of justice. I know, if my date was next week, I wouldn't get any mercy either. They are going to execute me someday. The only way I'll walk off of death row is if they (Ohio) end the death penalty all together. And I don't see that happening any time soon. Oh well, 'que sera, sera', eh? I used to have to play that little tune – I didn't mind, in fact I enjoyed it because the people enjoyed it. I love to make people smile and feel good, don't you? Yes, I know you do. I think all musicians do; that's one of the perks of playing music – i.e. making people feel good or feel something inside of themselves anyway.

Yes I would love some good books to read. One book I would like to read: "A Painted House" by John Grisham. If you want and can; thank you. Yes I'm getting my weekly Newsweek magazine I love that! Thank you my friend. You are very kind to me. You're a good woman, Agi; I admire you and love you for just being you.

You're great.

Peace & love, God bless,

Rich

March 11, 2002

Dear Agi,

Hello my friend. I hope this letter finds you well and happy. The first day of spring is Wednesday, which should brighten your mood; it does mine, for sure.

In the local paper last week it said the state is going to try to schedule 10 executions this year. They already scheduled another execution for next month: April 26th. Rap my first lawyer back in 1997 told me "hey, don't worry, Ohio doesn't execute anyone." Boy was he wrong. This will be number four since I've been here. Oh well.

I'm having a hard time this week keeping my mind and spirit up. I'm wandering, my mind is, all over my life and about the end of my life. I guess it has hit home to me lately that the clock is ticking down on me

Love ya,

Rich

March 12, 2002

Dear Rich,

I know about John Byrd - I work specifically on the death penalty within Amnesty, so I hear about all executions. I wrote several letters on his behalf, to no avail obviously. I am outraged about his case more than some others. Yes, the man was innocent of murder, that's clear. It's beyond belief what's going on in this country on the death penalty scene. But we are working like carpenter ants – one day the whole thing will collapse. We are behind the civilized world: the US is the last first world country to kill its citizens. It was slow to abolish slavery, slow to stop discrimination of minorities and now slow to abolish the death penalty. The most glorious country!

You were not outside since October? God, that's awful. I hope they let you out now soon. Yes, I am waiting for spring also. Was glad when March came – and on the 8 we had the most snow of the whole winter! It is still cold and rainy, but it's good to have the certainty that spring will soon come, no matter what.

I sent you three Grisham, among them the "Painted House" I hope you got it. I bought it this time in a used-book store, I hope they don't object. You know, if you get it, I can send you a lot, that's cheap, and they have a lot of stuff. Just let me know what you want, don't worry my friend.

There is not much news with me. My Amnesty group is doing well. We have meetings once a month, but in April the annual general meeting will be held in Seattle, so a few of the members will come with me. These big meetings are interesting, usually a few hundred attend. It is held in a big hotel with several rooms for side-meetings and a big auditorium for the opening and closing plenary. I know a few people of the administration from past general meetings, including the US Director William Schulz, whom I admire: he is intelligent, a good speaker, a great leader. We will be selling my book there, along with another, written by one of my best friends here; it's about the WTO protest in Seattle. That should be very much in point, since the theme of this meeting is "Reframing Globalization" the dangers of corporate power for human rights.

Well, till next time.

Love,

Agi

March 20, 2002 (First day of spring)

Dear Agi,

Zippity do-da-spring is in the air. Can't wait to get outside. Maybe Saturday I can if it quits raining; it usually rains a lot in Ohio in he spring time. I got your letter of 3-12 and, yes, I got the three John Grisham's book, too. They didn't say anything about them coming from a used book store, so that's great because it will save you some money.

OK, I will let you know when I see a book in the paper or hear of one I would like to read. I actually have a bunch of'em already written down. Some of them are books I've always wanted to read but was too drunk to do it. Drunks don't read whilst in a drinking spree, and I've been in a drinking spree since 1976.

For example I've always wanted to read a book by Mark Twain and I never have gotten around to it. And there are others, too, that my whole life I have heard that are wonderful stories and I would say to myself 'someday I'm going to read that book but I'll do it tomorrow' and tomorrow never came…well, it did but I was either too drunk or too hung-over to read.

So death row does have a few perks…"time," time to read, time to reflect, time to repent, time to pray (not good at that) time to know God…well at least read about Him, anyway, and time to read and study the Bible. (That I enjoy a lot, it does bring me some peace.)

I like it too when you pick out books for me. You have good taste, and you have introduced me to writers I wouldn't have known about, especially Isabel Allende and Kent Haruf. I love both of their books "Daughter of Fortune" "Plainsong" respectfully. These are indelible stories to me.

So you are going to Seattle in April for a meeting, huh? Will you drive or fly?

That's all for now. Thanks again, Agi, for the books; I'll let you know how they were.

Love,
Rich

March 30, 2002
Dear Rich,

Thanks for two letters and a card. Your letter greeting spring – zippity do-da! – was funny, because that day <u>it snowed</u> here! March was the worst winter month by far. It was cold and snowing four or five times. Now since the 23rd it's finally more spring-like. I am working on my property, gathering fallen branches, there's an awful lot of them. Yesterday I burned a huge heap!

I'm worrying about my dog who is not eating well for several weeks, lost a lot of weight and the vet doesn't know what's wrong with her.

I will drive to Seattle taking two of the members of my group. It's only 80 miles from the ferry. The ferry ride is about an hour; the only annoying thing is the waiting for the ferry – you have to get in line ahead of time, otherwise you might miss it. It's especially bad in the tourist season, during the summer.

I will look for more books for you soon.

Till next, cheers!
Agi

April 11, 2002

Dear Agi,.

I still haven't been outside yet. If I want to get outside rec I have to go at 6;00am and I am not an early bird – I 'm nocturnal. The way they do outside rec for my pod is weird. For example: I can have rec outside only on days divided by four on the calendar ie 4th, 8th, 12th, 20th etc. So this month I have seven days I can go out but only at six in the morning; the top tier, this month, gets outside rec at 2:00pm. Next month (May) I will get outside rec at 2pm in the afternoon and the top tier will have to go at 6:00am. Each month we switch back and forth like that.

Later in the summer, when it's warm at 6:00am, I will get up and go out, but right now the temperature at six am is still cold (high 30s, low 40s.)

Well it took one year and two weeks and nine visits but I finally got my dentures. A whole top plate. They feel weird right now but I'll get used to them. I was worried they'd look like horse teeth but they don't; in fact, they look real nice with no gum showing. I do need to get some denture cream or Efferquip or something from commissary, because I cannot eat with it because the plate moves too much. OK, enough abut my teeth, eh? At least I can smile again on days I can find something to smile about. In truth, I still smile and laugh. I just don't do it as much as I used to.

Prison is weird and the people become weird. Too much laugh and smile is frowned upon like "kindness is weakness" thing. Stupid, huh? Most inmates put on a face of meanness or sadness or just indifference, like an actor – it's not real. (When in Rome be a Roman.) So I mostly smile and laugh whilst being alone.

Coda: Thanks Agi, for being there for me. I love our friendship. When one of your letters comes under my door, I smile.

God bless.

Love ya,

Rich

April 15, 2002

Hi pal,

Got your letter today. Hell, you didn't have dentures for more than a year? I remember asking you long time ago and you didn't answer my question, so I thought it was all right. How did you eat all this time?

Listen, my friend, Janet, is pestering me to ask you to send <u>all</u> my letters. She seems to be serious about trying to publish a selection of them, of our correspondence. <u>It would do good to our cause, the</u> <u>death penalty</u>. Reading the very humane, loving letters of yours must do some good. So, do it friend, I promise to send them back very soon. I will copy them right away. OK?

So you smile and laugh all alone – but this is wonderful. It's sad you have to do it alone. Maybe I should send you books which make you laugh. By the way there are 4 books here ready to go: 3 Mark Twain and a big volume of Hemingway's short stories. I hope you will enjoy them.

The AGM – Annual General Meeting – is coming up this weekend. I am quite excited about it. I will tell you all about it afterwards.

After a few nice days it is again goddam cold and raining. But the hummingbirds are here, so it's spring after all. They are swarming at my windows – I have two feeders and have to refill them 2 or 3 times a day. They arrived about two weeks ago and they certainly remembered my feeders. I love them, they are so beautiful. They gobbled up already about two pounds of sugar.

Love,

Agi

April 25, 2002

Dear Agi,

I got your letter of 4-15; always good to hear from you. Here's all your letters and two cards. You keep them and no need to make copies to send back. I made notes in my notebook and I know what you wrote and it is stored in my heart.

Every six months or so I will send 'em back to you. I really do prefer that too, because if anything would <u>happen to me,</u> I would hate to have the prison to just destroy them, which they would or will someday.

It has been stressful in my pod the last month. We have new 1st shift C.O.s. They are young and gung ho, and they like to show off by showing their authority over us.

In the last few weeks, I've had two cell inspections (three for the year) which is quite unusual. The whole atmosphere is unpleasant and somewhat contentious. I hold my tongue (thank God) or I'd be heading to the hole. If I was drinking, I would already be there. I don't like taking arbitrary, capricious, and definitely unnecessary crap from small minded people – hell, nobody does. But, in here, you have to (hold your tongue) or they just make it harder on you.

I finished "Street Lawyer" which was pretty good. Now I'm reading "A Painted House" which is wonderful – I like this one a lot – John Grisham's best, I think. Question: Have you read any Grisham? Do you like his books?

I got up yesterday and went outside for the first time since October. It was a bit chilly at 6, but it felt good just to breathe fresh air. They put 5 of us in a cage and we shoot basketball. I grew up in Indiana; I grew up playing basketball. Before I fell in love with music, I was crazy about the game of basketball. Someday I'll have to tell ya about my athlete days in school. I look back on those days and smile.

Coda: I'll let you know when I get the Twain & Hemingway books. God bless you Agi, you're a wonderful friend.

Love ya,

Rich

May 14, 2002

Dear Rich,

Got your letter about the unpleasantness – more of it – in your pod. I'm glad you're clever enough to shut your mouth, that's the way you should act, of course.

I have two news, a bad one and a good one: the bad one is that my great dog, Kali, died of cancer. The vet didn't recognize it until the last few days, but I knew something was wrong for several weeks. When a dog stops eating, it's a bad sign. I won't describe all the agony about this. At the end she was so miserable that I let her be put asleep. I still feel strange – it happened almost two weeks ago – but I still expect to see her. She was wonderfully affectionate. I rescued her from a bad home, neglect and abuse and she was very grateful, loved me very much. It's like losing a baby.

But let's get to the good one: tonight I wrote passionate letters to the Governor and stuff of Maryland about a man who was to be executed next week. Finishing the letters I checked my e-mail – and there was a message: Maryland <u>declared moratorium</u> on executions!! They expect 14 more states to do this year and Ohio is one of them! We are winning, slowly but surely. One reason of this is that the international community puts a pressure on the US.

It begins to dawn on people that something is wrong about the death penalty; if, for many people, not the mere fact that killing is wrong, whatever the motive is, but they begin to see the whole picture of racism, the role money plays (inadequate defense, as in your case) and all the other dirty tricks prosecutors do, etc. They just released the 100th person who was sentenced to death and who was found innocent. The whole edifice is crumbling, the carpenter ants will finish it!

I am glad you enjoy the books. Answer: I read one by Grisham, he is a very skillful writer and has a good mind.

I am attending a writer's workshop, starting to write an autobiographical novel.

Well, that's it for tonight.

Cheers friend,

Agi

PS There was a huge fire today in Friday Harbor, in the middle of downtown – several shops were destroyed. Thanks for the letters!

May15, 2002

Dear Agi,

Hello my friend, my Earth Angel. I got your letter of 5-7.Thank you. You are sweet and very kind to me.

So sorry to read about Kali. No doubt, it's hard to lose a loving dog. They become such a big part of one's life. Sometimes your pets are closer than people friends. No matter what, they are always loyal and loving and forgiving. I think the reason a dog always has friends is because he wags his tail instead of his tongue.

I'm still holding my tongue and, if I did have a tail, it would not be wagging; these new, gung ho C. O.s are tough.

Hold up sending books for awhile. I'll let you know when it's cool again. OK.

I finished Grisham's "A Painted House" and I really enjoyed that one. That's the best book he's written so far. I just started Mark Twain; more on that later.

Glad to read you received all your letters back. A few of them are torn from the mail room workers here at Manci. When they open incoming mail they must use a blade of some sort and they sometimes cut the letter too with the envelope by accident.

For sure, good news about the moratorium in Maryland, and maybe here too, huh.

I do admire you for the letter writing, fair booths, bazaars, monthly meetings, and you support me personally, unconditionally, and you are always there for me. I do have a hard time putting words on paper to express how much you have touched me.

Like a song, I can feel the vibes and you have a heart of perfect pitch.

A (as in Agi) equels 440.

Be happy. I love you.

Rich

May 29, 2002

Dear Rich,

Thanks a lot for your awfully nice card and letter. You make me feel good and I am so glad to be able to help you a little bit.

Well, I would like to help you more. My friend Janet – she again! – gave me the idea of talking to your lawyer. It can't hurt to try. So, would you mind giving me his name and number?

Another idea would be to get a good lawyer, at that Amnesty might be helpful.

My news is that I am getting a dog – I didn't look for it so soon after Kali's death, but somebody offered me a wonderful deal. It is a Hungarian sheep-dog I always wanted to have, but it's very rare and expensive kind; and they give it free. The breed is called kuvasz, they are big white dogs, intelligent and beautiful. I'm getting a puppy nine weeks old. There will be trouble and work with it, but I decided to get it. One of my friends told me before Kali died that she will send me a dog. Maybe she did.

I fund these maps in my phone-book – I remember long time ago you asked for a map of the island. Well, here they are.

Cheers friend

Agi

June11, 2002

Dear Agi,

I hope this letter finds you healthy, happy and just feelin' good.

Yes, I got your letter of May 29. I am so happy to hear you are getting a new dog. I don't know what a Hungarian sheep-dog looks like so maybe someday this summer you can have a picture taken and send me one. Is it a male or female, and what will be his/her name?

I love where you live. That's so hip to live on a small island like that. Peace and serenity away from the hustle and bustle of city life which you have experienced plenty of in your lifetime.

I loved Orange County but it sure was fast and crowded. Once in awhile I'd get a gig up in Big Bear Lake, which is a ski resort in the San Bernardino mountains (50 mi east of LA, 10'000 ft.) anyway, I always enjoyed the serenity and peace and quiet Big Bear had – a surreal contrast to Huntington Beach and the freeways taken to work. There (Big Bear) I'd walk to the gig from my lodge, which was a log-house. Man, I sure miss things like that.

I finished "Mysterious Stranger," short stories of Mark Twain. I like Twain. He's smart, funny, witty, clever. Twain is dark and depressed in his writing and his real life too.

At the used book store, look for or watch for: "Huckleberry Finn." I really want to read that someday. (Please) Don't send now but later when I let you know it's cool again. This week I'm starting "The Partner" by J. Grisham. (More later on that.)

How is Janet, your friend?

I'll respond to my case later this month when I'm in a better mood to write, esp. on that subject (my case) which is a downer to me. Note: Only a

<u>judge</u> can give me a new trial and that won't happen (long story –explanation etc.)

I'll be back soon.

Peace & Love,

Rich

June 17, 2002

Dear Agi,

Hello my friend. I feel like writing, so I thought I would talk to you. I want to respond to your last letter of May 29.

<u>News on my case:</u> Right now, I <u>do not</u> have a lawyer assigned to me from the Public Defenders, Office down in Columbus, OH. My last two lawyers both moved away – one to Alaska and one to California – and I don't blame them, 'cause Ohio sucks!

I was born in the Mid-West (Indiana) but, for the record, I hate the Mid-West. My favorite part of America is the West, and also Hawaii.

My case right now is up in Wash.DC at the U.S. Supreme Court. Note: I have already been through my "Post-Conviction" and the Ohio Supreme Court and lost both of those - just about everybody does. (And my lawyers, beforehand, told me I would.)

The U.S. Supreme Court will not hear my case and they will kick it back down to the Ohio Federal Courts and, if I am going to win a lighter sentence, for some reason, that (Federal Cts.) is where it will happen.

To get a new trial or have the robbery charge dropped would indeed be wonderful, but that will be up to a Federal Judge. (Note: getting the robbery dropped should have happened<u> before </u>my original trial took place – i.e. a good defense lawyer on a death penalty case costs between ten to a hundred thousand dollars, and only rich people can afford that. You do not see any wealthy people on death row, or not many anyway.

Anyway, a good lawyer would have gone to the prosecutor and made a deal for me <u>before</u> my trial and conviction. My public defender said he did talk to the prosecutor but no deal was made because the prosecutor did not make deals on death penalty cases, he said. This prosecutor, whose name is Joe Deters, is now Ohio's State Treasurer. In other words, he's a politician and the men here on the row from Cincinnati (Hamilton County) we are his trophies in his showcase of his personal, political career.

Note: Fact / There are more men here from Hamilton County (Joe Deters) than from any other county in Ohio. And Hamilton County is not the biggest nor the most populated, neither! It is out of proportion, out of balance, when you compare and discern the statistics of how many men on the row vs. how many from Hamilton County (Joe Deters). I don't know the exact figure but it's something like: 201 men on the row and 60-70 are from Joe Deters – something like that. Way out of proportion and that fact is one of mine and others' argument for a lighter sentence or whatever.

If I would have been in another county or state, I probably would have gotten, through a deal, which everybody gets usually, in such cases, and I see them all the time on TV – news coming from Cleveland – where a man kills his wife in a rage and gets charged with murder and through a deal it gets lowered to manslaughter, where the guy usually gets 8 to 15 years.

I see cases on TV all the time where a person kills two or more people and get life and not the death penalty – man(!) that does bug me. Oh well.

Anyway, I can't give you a name or number because I don't have one myself, neither. There's nothing happening right now anyway because my case is sitting up in Wash. Which is fine with me. I'm in no hurry to make something happen – let'em take their time and drag out as far as I'm concerned.

Keep up your work with Amnesty and hopefully Ohio and other states will stop executing people.

More later.

Love ya,
Rich

July1, 2002
Dear Agi,

I got your letter (6-24) so I shall respond as best as I can.

You asked: why is my case a downer? Because I don't think I'm going to be saved from being executed – and that's a downer to me.

You asked: what is the <u>long</u> story, explanation? I have a box – thousands of pages – trying to tell (explain) my case from both sides; ie. the defense vs. prosecution's and for me to write it out and tell you everything would take me …well, I just couldn't do it, it's too complex, and even I do not understand it all myself – (e.g.) all the legal talk, jargon, parlance etc.

Yes, a good lawyer can make all the difference. I needed a good lawyer at my trial; now it may be too late, because I'm so far, <u>already,</u> into my appeals. You can't go back and start over. I wish I could but I can't. I guess now what I need is an appellate lawyer who knows Ohio's laws, etc.

Enclosed is my case as presented to Ohio's Supreme Court. Read it, make a copy and <u>send my copy back</u>, OK? OK.

The dissent <u>on page 53 </u>is really the true picture of it, in my opinion.

If you should talk to a lawyer, this will be some help in where I stand in the system.

<u>Truth!</u> I'm not crazy about you spending your money on a lawyer for me. I don't trust lawyers and you could get taken for a ride because neither one of us know about these things. Bottom line: how do I (we) know that a paid lawyer – at this <u>late</u> time, where I'm at in the appeal process can be any <u>more</u> help or better help, than a public defender can be? It looks like a perfunctory job at this point, but I don't know – I really don't!!

We'll talk more later. Don't forget, make a copy and send mine back.

Love ya,

Rich

PS I really, really appreciate your offering to hire a lawyer for me – I do! But <u>please</u> don't do it before we talk some more on this. If you can talk to a lawyer for free, that'd be great, but don't spend any money on <u>this late</u> in my game, I'm not sure a paid lawyer can be any more help than what I'm getting now from the public defender's office. I wish I was a smart man but I'm not. I'm only a piano player.

Rich

Keep the faith. You're my Angel

Tuesday, July 1, 2002

Dear Agi,

I got your letter of (6-24). So
I shall respond as best as I can.

You asked; why is my case a downer?
Because I don't think I'm going to be
saved from being executed — and that's
a downer to me.

July 7, 2002

Dearest Agi,

Well, are you enjoying your summer? I do hope so. How's the new dog doing? Did you get him/her yet?

I saw your beautiful island on TV last Sunday. I got all excited seeing Friday Harbor. On Sunday mornings at 9-am CBS has a nice show on for 1 ½ hrs called Sunday Morning. It's well done and one of my favorites to watch, which I do every week.

Anyway, last Sunday they did a piece on Orca whales, and it was filmed right there in the San Juan Islands. They were interviewing a man who's involved with saving the whales, right there in town, Friday Harbor. I could see all the tourists walking and shopping on the street. Real nice. I was wishing I was there. It's a beautiful place. I'm glad you live there; peaceful, serene, and safe.

I miss the ocean. I lived one mile from the beach for six years. I didn't go swimming in the ocean very much, because I prefer swimming in a clean clear pool, and I never went surfing either. But, I would jog on the walkway and then sit and just look out at the sea and wonder about God and life and why are we here, where does God live, is there life out in space (yes 😊) and stuff like that – we all do that, huh?

I believe that in general people who live by the sea are healthier in spirit, mind, and body. We came from the sea, some say. Maybe so – I don't know.

I finished "Partners" by John Grisham. Excellent!! It got me out of here for a while. I'm starting "Life on the Mississippi" by Twain.

I miss my river, the Ohio River. I grew up on the river; Aurora is a river town. Heck, I miss all kinds of stuff. It's pretty hard living in a box. But I let my mind wonder upon the wind and I leave here all the time – Man C I just doesn't know it.

You're a wonderful friend and I cherish our friendship. Love always,

Rich

July 10, 2002

Dear Rich,

I got your trial document and gave it right away to a lawyer here, for opinion. I am worrying – how come it is so late a stage in your case, as you point it out. The average time, before it gets serious, is 10 years, so I thought you have a lot of time. Why is your case going so fast? Hope it's not too late to do something – see what the lawyer says.

Here is a picture of Prince, my beautiful Kuvasz-puppy. He is adorable but he is a baby, a lot of trouble. The worst thing is that my cat is afraid of him and is practically living in a closet, hiding. Before she slept on my bed, now her life is ruined – hopefully it will change.

Another trouble: my car broke down and it will cost me a fortune. Oh well, nothing is as serious as your trouble, my poor friend.

You certainly know that people who were sentenced by a judge rather than a jury are now out of death row. I suppose it doesn't apply to you or you would have told me. In any case we are chipping away the death penalty – I wish it would go faster. Tell me, how close are you to be in real danger?

Till next, write soon.

Love,

Agi

July16, 2002

Dear Rich,

Here is a letter to you by the lawyer I gave the script to. You will like it. I also talked to Mr. K who had an idea about a lawyer. I am sending him a copy of your document and hopefully things will go from there.

Sorry about the original script, the copy machine did some damage to it.

This is all for today. Cheers,

Agi

July 22, 2002

Dear Agi,

Hello my friend. I got two letters, a picture of Prince, my Ohio Supreme Ct. opinion, and a letter from lawyer Lawrence Delay last week.

Thank you, Agi, for your loyalty, your efforts, and your steadfast friendship.

I liked what Mr. Lawrence had to say, and I will show this letter to my next lawyer for sure, and maybe it will be of some help when my new attorney prepares for my Federal Appeal.

You asked: why my case is moving so fast? Well, I'm under a new law or system of 1996, where my appeals are running concurrently, to cut the average time of stay on death row from 10 to 20 yrs. down to 5 to 10 yrs., they hope. That was the purpose of this '96 bill, to cut the time half or at least speed it up.

So, yes, I'm moving through very fast. I have passed up guys – through the appeal system – that have been here over 10 years. It will be 5 years for me on Dec. 23, 2002 (this year). How much time do I have left, I don't know, but I would guess…I don't want to guess 'cause I really don't know – no one has been through the new (1996 Bill) yet. (At least a few years, I would say, hopefully, I have left.)

Mr. Delay is a smart man, and I bet if I would have had him as my lawyer from the very beginning, I would not be on death row at all. Guys like that S.O.B. in Stanton Cal. who took that little girl and raped her and then killed her needs to be executed, that's for sure! OK, change the subject, Nields, I'm getting down, riled (?) and upset, and frustrated.

Hey, Prince is beautiful! I like him, and I do hope things work out OK for Zizi, the cat, too, living in a closet, hiding, I'm sure is hard on her and you. In time, as Prince gets older and mellower, I'm sure Zizi will get used to him being around.

Peace & love,
Rich

PS You are correct: 2 New Supreme Ct. ruling Judge decides, and mentally retarded issue, is N/A to me. Keep the faith my Angel. Enjoy your summer.

July 26, 2002
Dear Rich,

I just got your letter. I knew you would like Mr. Delay's letter – he was really outraged after reading your document. Too bad he is here and can't be your attorney. He is kind of a friend, his wife is my Italian teacher – maybe I told you I am studying Italian just for fun, it's such a beautiful language.

It's my fifth, because of course I speak French and German – I lived there – besides English and Hungarian.

Right now I have a lot of worries and troubles: my car is in the garage for almost 3 weeks: transmission trouble and they don't seem to be able to fix it. A few days I was stranded, then I rented a car, then they lent me one which didn't work, etc., etc. And it will cost me a fortune. Hell!

Also, I am worrying about my friend the cellist who has cancer. First it looked like he was pulling through and now I hear alarming news about him.

Prince is adorable but also a goddam nuisance, doing a lot of damage around and sometimes really exasperating. And the cat is still in the closet. Well!

Other than that, summer is much better than last year, really warm. I wanted to swim, but the nearby lake is overgrown with seaweeds, no way to swim.

I am complaining to you who sit in a cell and think about getting killed. This is human nature, when things are normal one is upset about minor things.

I will subscribe for Reader's digest.

Till next, my best, pal

Agi

August 3, 2002

Dear Agi,

Or maybe I should say ciaou, my friend, eh? Gosh, you're learning your fifth language and I'm still working on English, especially when doing crosswords; my spelling has improved but not as good as I'd like it to be.

When I was a kid going to St. Mary's, two things I really hated: spelling bees, where the whole class would stand up around the classroom and the nuns would asked us to spell, by ourselves, out loud, different words; and I'd be nervous and misspell simple words like I'm doing in this letter (ha-ha) and would end up sitting down pretty quick in the spelling contest. And, also, I hated when I would get called upon to go to the black-board to write out sentences – damn! I hated that. The nuns made me so nervous I couldn't think. Hell they made me so nervous I wet the bed until I was 12 or 13 yrs. old. Yeah, I was a bed wetter. I didn't think I'd ever stop peeing the bed. It made it hard for me to go on camping trips with the Cub Scouts and Boy Scouts.

How did I get on this subject? Anyway, kudos to you for learning Italian.

I did learn a new word last night from my crossword book: soliloquy – man, I can relate to that, now that I live in a box by myself. I soliloquize a lot, I talk and laugh by myself, and I'm cool with it as long as I don't get in an argument with myself everything is <u>copasetic</u>. (not in my dictionary) Question: is the word <u>copasetic</u> Italian or French?

Patty was Italian. What a temper she had; she liked to throw things at me. When I was drunk I would laugh and, of course, she would get even madder.

Three weeks to fix your car? That doesn't sound right but I hope they do get it fixed correctly. I always hated car problems because I don't know much about cars. My criterion for buying a used car was: "How good does the radio sound?" (I never owned a new car in my life.) I do love the smell of a new car, don't you? Thank you for getting Reader's Digest for me. I'll let you know when it starts coming in.

To coda: One of my favorite film composers is Henry Mancini. I love the song "Moon River." Be happy – keep the faith.

Love always,

Rich

August 10, 2002

Ciao amico,

Salut ami,

Servus Freund,

Szia baratom,

Hi friend,

Well, I have an idle evening, having my gin and tonic and being silly. I got your letter about your bed-wetting. Hey, don't do it any more, pal.

It's now Fair-fever, and I didn't do anything about Reader's Digest yet. Fair is next week and there is accordingly a mess in my study and next week I will be going crazily busy.

I still don't have my car! Now they sent the transmission to a Mercedes-place – I have a second-hand Merc. – so it will take another week or more. Meanwhile the borrowed car broke down in the middle of the road because they didn't tell me it operates on Diesel and I put in regular gas. Goddamshit!

Prince is adorable, chewed up my reading glasses – costs me $182 – I had to clean my carpet because it was getting dirtier than tolerable. That's an expensive dog.

Mr. K. just called me – we are getting a good lawyer for you! Hopefully.

Tell yourself some jokes, play chess, do crosswords and say to the world my motto: fuck'm all!

Cheers,

Agi

September 3, 2002

Dear Rich,

I was going to write you tonight in any case, but I just got your letter. I am planning two trips in October: one to the Grand Canyon with my stepdaughter and her baby, and one to San Francisco to see an interesting opera and see my friends.

The Fair was again a success – over $ 900! – and it was interesting too. We always have petitions and this year it was for the moratorium on the death penalty. There are still people in favor and there were some arguments, but a lot of people eagerly signed it. We filled 15 pages. The tide is turning. I did some educational work about it, distributed lots of brochures and talked myself hoarse.

Do you play chess, do crosswords? Read? Want some new books? "Huckleberry Finn" is already here to send it.

What do you think of our goddam President wanting to start a war in Iraq? If he is in the White House too long, he will fuck up everything.

Well, cheers friend,

Agi

September 3, 2002

Dear Agi,

And how are you today, my sweet Agi? I do know you have been very busy the last few weeks taking care of business.

How did it go at the Fair? Good, I hope. Did you work the booth? I'm sure you did – I admire you for that. You walk your talk. You walk your heart's convictions, like my activist Angel you are to me. As James said, "Faith without works is dead." Touche.

Just curious. Do you ever take your violin to the Fair booth and play music for the people?

One of my favorite movie themes is from a French film called "A Man and a Woman." I used to play it every night for myself I enjoyed it so much. (The movie and the tune are same title.) Have you seen this love story between a race car driver and a woman? It's a French movie from the 60s?

I also played the tune "Charade" from the movie w/same title: (Hollywood production but filmed in Paris.) Tune written by Henry Mancini. I haven't seen a lot of French movies in my life, but the few I have, I noticed the film score had a jazzy flavor to it.

Also, I love French toast, French fries, and the mellow as a cello, French horn.

I always wanted to visit Europe. I actually had an offer once to go and play for U.S.O. clubs in Europe but I turned it down. Now I wish I'd gone.

Hindsight is 20/20, huh? Hindsight is like foresight but without a future, as in my case. In prison, you sure do take your life apart in thought and it can be painful. Now that I'm sober, I can see all too clearly what a fool I've been all my drunken life. (Not feeling sorry for myself, just sharing.)

I can be cynical and go to rot, or I can remember and share and keep on hoping. I choose the latter. I have always accented the positive – albeit sometimes in a syncopated way.

Keep the Faith, my Angel – I am.

Peace & Love. Ciao,
Rich

September 18, 2002
Ciao Riccardo,

I wrote this to the newsletter of the NCADP (National Coalition to Abolish the Death Penalty) I hope they will publish it. On the phone they already said they were interested.

I gave away my beautiful puppy! He was absolutely unmanageable, and struggling with him I hurt my hands. I couldn't walk him for the same reason. And I felt terrible about my cat whose life was ruined because of him. But there was a lucky solution: he is living now with his brother here, on the island, has a good home and can play with his brother the whole day long. He did a lot of damage in my house and outside.

Cheers,
Agi

September 19, 2002

Dear Agi,

Hello my friend, and thank you. I got two letters from you since the last time I wrote. Sorry to hear about Prince having to leave, but it's probably for the best for you and your house and him too and most of all for Zizi.

The letter you wrote to the NCADP is very good indeed. Also 100% correct. I see cases all the time on TV of crime of passion, which is what mine is, but they get murder dropped to manslaughter and 6 to 10 yrs. or something like that; man, oh, man, if I didn't have any bad luck, I'd have no luck at all, as the Blues man sings his 12 bars of blues in the key of F cause I got fu…!! (No pity-pot talk, just sharing.)

I must say it is encouraging to read in your letter that you got 15 pages of signatures calling for a moratorium on the death penalty – that's real good – and, yes, I do believe (slowly) the tide is turning on capital punishment.

I'm really hoping in our governor's race here in Ohio in November that Governor Taft, a Republican, is beaten. The polls say it's real close right now between Taft and the democrat Hagan.

Oh, yeah, we are having another execution next Wed. 25th. A Mr. Robert Buell. He's been here since 1982. He's under the old appeal system, that's why it took this long.

I'm happy for my Angel. You get to go away for awhile to two great places: San Fran. and the Grand Canyon. Yeah! That's wonderful. It will be nice to see all your friends down at the opera, huh?

I think about my musician friends from California and wonder what they are doing now and where they are etc etc. "If music is the food of love, play on," eh? (Shakespeare) Of all the things I miss the most is my music and my music friends without a doubt.

In truth, I know you're the greatest musician I have known, and I'm truely honored that you are my friend – I love you for that.

Coda: Yes, I would love to read Huckleberry Finn – send it when you want to. Remember, it has to come from the store. Be happy, be safe.

Ciao,

Riccardo

September 28, 2002

Hi Rich,

Tomorrow I am off to SF, coming back Wednesday. The performance I want to see is on Tuesday and the orchestra's "black" day is Monday, so I hope to see a few friends. The opera is "St. Francis of Assisi" by Olivier Messiaen, one of the greatest of the 20th century. He was a great catholic and loved birds, so his choice is pretty obvious. That's his only opera; it lasts 5 hours (!) and there is not much going on on the stage. It requires a huge orchestra. It is of course rarely performed – it will never be a popular opera. They say that people from all over the country, or even from abroad, are coming to see it.

My other trip, to the Grand Canyon, is cancelled. I found out it was too expensive and was about to cancel when an emergency happened: the husband of my stepdaughter got very ill. He is recovering now but it will be very long, so she couldn't have come anyway.

What you say about the governor race in Ohio is another good sign that the tide is turning about the death penalty. Even a year or two ago, if a candidate would have expressed opposition on the death penalty, he would have ruined his chances. Now the race is close. Let's hope!

Till next, ciao, Riccardo,

Agi

October 7, 2002

Dear Agi,

My mood is a tad sour. Sorry about that; I'll get back up real soon.

When they do an execution it bothers me more than I want to admit. It brings home to me that someday it will be my turn to walk into that chamber.

I'm really hoping Hagan wins in November, needless to say, I'm sure.

Life is strange. I've never been involved with politics at all; hell I've never even voted in my life. Now in a way, my life – to live or die – could depend on who's the governor in Ohio. Come on Hagan. (Last I heard he's behind only 6 points.)

I did get your letter of 9-28, which always makes me feel good. How was your trip to San Francisco? I'm sure it was great, huh? Did you fly or drive?

Man, oh, man, a 5-hour opera! That's a lot of music to play.

Maybe next year you go to see the Grand Canyon. I hope your stepdaughter's husband is doing OK.

How is Zizi doing, is she back to normal?

Sorry (again) I know it's a boring letter but my mind and soul are lost in a haze of shame, fear, disgrace, anxiety.

I'll bounce back up; starting tomorrow I'll start my exercise program again to rev up my metabolism; improve my outlook, boost my moods, and, get my endorphins kicked in. And the beat goes on.

Ciao, my wonderful friend,

Rich

October 17, 2002

Dear Rich,

Thanks for your nice card and sad letter. I hope you got back up since. Did you get the books?

My SF trip was awfully nice. The first night I stayed with my ex-stand-partner, a gay man, and the two others with a couple; she is a cellist, he a violist, good friends. And a third colleague picked me up when arrived. The weather was great and it was nice to see the city; I think it is the most beautiful of this country. And when I walked in backstage before the performance, it was heart-warming to hear cries: Agi!! Hey, goddamshit, how are you? You look great! Etc. It's almost nine years I retired and they still love me; that was great. And I loved the opera. It's something else, nothing like any other one. A great modern masterpiece, with unusual instruments. Besides the usual orchestra it requires three xilophons, a marimba, and several other keyboard instruments called <u>onde martinot,</u> which have eerie sounds like an extremely low tuba. It was great. And a marvelous production.

Next week I am going to Denver to a Western Regional Conference (Amnesty, of course.) I didn't want to, because of expenses, but my group urged me to do it, and I got financial help from Amnesty. So I am exited to go.

Now something else: Janet and I will start working on our project, the play about you and me. We will use classical music for me and jazz for you. So, please make a list of your favorite songs, maybe eight or ten and send it with your next letter, OK? We have one common one: "The Man I Love" (By Gershwin)

Ciao Riccardo,

Agi

P.S. Zizi is back to normal and happy. And I am thinking to get a dog soon.

October 20, 2002

Dear Agi,

Hello my friend. Are you feeling good today? I hope so. I feel better than I did a couple of weeks ago. Not as blue anyway. I started my exercise program and I'm doing pretty good. I could do better but also I could be doing worse; the last 14 days I have worked out 8 days and 6 days I didn't. What do I do? I do some yoga stretching and then I do a half-hour of cardiovascular exercises-i.e. 200 to 300 jumping jacks 200 to 300 jump rope, without a rope, step aerobics- 200-300- (I step up and down on my metal footlocker) pushups, squats, and dips.

If I do it right – go for the burn – after I finish and take a hot/cold shower, I sometimes feel that 'runners high' which of course is just some endorphins kicking in or being released, or whatever you call it. It just feels good.

I got my first Reader's Digest, too. Thank you again. That's a good magazine, I think. It has a little bit of everything in it: stories, real & fiction, new word puzzles, some jokes & comics (most are corny but some are cute too.)

Did you get your car back yet? Surely by now you have. When I thought about it I was a little surprised that on your island there was a garage that could fix a Mercedes, (oops) I forgot , they sent it away for repair – the transmission – that's right. OK.

I got some sad news (nothing to do with me but an inmate in my pod 3 cells down) but I'll share it next time. My last letter was a downer I remember and I don't always want to bring you <u>down</u> every time I write. I worry a little about my bad situation wearing you down, where you'd get tired of me.

But then I remember your book, your story, and realize man, oh, man, Agi's a woman with true grit, courage, conviction, and panache. You're a woman of strong character. I do admire you and I'm proud of you and happy that we are friends forever.

Peace & love, my friend,
Rich

October 23, 2002
Dear Agi,

Well, we got a small problem. The books from Serendipity are being sent back because of a, to me, stupid rule, which I didn't know about either. They are being sent back because there was no receipt or bill from the store with the books that would show you <u>purchased </u>the books there.

Anyway, I can't believe they also charged me $ 5.75 to mail two books back. That seems like a lot for two paperback books.

So, you might want to call the store and see if they are back yet and either get your money back or the books back or you can have them send 'em back but with a receipt this time. You do what you want – I'll understand. Hell these used book are costing more than new ones now, huh? <u>So sorry</u> for all this trouble. Next time we'll know to make sure that the sales lady at the store puts in the receipt with the books.

Also, I'm sending back a few of your letters for safe keeping.

I'll write a chit-chat letter this coming weekend. Now I just wanted to let you know what happened with our books.

Harry Truman said "Friends don't count in fair weather. It is when troubles come that friends count." I thought of you when I read that. You are a <u>wonderful</u> friend – you always chase the clouds away for me. You have taught me much.

I'll be back soon.

Love & peace. Ciao,

Rich

P.S. I love Richard Harris. One of my favorite actors. In case you don't know he died last week. Anyway, do you want to see a real good movie with good acting? Rent this video: "Wrestling with Hemingway" with Robert Duvall, Richard Harris and Shirley McLaine. This is Duvall and Harris at their best. "And in the sweetness of friendship let there be laughter, and sharing of pleasures." (Kahlil Gibran)

This film will bring you some smiles and pleasure – and touch your heart – it did mine.

October 24, 2002

Dear Rich,

I just got your letter and I just finished a conversation with Mr. K., so I have to tell you right away about it. First: he said you have now a <u>good</u> attorney. Second: you have still a lot of time before real danger, maybe two years. Third: I offered to pay any expenses the lawyer might have, like refuting the robbery charge – that's the key of your case I think.

Is the sad news about Mr.Udall(?) who was executed? Of course I know about it, I wrote letters on his behalf, (to no avail, hell.)

The clipping you sent me doesn't look good for Hagan, but the press is <u>Republican</u>. People feel very strongly against Mr. Shrub, our fucking president. So, maybe there is still hope. The November elections will be very important.

Rich, you are silly. You are afraid to "bring me down?" and get tired of you? Ridiculous. My God, just pour out your heart to me. Hell, you are sitting in a cell and I am free and have a good life. Don't be afraid to tell me about being depressed, it's more than natural, my poor friend.

Go on with your exercises, read, play chess, do crosswords, tell jokes to yourself.

Love,

Agi

P.S. Of course I got my car back a while ago. They didn't send it off, just got parts for it. It works now alright.

My friend, the cellist who lived near you, died of cancer. I feel terribly sorry for his parents who live here.

October 28, 2002

Dear Agi,

Hello my lady and how are you today? Good, I hope. I feel good, too. Doing exercise no doubt does help with my mood. But the persevering, to keep on keeping on, is the hard part. Like my piano studies, I enjoyed improv over the chord changes a lot more than I did doing scales and arpeggios. I've always been a discipline person up until the drinking and smoking pot took over my life; then, I became a diligent drinker and smoker – no problem – that I could do everyday, off and on all day and all night.

I got your letter of 10-17-02. I am so happy to hear you had a good time down in San Francisco. You went to the Opera (such a worldly and classy lady you are) and saw all your friends and a great opera and enjoyed the ambiance (I agree with you) the most beautiful city in America.

When you're happy, I'm happy. Mark Twain said "Sorrow can take care of itself, but to get the true benefit of joy, you must share it."

That's what we are doing, sharing. It does feel good to share, huh? I enjoy writing letters of chit-chat more than letters of news, because 'news' letters usually are downers from death row, and I want to make you smile more than anything.

In truth, there's never a good day on death row; it just that someday are not as bad as others. But if I can write or share something that brings a smile to your face, well that makes it a better day for you and me. If you smile when no one is around, you really mean it, eh?

A few tunes I like: As Time Goes By, It Had to be You, The Summer Wind, Stardust, Night & Day, Mood Indigo, Moonglow, Meditation, Poinciana, Rhapsody in Blue, and let the dance begin w/Begin the Beguine. Keep on dancing and keep on smiling the show will go on. Keep on swingin.'

I have so many favorites it's hard to choose just ten. I sure miss the feeling of beauty I can achieve by playing music, you understand I know.

Peace and love, ciao,

Rich

November 7, 2002

Dear Rich,

So, the bastards sent back the books, hell! The bookstore called me, they will send it again.

Last week-end I went to Denver for the Regional Conference, and it was a success. It was wonderfully done, the panels and discussions were great. And I made money for my group selling T-shirts and my book. They ordered more shirts, which one of the members of my group makes, so we will have more money. Did I tell you that my group is second in the whole country for fund-raising? I am pretty proud of this. This year we donated already $ 750 and our "Bizarre Bazaar" is still coming next month.

I talked to a famous abolitionist there about you. He named two good lawyers at your place. Is your new lawyer's name is David Stebbens? Did he come to see you? Please, answer this!

Thanks for the tunes. We start working tomorrow with Janet. This afternoon there is the monthly Amnesty meeting, and afterwards one of my best friends here comes to dinner.

Till next, ciao Riccardo,

Agi

November 10, 2002

Dear Agi,

Hello my friend. I hope this letter finds you healthy and happy. I'm doin' okay myself.

Since I have written, I have received two letters from you, (10-24, 11-3) so I will respond to those.

Yeah, Hagan lost, too bad, huh? I know we both wanted him to win but we knew in our heads he didn't have much of a shot.

The bad news I spoke about a few weeks ago (sad news) is that an inmate that lives three cells down from me, a man I play chess with, well his time is up and all of his appeals are spent. The pod gossip is that he'll probably be executed next year. His name is Richard Fox. (If Hagan would have won, Fox's sentence would have been commuted to life, but not now because Taft is governor. Sad, huh?) He's been here around 10 years. The prison priest has been going to his cell for a one-to-one talk once a week. I guess if he hasn't, now is the time to repent.

Truth be told, I think it's strange, weird knowing when you're going to die. I would rather not know because, in all humility, in truth, I'm chicken. Oh, yeah!

I always thought (kind of) I'd die drunk and I wouldn't know it, but to die sober and to know it's coming and they won't give me a drink at my last meal...man, oh, man that sucks, to me. (Spoken to share but not to bring down.) Like you wrote (10-24) "just pour out your heart to me." OK, I will. Thanks for being my friend.

Sorry to hear your friend, the cellist, died. I hate cancer and I wish doctors could find a cure for that horrible disease and AIDS, too.

Glad to hear your trip to Denver was a success. How do you like being a mile high on the ground? To me, being in the mountains was always a spiritual feeling – really it was. I used to play at Big Bear Lake down in Southern California once in awhile, I loved it there.

David Stebbens? No. I do not know him. I haven't met 'em yet but my two new lawyers are: Kyle Timken, Dave Hanson. I'll let you know when I meet with them, which should be very soon. I'm very proud of you and your group. Second in the country for fund-raising!! You're an angel.

Love & Peace to you, Agi.

Ciao,

Rich

November 20, 2002

Dear Agi,

Hand on heart, I'm so proud of you! You're on the cover of AI's mag. With a short bio and a wonderful picture of you; plus, your story on page 3 of the general meeting in Seattle was/is real good.

I have never known anyone like you in my whole life; I read about people like you (i.e. activist, humanitarian, philanthropist, virtuoso) but never personally knew any that called me friend. I'm honored and blessed and, if I had a tail, it'd be wagging at ♩ =200 (beats per minute.)

Yes, I got the books this time. "Huckleberry Finn" and "The Evening News." I have never read a book by Arthur Hailey, so I'll let you know if I enjoyed it after I read it. Thanks, Agi.

I'm enclosing one picture and one old business card. The picture was taken at my sister's house on Xmas day 1990. The card is from '89-'90. Man, oh, man time sure does fly by fast. Even in here time is going by quickly.

So Bartok and Goodman played together, huh? I didn't know that. I'm not real hip to Bartok, the man nor his music, except for an album a friend of mine had his string quartet of Hungarian folk-music. I remember I liked it. Question: What instrument did Bartok play? Violin?

As I'm writing this my shower is stuck on and probably will be until tomorrow morning when 1st shift comes on. We have a push button system where you push the one button and the water comes out for 30 seconds, and then the water pressure pops out the button, and the water goes off. Well, when I pushed it the last time the button went in way too far – the spring broke– oops! So now, since I live in a dysfunctional bureaucratic system, it will take about 15 hours to get a maintenance man over here to fix it. I'll just pretend it's raining and maybe like Gene Kelly I'll do some "Singing in the Rain."

That's all for now, I have to go pee; running water does that to me.

Peace & Love, Ciao,

Rich

November 29, 2002

Ciao Riccardo,

I just got your letter, hope your shower is fixed and you don't have to pee all the time. Got your pictures, too. This time I will copy them and send them back.

I had an awful trip to Seattle last week. There was a "summit meeting," that means that all AI groups of Washington meet. None of my members wanted to come, and I have zero sense of orientation and I got bad directions. Going there was not too bad, I found the University where it took place, and I found a parking lot, but I had no idea where the building was. Finally a girl took me to the building. I was late. The meeting wasn't any good; it lasted till 4.30. Then I didn't find my parking lot. Then I didn't find the highway. By then it was dark and traffic was terrible. Finally I was on the highway, then, in the heaviest traffic it was pouring rain. Man oh man – to quote you – I was surely glad when got home.

Zizi decided there was something wrong with her box and now every morning I find a pile of shit right next to her box. Shit – well, that really is shit.

The "Bizarre" is coming up next week and accordingly I have already a holy mess in my study.

But last night I had a nice dinner party and card game. Did you play card games? I confess, I am a game addict. Chess, canasta, jigsaw puzzles; I have some kind of need to shut up my mind which otherwise is racing around too much.

Answer: Bartok was a wonderful pianist; he toured a lot in his earlier years. I love his music and was a noted interpreter of his works.

I bubbled enough for today.

Bless you,

Agi

December 3, 2002

Dear Agi,

Hello my wonderful friend. I hope all is well on the island and the home-front.

I want to try to write "up" stuff through the holidays but, truth be told, I am a tad blue. Why? Well, remember a few letters ago when I told you about my chess buddy? Richard Fox? Well they took him out last Friday. They took him to the hole because that's what they do when you get your date. He's going to be executed February 12th.

This is the first time since I have been here that someone I actually know, from my pod, is going to be killed.

It sure was surreal – for lack of a better word – seeing them come in and take him out; he turned white as a ghost with fear – as we all will, I'm sure.

They put inmates in the hole after you get your date, just to keep you isolated, so you won't freak out and kill somebody or kill yourself. Then a few days before your date (with the devil or an angel) going for some wry humor – laughing beats crying – but I'm not doing neither... hell, I'm going stoic, apathetic with this act; anyway a few days before the play is over and the curtain comes down, they take you down to Lucasville; that's where they do the killing, not here in Mansfield.

So Fox is gone because Taft won the election and he will not (like Bush) show mercy. What did Fox do? I don't know. He never told me or anyone. Most guys in here don't talk about their case and I don't ask because you just don't do that.

Sweet Agi, yes, I'm a tad blue but I'm not whining. This letter is just matter-of-fact and not woe-is-me, OK? OK. I'm just sharing because that's what we do, huh? There is nothing in my life today more satisfying than <u>our</u> friendship. Smile. I am.

Peace & Love.

Ciao,

Rich

December 11, 2002

Dear Rich,

I got your "blue" letter yesterday. It is awful. I don't know what to say. People who support the death penalty should live only one day on death row, it would teach them…maybe. Human stupidity and cruelty is the plague of this world and we, who try to fight against it, are not enough in number.

Try to escape – it's easy to say. Maybe I will cheer you up a bit: next to me on the couch there is a tiny black creature named Lucky. I got him two days ago. It's an adorable 9 weeks old mix of black lab and something else. He is remarkably calm for a puppy, already attached to me, wanting to sleep with me, wanting to crawl on my lap: a sheer joy (except for not being yet house-broken.)

Another good news: at our "Bizarre" last Saturday we broke the record: we made $ 1,000! With that money – after sending some for AI – my group will probably send me to the next Annual General Meeting in Pittsburgh. That will be in April.

I just finished a series of the music class, we will continue in January. We agreed to concentrate on the great 20th century composers more in depth, and talk and demonstrate about interpretation. We did some of it already and it was fun: comparing different CDs and videos of the same piece, things like that. There are only three ladies attending the class, but they are really interested and enjoying it. It's fun.

To finish I tell you a Hungarian (political) joke. It was told during the Communist regime, but it's very up-to-date now here: Two men are sitting on a bench in a park. They don't talk. One is spitting. The other sighing. Silence. Then one of them says: "Let's don't talk about politics."

So let's don't, because you – and I – will get depressed.

Cheers, friend,

Agi

December 15, 2002

Dear Agi,

Well how's the weather out there on your island? Back here all week off and on snow, but no accumulation. I like watching it snow, don't you? I hate driving in it though; I guess everybody does. Does it snow much on your island to where you get inches or feet of accumulation?

I bought myself some Xmas cookies and man they are delicious – hum-hum good! You are lucky we aren't allowed to have food boxes, because if we were, I'd be buggin' you crazy with requests to make me some cookies and other sweets. Yes, I have a sweet tooth. I think most alcoholics when they get sober, do crave sweets. I know I do, anyway.

Yeah, I'm enjoying the novel "The Evening News" a lot. Not only is it a pretty good story, but, also, it's enlightening to know how the network news works.

I like the world of music, musicians, the best. I wasn't made to do anything else in my life except play music. I sure miss playing my gigs. I even miss playing Xmas tunes – a little bit though I'm not real crazy about those tunes. Truth be told, I never practiced those so at first I would kind of stumble – well not stumble, just be "tight" with 'em, and by the time they started swinging, hell, the holidays would be over. (Ha-ha) When I say swinging I mean no longer "reading" it, the sheet music; i.e. read it, learn it, and now put the sheet away and just play it my own way. That would take me around 2 weeks and by then Christmas was over…oops oh well, maybe I should start now my Eastern tunes. What the hell am I talking about?

Love,

Rich

January 2, 2003

Dearest Agi,

Hello my Lady and a Happy New Year to you. I wish nothing but the best to you in 2003, filled with love, peace, good health, prosperity, good friends, good food and good booze eh?

You know King Solomon, the wisest man who's lived on the planet, actually did say, "…for there is nothing good for a man under the sun except to eat and to drink and to be merry." Ecclesiastes 8;15.

I'm sure his parties were something to see, huh?

Every new year's eve since I've been here, I watch the parties on TV and I think back through all the years and try to remember where I was playing, (I do it for fun, not to feel sorry for myself.) I can remember a few of them and a lot, of course, I don't. I actually enjoyed the ones where I didn't have to play more than the ones I was working, but there was only a few of those. (Man! My letter writing is rusted. Sorry.)

Do you realize you and I are going on our 4<u>th</u> year of friendship and sharing!

I love you Agi. You're a wonderful, loyal, spirit-lifting friend. And, truely, you are making this situation I'm in a whole lot less daunting. Thank you my sweet Agi; you are always deeply in my mind and heart. I will always cherish you.

Yeah, glad to hear about Lucky the new family member. Hopefully Zizi will get along with him too. I had a Black Lab, 'Solo' was his name, back in '71-'75. He was a real good dog, well behaved and super friendly, and smart too.

I finished the book "The Evening News." I thought it was pretty good.

I saw my lawyers last week on Christmas Eve for 3 hours. One of them is a part-time musician too, he plays guitar in a band on weekends. Gives us something in common anyway. (More on this later.)

Jolly good show! You raised $1,000 at your "Bizarre", huh? I think that's impressive being on a small island at that!

You're one in a million. Stay happy. I'll be back soon.

Peace & Love,
Rich

January 6, 2003
Dear Rich,

Thanks for your nice letter. I wish you the best for the New Year, too. I am glad you have seen your lawyers. What was your impression? It's fine one of them plays music but that's not what I'm interested for, man! Come on, tell me and let me talk to them, or one of them, will you, goddamshit! It's so nice what you write and you love me, so why don't you let me help you, heh?

Did you get the little sign? I am a bit worried about it because it has a little magnet and it might be suspicious for the bastards there. Let me know if you got it. I have seen it in the store and I had to send it to you.

Yeah, it's our fourth year, amazing, what? Actually we started in May '99, so it's well into the fourth.

Lucky is adorable, but of course some trouble too – like doing puppy-business, trying to chew everything he can get. And still peeing here and there, especially when there are guests, being excited. But it's nothing like Prince, Zizi is not afraid of him. Lucky is trying desperately to be friends with her, but she is aloof, probably wisely, because the puppy has sharp little teeth. They will be OK later I hope.

I had a few parties during the holidays but nothing like King Solomon's, I'm sure. Yesterday I celebrated my 74th birthday with a canasta game after an Amnesty meeting. By the way, when is your birthday?

Want more books? I will go soon to the bookstore – if you have any special request, let me know.

Love,

Agi

January 13, 2003

My dear Agi,

How are you today? Happy, I hope. I'm doin' OK. I just finished exercising and I worked up, revved up my cardiovascular system and ba da boom-ba da bing I feel free for the moment.

Thank you for the small plaque of H. B. Stowe and I promise to you that I will <u>never</u> give up – <u>NEVER!</u>

Sure it's OK if you talk to my lawyers. I'm enclosing their names, address, e-mail, telephone number for you. What was my impression, you asked. Truth be told: I'm not good at first impressions with lawyers because I do not like lawyers. I don't trust them and I do think they just tell me what I want to hear to make me feel better (sometimes) so I never know what to believe. (Hell my first lawyer told me I'd get 15 years at the most; now I sit on death row.)

One thing we do want is for them to prolong this process as long as they can. I'm in no hurry as you can understand.

Hey, Lucky is a cutie I like him. And yeah, he'll mellow out as he gets older.

Happy belated Birthday to you, Agi. I would have sent a card but I didn't know.

I was born May 19, 1950. I'm 53 but I don't feel it or think it. I've been told by a few people (before Mansfield) that I have 'Peter Pan' syndrome, whatever that is. (A man that hasn't or doesn't want to grow up?) Well, maybe a little bit. Ha-ha

In truth, I was always trying to escape somewhere else rather than be in reality, I suppose.

I loved the 'high' of playing, especially in a good band, and it was cookin' and grovin' and the feeling is so good you don't want it to end. You know what I'm talking about, I know. I guess I just wanted my whole life to be that high, that inexplicable feeling that music brings to a player. I guess I got lost in the high.

That's all for now. I'll be back soon. Call or e-mail my lawyers, that's A-OK with me. Be happy – keep the faith.

Peace & love.

Ciao,

Rich

Thank you for the small plaque of H. B. Stowe and I promise to you that I will never give up – NEVER!

January 20, 2003

Dear Rich,

I talked to David Hanson and he sounded pretty good to me. He said he is not yet completely familiar with your case, he can't say at the present too much, but he completely agreed that the robbery charge is absurd. And he said there is hope to reverse the verdict. We even exchanged e-mails after the talk: as an afterthought I told him a bit about myself and he answered saying it's good you have support. And, of course, it's the best thing to go as slow as possible, because time is working for you, working for us, about the death penalty altogether. You probably know about our latest triumph in Illinois.

I participated in a peace walk here; for Friday Harbor it was a big crowd, about 300 people.

I have to tell you a joke: three surgeons get together and brag about their achievements. One says: there was a pianist who lost seven fingers —I reattached them and hey, tomorrow he will play a concerto with the Cleveland Orchestra. The second: that's nothing. I had an athlete who lost both legs, I reattached them and he won seven gold medals as a runner. The third: that's nothing. There was a terrible accident: a cowboy riding a horse was completely destroyed in a train accident. Only the horse's ass and a hat remained, and now it's sitting in the White House!

Lucky is adorable and a goddam nuisance, but I love him. Zizi is still shitting on the floor – I'm really blessed with these animals. Tonight I will try a new method: I will lock out Zizi, because I don't like to step on shit first thing in the morning.

My recital is coming up in three weeks. I will see the pianist in Victoria only a week before.

Bless you, my friend.

Agi

February 4, 2003

Dear Rich,

Lucky chewed up your last letter, but I remember it. I did go to the bookstore and sent you an I. Allende but didn't find a K. Haruf, instead I sent a Grisham, which I hope you didn't read.

I completely agree not to go to "psych" doctors and to give a thought to your feelings and emotions. You are a great guy!

And it's better not to comment about R. Fox and his father because my language would get very nasty indeed. You know by now how deeply I feel about the cruelty and <u>pointlessness</u> of the death penalty. You know there was something like 12,000 murders in this country last year, while in Canada, where there's no death penalty, there were 89. Well!

My news is that my recital was cancelled – because the Victoria-Friday Harbor ferry stopped on Feb. 1 and I couldn't get together with my pianist. It will reopen in April and my recital is tentatively scheduled for June 6.

I m sorry you are that cold; I wish I could send you a heater – I know I can't. Here the winter was so far incredibly mild, no snow at all, some gloriously mild, sunny days, and some rain. I wonder if we go through winter like this, probably we will get it in March!

I am involved in the anti-war movement, getting tons of e-mail, signing tons of petitions, letters, etc. The whole thing is a nightmare and if that madman will do it anyway, we will get a bomb on our head, I'm sure. Human stupidity will destroy this world. Human stupidity is limitless.

Well, I don't mean to depress you, sorry.

More soon.

Ciao,

Agi

P.S. Dear pal, you spell "truely" like this: It's spelled "truly." It's true. (What nerve, a foreigner tells you about English spelling, what?)

February 6, 2003

Dear Agi,'

I hope this letter finds you well, happy and warm.

I got your nice letter of January 20th and it made me feel good knowing you talked to David Hanson. Indeed, having support does feel good. It keeps my morale up just knowing you are there for me.

It's been a tad melancholy for me this past week: thinking of Fox waiting for his time to walk into the death chamber knowing he is going to die – man! That's weird, to me.

Truth be told, I'm not good at praying but lately, the last few months, I have been working on my praying technique. I grew up Catholic and I went to Catholic school for 9 years (I flunked the 4h grade) so back then I learned how to pray and say the rosary the Catholic way; i.e. repeat Hail Mary's and Our Father's and the "net of Contrition" and so on. To me, and this is just my opinion, I don't think repetition of prayers mean much to God. Although I could be wrong; I've been wrong most of my life (a dry smile) Still, keeping my sense of humor – laughter is music to the soul, eh?

By the way, I'm not Catholic any more; they kicked me out a long time ago. I'm not a part of any organized religion. I just enjoy reading my Bible and talking to God – to me that's prayer –ie. talking is praying to God and meditating is listening to God. Anyway, you know what I mean.

Kudos to you my activist angel for being out in the streets and marching for peace. The immortal words of John Lennon are still the right melody "Give Peace a Chance."

Truly sad about the space shuttle, isn't it? Now I hear that Columbia might have started falling apart over California. No doubt it's those tiles, that's the problem. NASA will fix it and space exploration with humans and robots will go on and it should. Personally, I believe there is intelligent life out there somewhere but on this planet I'm beginning to wonder. Look who's in the White House. Man, oh, man, eh?

Have fun on your recital – I know it's any day now. I'm glad you still keep playing gigs. It will keep you young at heart and warm-hearted.

Be & stay happy.

Ciao,

Rich

P.S.   I used to enjoy playing the tune "Young at Heart" one of my favorite Frank Sinatra tunes.

February 16, 2003

Dear Agi,

And how are you today, my lady? I know you are keeping busy with the death penalty and now the anti-war movement issues.

I saw on TV yesterday (Saturday) that millions of people all over the world were marching and protesting against the war. We're looking like the bad guys now, the aggressors. Sad situation, indeed.

Well, they executed Fox last Wed. I found out what he did because that was on TV on the local news. Another sad and horrible situation, but killing Fox didn't make a positive out of a negative, it's just another murder, this time by the government.

It sure did bother me though, more than I thought it would, when the day came for them to come in the pod and take someone I know and take him down to Lucasville to kill him. One day you're playing chess with a guy and tomorrow he's stretched out in a coffin; life is precarious, eh?

OK, I'm changing the topics to a new key. No more downer stuff – let's get happy and enjoy life, our sharing, our wonderful friendship we have.

By the way, thank you for correcting me on truely vs. truly. I bet I've been misspelling that word since the 4th grade (ha-ha).

If you see any others, words or punctuation, correct me please; I still like to learn.

Stupid question: How do you get off the island, if you need to with your car, if the ferry is closed Feb. until April?

Thank you for the 2 books; I'm looking forward to reading them both. And, no, I have not read the Grisham book, so that worked out A-OK.

The weather is a little warmer but it's snowing a lot. I'm looking forward to being able to go outside for rec.

So how is it working out between Lucky and Zizi? I'm hoping they're getting along with each other. Are they?

I'll be back soon; right now I think I'll get back in bed and start my J. Grisham book.

Peace & love, my friend.

Ciao,

Rich

February 17, 2003

Dear Rich,

You started your last letter saying you hope it finds me well, happy and warm. Well, I am healthy and warm – but happy?

I couldn't get my nice pianist for the June date for my concert. I got back to the Victoria pianist – of whom I have some misgivings – and we are trying to get a date in May. But…I was struggling with some technical problem for a long time; I didn't play as well as I could. Now I begin to see the light at the end of the tunnel, and…I started to feel pain in one finger on the left hand: arthritis. That's the end of my playing. I still could do that concert, I think, but it will be probably the last one. Of course, what the hell, I'm 74, what do I want? But I'm not happy.

About your praying and being Catholic: I'm very sure you are right: repetition and Hail Mary's don't mean much to God. I would go even further: being Catholic or Protestant or sun-worshipper or whatnot, means nothing to God. Religions are <u>man-made.</u> <u>Talking</u> to God is the only way to help yourself. This is my opinion – I hope it doesn't hurt your feelings.

As you know I have no religion but I have tremendous faith. I know there's something out there and this life is but a visit before going home.

It's absolutely beautiful what you saying: "talking to God is praying and meditating is listening to God."

You are great, my friend.

Love,

Agi

February 23, 2003

Dear Agi,

What's up?! Don't you just hate that expression? I'm sure you do; I know I do, and I have to hear it all day long, not just from the younger inmates, but the younger guards, too.

Always good to hear from my friend; I got your letter of Feb. 17th. Truly sorry to hear about your arthritis on your left-hand finger.

Even if your playing days are over, you can still teach music if you want. You have been playing a long time, huh? I am very proud of you. Being a musician, doing it for a living, is hard, I know. But, being a serious classical musician, I think, is harder. Actually, I know it's harder. So many obstacles to deal with – i.e.: less jobs, tougher competition, and highest degree of musicianship to maintain at all times. I would be drinking between songs and during breaks smoking pot; classical players play it straight – then they go get drunk and smoke pot, eh? (Goin' for a laugh.)

The newspaper article I enclosed sure makes me feel up with some hope. I had heard about this study but by the time I finally got a paper someone cut out the article, so I never got to read it. So, I wrote the library here and they sent me this.

George Franklin (# 8) he lives two cells down from me and he is getting a new sentence. He went through the Fed. Appeal Ct. last summer and the Fed judges said "new trial or new sentence." Very seldom do they want to have a new trial because of the cost, I guess. Most of the time you get life in prison with no parole. Maybe I'll get that too. Then I can ask myself "what is better, bondage or death?" That's a tough one, huh? Right now I'll take bondage because I'm chicken ha-ha-ha…well, hell, at least I'm honest.

Like the Old West adage, "Don't shoot our piano player; he's doing the best he can."

It always feels good to talk with you.

Peace & Love, my friend.

Ciao,

Rich

February 28, 2003

Hey Riccardo, that's wonderful! I'm sure your lawyers will be able to use this article to get you a new trial. Tell them, but hopefully they are clever enough to do it. Did you realize there were three cases with obviously lesser crimes? You and two others who killed one person with no aggravations, all the others involved robbery and rape or other things (like the father who beat to death his 6 months old child? God!) Of course, you are charged with robbery, but the others did the killing during a robbery, that's different. Well, I'm thrilled. Maybe I will call D. Hanson to get sure he uses the article – and the support of law students!

The enclosed article was in the Moratorium Campaign's newsletter, you might be interested to get some of those writings, maybe it will inspire you... If you want me, I will subscribe to it, I donate anyway to these causes.

And don't think of a life-sentence. You should get a few years only if there's justice.

To answer your "stupid" question: the ferry stopped only from Victoria, you still can get to the mainland and the other islands. They can't possibly stop the ferry altogether. By the way my concert is rescheduled for the 13th of May.

I have seen an Ayurvedic doctor, that's a doctor who uses only natural ways to cure. I went twice on the mainland, he was a little further than Seattle, and now I'm inundated with herbs and he changed my diet a great deal. We will see what it does. In any case, I think I still can do that concert. I have been playing a long time, you can say that: started at the ripe old age of 5, so that makes 69 years!

Lucky and Zizi are quite a riot: Lucky pesters Zizi all the time with his love, she hisses and runs away, he after her. And there are still "accidents" by both – am I blessed! I'm looking forward to a time when Lucky will be grown up and reasonable to change my carpet and couch, because they are disgusting.

Once more, I'm very glad about that article. And spring is coming, almost here! It still didn't snow here, but it was a bit colder the last few days.

Cheers my friend,

Agi

P.S. I kept the copy of the article.

March 9, 2003

Dear Agi,

Well, my friend, how's it going? I hope all is well on the island.

Myself, I've been sick and in bed for 12 days. Man, I felt bad! That was the first time I've been really ill since I've been here at Mansfield. I had the flu and for a few days a high fever; so high at night I was hallucinating.

I'm on the 'upswing' now. I'm weak but my appetite is returning, so I should be back 100% in a few days.

I got your letter of Feb. 28 with my article, thanks for sending that back, and your article on Compassion, Dead Man Walking Opera and Election Results etc.

I get "Compassion" for free – we all do here at Mansfield. I also get one from New York, but I can't think of the name of it. There are some good articles in Compassion, written by inmates, once in a while. In truth, some I enjoy and some of it makes me depressed. I really don't like to read too much prison stuff; i.e. from it or about it. I don't even watch TV shows that the theme is taken inside jail or if it's too much crime.

In my opinion, there is too much crime/violence on TV and in movies and music and those video games. It's like they (Hollywood) is saying crime and violence is cool and it's not, of course. No wonder kids today are so screwed up and take guns to school.

Man, I sure can't wait to get to go outside. I haven't been out since Oct. (5 months!) I hate living like this – it's hard.

Sometimes I just don't feel like I'm part of the world anymore. Some days I'm very lonely inside. Loneliness is something I used to fix by my drinking. When I felt lonely, I'd just go to the bar and be with all the other lonely people and drink. I'm a people person.

Peace & Love my friend,

Ciao,

Rich

March 18, 2003

Dear Riccardo, my poor friend,

I am so sorry you were sick – I knew it because your letter was kind of late. Did you get medical care? Is there a doctor for the prison? I'm glad you are better, maybe quite well by the time you receive this letter.

You couldn't be more right saying that crime and violence on TV and movies do an awful lot of harm and is responsible for many of the crimes committed. And the music! Yes, I absolutely loathe rock and "bad music" as you say. Millions of people grow up listening to that crap all the time. A mad, mad, mad world.

And that madman – the horse's ass – is going to do the war, no matter what. There was another peace walk here on Sunday, quite a lot of people and we walked up and down on the main street with candles and signs against the war. Do you realize that the madman didn't let finish the inspection, so if there's any weapon left, they will use it to us! Man oh man – to quote you – human stupidity will destroy this world. I am glad I am old, maybe I won't live to see a total disaster.

I sent an e-mail to D. Hanson about the article and pointed out that you were one of only three of lesser crimes. Now you have that article, the dissent of Judge Pfeifer and the letter of Laurence Delay. The lawyers have a good back-up to get a new trial – I hope to God they are clever enough to make good use of all this.

On March 29th we will have an event of Amnesty: a famous photographer who {Phil Borges} is connected to Amnesty is coming to give a lecture and sale of his books and photos, of which we will get some money. And right after that – the 3 of April – I'm going to Pittsburgh for the annual general meeting.

Tomorrow I go again to "America" – people here call that to go to the mainland. I go to see my doctor about my arthritis. I changed my diet and swallowed 15 pills a day and it looks like it works. My concert is now scheduled for the 13th of May.

Take care, my friend.

Agi

P.S.   It did snow here on the 8th of March, as I predicted. It looks like the only snowing in the winter. But it didn't stick and was completely gone the next day. Trees are blooming and I have daffodils out at my house.

March 22, 2003

Dear Agi,

Hello, my Lady, how are you? I hope everything is okay; it's been awhile since I heard your voice.

I'm feeling a lot better now except for my chest which is a tad sore from all that coughing I did for two weeks.

I just finished reading the John Grisham book you sent me, "The Brethren," and I enjoyed it a lot. I passed it on to the other guys in here. J. Grisham and Stephen King are very popular in prison. Myself, I don't care for S. King stories because I don't like horror stuff. Hell, my dreams sometimes at night are scary enough and my reality is the pits, so I don't need King to get my imagination going into a negative vibe, a discord so to speak. I want peace, love, serenity, harmony and spirituality in my isolated life. I guess we all do, huh?

Well, I've been watching the war on TV. The last 2 days they sure have bombed the hell out of Baghdad. Even though I'm against the war – any war – I'm glad that Saddam Hussein will be gone from Iraq; he's pure evil, and his sons, especially Uday, from what I have read in my Newsweek and seen and heard on TV.

I thought of you as a little girl going through that yourself – feeling bombs dropped on your city. Man, oh, man I'm sure there are no words to describe the horror of being in that situation – a true living hell.

So you are going to play your concert on May 13th, eh? That's great. Are the herbs and new diet helping with the arthritis problem? What music are you going to play at your concert?

Are you back teaching your class at the College? I never taught at College but I played a jazz concert at Berkeley back in '77. We, the band, stayed the whole weekend and we were always riding BART back and forth to and from San Fran. Love the Bay area.

I saw on the news someone jumped off the Golden Gate Bridge to protest the war.

Be happy. Peace & Love.

Ciao,

Rich

P.S. Write soon.

March 26, 2003

Dear Agi,

Hey, I just got your letter of March 18th, and it's always good to hear your voice.

I see you are staying very busy these days, huh? I admire you and I am truly proud to know you. Not only are you a loyal and wonderful friend, but, indeed, a beautiful human being, that planet earth could use a billion more of like you.

Yes, I'm feeling better, a lot better, and yes I did see the doctor. We have a doctor that comes over to our pod on Tuesdays. He gave me some medicine which did the job. Also, there is an infirmary on the compound but it's a real drag to go to, believe me, I've been there once and I told myself I'm not coming back unless I am truly in pain.

The first summer I was here, 1998, I tripped and fell playing basketball and landed on my head – the back of my head – ouch! The bump on my head swelled up pretty big so the guards made me go to the infirmary. They, the doctors, kept me over there for 3 days and what a long 3 days that was! They put you in a room that's very cold with only one blanket, no pillow, no books, no TV, no radio, no smoking, no nothing; you just lay there! Man, I hated it!

They make it uncomfortable so inmates, especially inmates from general population, won't fake illness or injury to go to the infirmary to get out of work or whatever. I could not wait to get back to my cell on death row where my things are, my home is now. Weird, huh?

I could have gone to the infirmary the second day I was sick – and I felt bad, too – but I chose to wait (6 days) for the doctor to come to our pod the following week.

Truth be told, I don't trust the doctors here. Their bedside manner…well they don't have any bedside manner ha-ha.

Prison is a cold world , Agi, I really hate it. Thanks for being my friend; you do bring me some warmth and hope. I cherish our friendship. Have fun on your trip to Pittsburgh and stay safe.

Godspeed, Peace & Love,

Ciao,

Rich

March 31, 2003

Dear Rich,

I am glad your sickness is gone, and hope you can go outside soon. How is the weather there? Here it's OK but I wish it would be warmer. Well, it will come soon.

Last Saturday we had a wonderful event here, organized by the group: a famous photographer, who is connected to Amnesty has come and gave a lecture with slide-shows. He takes pictures of remote tribes of the four corners of the world – it was very interesting and his personality I liked a lot, a wonderful guy with warm heart who cherishes all the values I do. It was the most successful event we ever had, jam-packed, and we also made a lot of money. He sold his books of which we got a good percentage.

Next Thursday I am off for Pittsburgh to the Amnesty General Meeting, come back Monday. My poor animals have to go to the Animal Inn.

What I play at my concert you ask. I will start with a short French Baroque piece, then a Mozart Sonata and a Brahms Sonata. The second half will be kind of ethnic: two Hungarian, two Brazilian and two Spanish pieces. My new diet and herbs work all right, I feel very little my finger, that's good.

The war…very upsetting, even though Saddam Hussein will be probably gone. It looks like the Iraqis have more resistance than expected. Blood and tragedies to satisfy the whim of our charming President…

I will start teaching a course in the College in April and already started my private one.

Do well my friend. Did you hear anything from your lawyers?

Love,

Agi

…"peace, love, serenity, harmony, and spirituality"…You say beautiful things my friend.

April 8, 2003

Dear Agi,

Well how was it in Pittsburgh? Did you have a good meeting? What was your impression of the city? What did you talk about at your meeting? When you're in the mood, write about your trip if you want to, I'd like to hear about it.

Well it's like winter again back here with cold temperature, wind and rain, and some lite snow – unbelievable! I do not care for the Mid-West, never did. Not the people – though they're not my favorite either – but I try not to judge people (but I do anyway, sorry) hell we all do, huh? (ha-ha)

The weather and geography of the Mid-West is what I hate. Both are ugly; give me the West & West Coast, oh yeah!!

Anyway I did get three days outside last month and needless to say it did feel great to get some sunshine and fresh air. I get to go out, when it's nice, only on day you can divide by 4, because our pod shares the same outside rec cage with 3 other pods, so we have to take turns. I usually get 7 days a month outside if it's not raining. And usually we are allowed to stay out for 2 1/2 hours.

I always feel like a kid in a surreal nightmare when the guards march us out to rec and back, like I did back at St. Mart's when the nuns marched us kids to recess and back; however, at St. Mary's I wasn't handcuffed – ha-ha.

Our VCR system has been broken since November. Mansfield used to show us 2 or 3 movies (videos) a week. I miss not seeing new videos. I would like to see "The Pianist." Question: is there a movie theatre on your island? Do you ever go see new movies? I used to go to the theater by myself a lot in the middle of the week during the afternoon when kids are in school and normal people are at work I enjoyed that. I like the movies.

I'm reading Isabel Allende and once again I love it. She's definitely a good writer and storyteller. (More on this later.)

I'm sure Lucky and Zizi were happy to see you, huh? Me too I'm glad you're home on your island.

Write soon. Ciao.

Love,

Rich

April 11, 2003

Dear Rich,

Thanks for your letter and lovely card. I am back from Pittsburgh. It was a good trip and the meeting was good, as always. Mr. Schulz again made a great speech, very outspoken about our charming President and the human rights abuse. AI can't have a stand about the war but he pointed out the shit it's happening in this country. This administration is destroying everything good in this country. We desperately need a strong democratic candidate for the next election. Here, in little Friday Harbor an organization was formed to work on that. There was an open meeting, about 200 attended, and we discussed how to get rid of GW. They have somebody in mind: Governor of Vermont, Howard Dean.

There were three events about the death penalty: a table discussion, a big panel, and candle vigil on the streets. At the panel one of the panelists was from Ohio, so I grabbed him afterwards and told him about you. He probably can't help; he doesn't deal with Ohio cases, but took your name and story. The more people hear about it the better.

But the trip was goddamn long and when I arrived there was a big mishap. I was going to stay privately and I went to the wrong place – wow! It's a long story, some day I will tell you – I was out in a deserted place late at night, couldn't get a cab… well, finally I got it, about 1.30 am, and the place was so miserable that next day I just stayed in the hotel where the meeting was held.

Yesterday there was a lecture by a survivor of the Holocaust, a Hungarian lady who was in Auschwitz. You know my story, but I tell you I was lucky. I escaped the unspeakable horror of the death camps. It was nice to talk to her, we could talk a little bit in Hungarian – I don't have many opportunities to speak my native language.

So here I include some pictures about these events, and you can see Lucky grown a lot since he was a tiny puppy.

I hope you are well and gone outside a bit. Here the weather is finally getting warmer and the days longer. I love spring.

Ciao my friend,

Agi

April 20, 2003

Dear Agi,

Hello my friend. I hope this letter finds you well and feeling good. I'm feeling pretty good but I'm anxious, eager to get outside again in May.

I could go outside this month, April, if I want to get up at 6am for morning rec but, man oh man, that's way too early for me. I've never been a morning person, definitely a nocturnal man. Besides, it's still a tad chilly at 6am and damp. In June I might get up and go out. (Note: one month the bottom floor (cells) has morning rec and the top tier has afternoon rec outside; then, the next month the bottom floor has afternoon and the top tier morning rec outside on days divided by 4. Routine and rules until the day I die, oh my so contrary to the lifestyle I lead.

I've been reading "The House of the Spirits." Have you read this book? If not, you should. It's a wonderful story.

Did you know that Isabel Allende is a niece of assassinated President Salvador Allende? I don't remember if I told you, but I saw her on TV last year on 60 minutes being interviewed. I didn't realize (then) who she was until the interview was about over because I wasn't paying real close attention at first. Anyway, she's married now to some political or some influential rich guy I San Fran. But I forgot whom.

I love her books, her stories. I'm not finish yet because I'm reading slowly because I don't want it to end; I so truly enjoy my trip down to Chile every afternoon around 2 pm. I read about Esteban Trieba (?) and Clara, who just died, I miss her already, and now the story will continue with the grandchildren taking the main stage. I do like the family except for Esteban- but they, all of 'em, are a dysfunctional family to say the least.

In my life, I started out in a normal family but later on it also became a dysfunctional family because of my alcoholic father.

Do you think the dead can see us people on earth? Sometimes, I wonder if my mom and dad, and my two brothers, are watching?

We're having another execution next week on the 29th. This guy I don't know, he's in another pod. More later, my friend – write soon. I miss you.

Love,

Rich

April 22, 2003

Dear Rich,

Are you handcuffed when going to recreation? What a shit! It's very enlightening all you tell me about prison life, and I feel very sorry for you, my friend. You know I really enjoy our correspondence, I like to write to you – I guess you know it by now.

There was a cold spell, when I changed planes in Chicago coming from Pittsburgh; it was snowy, temperature 29. It was cold in FH, too. But it's over, I hope you have nice weather now, and I hope you have a little time outside.

Answering your question: there is a movie theater here, but I go very rarely, I'd rather watch movies at home. I rent movies sometimes, but more often than not I turn them down after 5 minutes. At night, before going to sleep, I usually put on one of my videos, something soothing, uplifting. I must have put on the "Magic Flute" by Mozart a hundred times. I have trouble to sleep and often my stupid mind races about and I have nightmarish thoughts and images. The "Magic Flute" is a fairy tale opera, where love and the good triumphs over the bad forces, and, of course, the music is divine.

Oh, I am just bubbling now. You see, I am just sharing some feelings and thoughts.

My best,

Agi

April 27, 2003

Dear Agi,

Hello, my lady, I got your letter of April 11th with the eight pictures. Thanks for writing and I'm glad you're home on your island.

About those pictures, I did not know there was a rule on limit but now we both know. I'm only allowed to receive three pictures per envelope. I sent the office an envelope to send five of 'em back and NO, I didn't get to see them. They kept 'em and just sent me a notice of contraband and to either send them an envelope to send back or they would destroy them; I imagine you have them back by now. Right?

If you want to, send 'em back three at a time in your next couple of letters.

Hey, Lucky looks real good. He's a beautiful dog with a beautiful coat, and he looks like a very friendly and loving dog, too. How is it working out with him and Zizi? I do hope they are getting along.

Well, I finished House of the Spirits by Isabel Allende. Down the road, if you see any other used books by her, I would indeed like to read them, too. Question: Have you read "House of the Spirits"? What's the last book (novel) you read that you enjoyed?

In each death row unit there's a kitchen. There are five units w/five kitchens...well not anymore. They closed all death row kitchens and now we get our food from general pop's kitchen, i.e. it's put on trays and brought over already prepared. Anyway, my point is: now there are less jobs for us to get which will be a drag. If you have a job, Mansfield pays $16 a month, no job you get only $3 a month. It's hard to live on only $3 a month.

I'll be back soon. Be happy.

Peace & Love.

Ciao,

Rich

P.S.   I'm glad your trip was a success, but it is a bit disconcerting you got lost/stuck by yourself until 1.30 the morning. (You got lost inSeattle, too.) I wouldn't worry if you had a traveling companion. Anyway, I'm glad you're back home.

May 1, 2003

Dear Rich,

Here is the loveliest month of the year and here is our fourth anniversary of friendship, isn't that amazing? I hope you get to go out sometimes. The weather is great here; I just went for a walk with Lucky. He will be a great dog when calming down a bit. He is loving a bit too much now: jumping at my guests, he can be a real pain in the ass. He is pestering Zizi with his love, too, but it's okay. And Zizi is still shitting on the floor; I don't know what to do about it.

I got back the 5 pictures, here are 3 of them. (To hell with them!) I mean the stupid regulations. So, 3 pictures are OK, and 5 are contraband? Stupidity is the greatest evil in this world.

I will look for other I. Allende novels. Probably not until after my concert of 13. What was the last novel I read? Well, it was a stupid whodunit – I read it in Italian to learn the language. Of course, they are easier to read than serious books. Otherwise I am reading a book of Hungarian legends and myths. There is a whole mythology of the Hungarians and the Huns – you know, according to legends there were two brothers, Hunor and Magyar, so Attila the Hun is our ancestor. The Huns somehow disappeared; there is no explanation of that. Or they just melt into the Hungarians, the Magyars. But I got annoyed reading about Attila, how great he was – my God, he was great killing many people and causing many tragedies. I hate all those "conquerors" (Napoleon, for example) who want to conquer the world. They don't change anything, just kill and kill. It looks like it's in the human mind and it won't change. It's the men – without men there wouldn't be any war. I am not a feminist by all means, but that's the truth.

Can the dead see us? That's an interesting question. I think they can but I believe they might not want it after a while; they develop, go into other realms, other interests. Although, according to near death experiences, relatives and friends greet them over there. Don't laugh at me, but sometimes I think Tomi, my brother and Zoli are watching over me. Oh well, never mind.

Enough bubbling for today, right?

Love,

Agi

May 8, 2003

Dear Agi,

Hello my Lady. I loved this letter (actually the last two) and believe me I cherish it when you're "babbling" —as you call it – I call it sharing from the <u>heart</u> and mind.

The pictures are great! I was showing them around and the guys got a kick out of them. Me, too. 😊 Odd request, I guess, from an odd man out. I would like to see Friday Harbor, like the store where you buy me books and the other shops and so on. If you enjoy taking pictures, I do like looking at 'em.

Hey, I'm impressed! Reading your book in Italian, huh? You're doing real well with that; i.e. learning so fast. You just started learning Italian a year or two ago, I think.

In truth, I'm losing track of time. I can't believe you and I have been talking and sharing for 4 years already. Well, Happy Anniversary, Agi. I truly hope there is something I have brought into your life that makes you feel good inside like you have me.

You have been a wonderful friend since day one. Just knowing you are out there being my friend and really caring – and I do know you really do care – makes me feel stronger and kinder in here. What do I mean kinder? Well, I have learned about kindness from you these past 4 years. Your walk, not just your talk. I don't want to share too much about all this 'cause it would take 10 pages and then I'd be babbling, and believe me I can babble.

I think prison would have made me an angry, bitter, resentful person if I hadn't have met you. You might not realize how much you have helped me and I'm not very good at writing my feelings from things of my heart without sounding mushy –I don't think you like mushy. (I don't either.) No, I guess I am a tad 'cause I am very sentimental; hell, I was watching "Forrest Gump" and my eyes were getting teary. (Rent "Forrest Gump." It's a good story; very clever.)

Our VCR is fixed. I'm glad. I do like movies. Like you though, I'm picky. Sorry, I know I got off my train of thought. Some days this place wears you down and it's kinda hard to stay focused. I will write again this weekend and respond to your last two letters.

I love you, Agi. You're a damn <u>good</u> woman. Well, putting like that didn't hurt, huh? You're the best!

Peace & love.

Ciao,

Rich

May 13, 2003

Dear Agi,

Hello, my Lady. I'm back again. I wanted to respond to a couple of things you talked about in your last two letters of 4-22 and 5-1-03.

You struck a chord when you mentioned that you have trouble getting to sleep (4-22). Man, oh, man I can relate to that! You know how you hear murderers say in the movies, or interviews or wherever "I thought about it (the murder) everyday in prison"... they are speaking the truth! The time between bed and sleep is the worst of the day. My mind, or actually my conscience, goes, "OK, time to beat myself up, punish myself." The past, all the drinking, all the mistakes, the misery, the could-haves and should-haves comes back with a vengeance and it's been like that all these years on death row.

By the way, I am rereading your book. No wonder you have nightmares! And, yes, I think that Zoli and Tomi could be there for you to greet you, say hello, when you pass on through to the other side. I feel as though, and I was told, that my grandma, my mother's mother, is there waiting for me. Who knows?

I like what you said and agree with you that people who have gone on develop and probably lose interest on earthly things – the Bible says we are not to love this world – it's only temporal. But I still like the earth, and people, music, wine and women, good books, movies, food, nice clothes, cool cars, hot beaches, cold mountains and serene islands.

I would like to buy a pair of tennis shoes. I really, really hate asking because you already do a lot for me. Please don't get mad at me for asking, OK-OK?

I'm trying to move to a new pod, DR-6, where there is more freedom. It's a new thing for death row inmates. The cell doors are opened, no cages, more rec inside and outside. Only inmates with no tickets, write-ups can move there. My prison record is clean. This new pod will have 34 inmates, 17 up and 17 down. I'm hoping and praying I get chosen to go there. There are 200+ inmates here and everybody is trying to go there. More on this later.

You and Zoli were like Forrest & Jenny, "two peas in a pod". You and I might be in different pods but we are on the same plant.

Love,

Rich

May 14, 2003

Dear Riccardo,

Yesterday, coming back from the dress rehearsal – the day of my recital – I was in a sour mood because I played like shit and I thought how nice would it be to find a letter from you in my mail-box – and there it was, your <u>damn</u> nice letter. (If you think it hurts me you are silly. I am the one using dirty words, much more than you, am I?)

My recital was a big success, cheering, standing ovation and all that jazz. But I know exactly how I played: the first two pieces were pretty bad, I was terribly nervous. Then it got better and better – so, I was showing about half of my capacity. But my capacity is pretty damn good, so I am halfway satisfied. Since it was probably the last concert, it would have been nice to have played a little better, but such is life. I went through hell because of a technical problem and I know why it wasn't better.

My dear friend, thank you for your damn nice letter. It gives me a wonderful feeling knowing that I can help you some and can give you human warmth. So, yes, you give me something, too. Our friendship became an important thing in my life and I'm always happy to receive your letters. (Am I getting "mushy"??)

I will take pictures of Friday Harbor for you (And send only three at a time, damn the stupid bastards!)

And here is my best birthday wish: a <u>new trial.</u> It will be probably late, but never mind. (I mean the birthday wish; you won't get it by the 18th. Sorry.)

Enough bubbling for today.

Love,

Agi

May 17, 2003

Dear Rich,

I just got your letter of 5-13 and I feel like responding right away.

About sleep and nightmares and mind racing – just like me – I take some mild, over-the-counter sleeping pills and it helps. It's called Sominex, could you get it? I take only one but it makes a difference. Don't punish yourself, you are already punished my friend.

I hope you get to the new pod. It's good your prison record is clean. Keep up your good behavior, it will help at your new trial – which I hope to God will happen.

Yes, I believe, am convinced, that the dead are alive and we will see them.

I watched "Forrest Gump" last night. Very moving.

And I started to take pictures for you. When the roll is full I will start to send them – 3 at a time, fuck'm. And I sent 3 books, 2 Allende and a Wilbur Smith, hope you don't know those.

Cheers,

Agi

May 25, 2003

Dear Agi,

Hand on heart, I truly do appreciate your sweet generosity and kindness; I am indeed a lucky man to have such a loyal and wonderful friend as you Agi.

Well, I am in a new pod   DR-6. Being here is a whole lot better. There are no rec cages inside or outside and man I hated those cages over in my old pod; I always felt like a monkey at the zoo hangin' out in his cage.

Anyway, check this out, I now get <u>4 days</u> a week outside rec. Man, I love that. My cell door is opened on one day 6.30 am until 1 pm and then the next day the door is opened from 2.30 until 8 pm, with a 45 minutes lock up for count. We, the guys on the top tier, (18 of us) alternate morning and afternoon rec with the 18 inmates on the first floor; i.e. one day we have morning then afternoon and the next day we have afternoon and they have morning.

In the pod, which is really big, we have an ice machine (I haven't had an ice cube for 5 ½ yrs.) also a microwave oven, ping-pong table, a small workout room w/Universal Equipment, a laundry room w/2 washers & dryers and my favorite: a small library.

Note: A lot of the books you have sent me over the years are in there. There are about 300 books, mostly paperback novels in there, plus a lot of religious books and a set of encyclopedias and magazines – Time & Newsweek (when my subscription of Newsweek & Reader's Digest is over don't renew them – maybe later I'll ask for something not available here to share w/other inmates.) I can even read the New York Times now and USA Today.

Outside we have 2 basketball goals, a handball court, a small track (9 ½ laps equals 1 mile) and beautiful, beautiful grass! Oh, it feels so good to feel grass and dirt – EARTH! For 5 ½ yrs my feet have only touched concrete. More on all this later. I think this is going to be 110% better.

Thanks, Agi, for being my best good friend. Without you in my life prison would be 110% worse. Yes, also I got the 3 books you sent. I'll read 'em & then share 'em.

Ciao,

Rich

P.S. Pleased to hear your concert went well, and I'm sure if even at one-fourth of capacity, your music would be still superb!

May 30, 2003

Dear Rich,

Hey my friend, what a good letter I got! I am happy for you – what an improvement! You can now play chess and ping-pong often, I hope. Do you play ping-pong? I love it and play tolerably well, but don't have many occasions to do it. I did play as a kid, and later on whenever I could, like in the castle (see my book.) You will maybe even find somebody to talk to sometimes - I mean a friendly human contact among the guys there. More freedom, ice-cubes, wash-machines, New York Times, wow! Great.

I will e-mail the IJPC to get their news and also tell about your case. For Jerome Campbell I already wrote a letter to Gov. Taft. I told you I hear about all the death penalty cases. At the next Amnesty meeting, which is this Sunday, I will let them sign the petition for him.

Thanks for the glorious picture of Budapest – that's the Parliament building and the cupola of the Basilica church. Yeah, it should be better than in 44, or 56.

Days are getting longer here, at 9.00pm is still daylight. Weather is slowly getting warmer, too. I like this time of the year.

Once more, I'm very glad to hear about your new pod.

Love,

Agi

June 8, 2003

Dear Agi,

Hey, I got two letters from you this week. One you wrote May 17 and one on May 30th. I shall respond.

Yes, I can get sleeping pills if I asked the doctor or psych-doctor. But now that I'm getting a lot more outside time and more exercise I'm sleeping better already; plus, since I can come out of my cell everyday to visit I'm not taking as many naps through the day. (Today I walked 4 miles around the track, in state shoes-boots.)

Clothes? Yes, the prison gives us clothes. We get 2 pair of pants, blue with a red stripe on the sides of the legs, two white tops, (smocks) one pair of leather mid-top boots and free underwear every 120 days, socks, & white T-shirts; also, one hooded sweatshirt.

I am very lucky to have you in my life. I guess God wanted us to know each other; you are my last friend and how wonderful and loyal you are. You are the kindest person I have ever met. As Forrest Gump said, "You are my best good friend." I'm glad you watched it. It is one of my favorite films; it touches my heart, as you do, Agi.

So you enjoy the game ping-pong, huh? Yes, I play it but it's been years since. A kid I grew up with had a table in the basement and we used to play all the time. It is a fun game.

Everything here is working out A-OK for me. I really like my new pod and all the freedom. The other inmates seem nice and we are all getting along fine. This is the best of the death row inmates. No fighters, and everybody is polite. I am making some new friends that I enjoy. In my old pod, I really never had a friend to relate to, I was very lonely – believe me.

You have to watch your p's and g's over here, obey the rules, which are <u>very</u> strict. You get into trouble here, you go to the hole; (one guy went last week) if you go to the hole, you can't come back here.

OK, all for now. I'll be back soon. Be happy.

Love,

Rich

PS The jokes/comics I send you made me laugh or at least a small chuckle or smile; I just want to share some of my smiles with you.

June 15, 2003

Dear Agi,

Hello my Lady. I hope all is well and you're feeling up and happy.

I'm doing great over here in my new pod. I really like all this new freedom and new friends.

I'm starting to get in this ping-pong thing. It is fun, huh? Also, there is a lot of chess players here, too – good ones! I am not the best, though I have and can beat the best, but out of 10 games he would win 6 and I 4 games. That's cool, because, in truth, I enjoy playing with someone better than me rather than playing someone I can always beat easily.

The weather here, in Northern Ohio, the armpit of America, has been lousy. Rain, rain and more rain…damn, I'm really ready for some hot sunny days and clear blue skies. I still go out (if it's not pouring) and get my daily walks around the track.

By the way, I got my tennis shoes (Wed.11th) thanks Agi, you are so kind to me. I wish I could give you a hug so you could feel how much you mean to me – I love you Agi – you're a wonderful and dear, dear friend – you have indeed touched my heart and soul. You also have taught me much about being a caring and truly beautiful human being. I hope that's not too mushy for you – I know you don't like mushy, but heck, you need love too, and I send my love to you even if mushy bothers you some, I don't care, 'cause I will always send my love, anyway. (I promise I won't always overdo it.)

Just sharing: I grew up in a family that never said we loved each other. I think today w/20/20 hindsight that's truly sad. The world and families and friends should express more love – if they feel it – as John, the Beatle said "all you need is love" and John, the Apostle said "God is love." Therefore I say our friendship is unconditional love, and, to me, that feels and is marvelous.

Wow! I feel better. Be happy.

Love,

Rich

June 18, 2003

Hi, friend,

I am so glad your life is more tolerable now and you find some friendly contact in your new pod. Watch your "p's and g's" – I know you will – and enjoy the more freedom, the grass, the sunshine, the ice cubes, and the New York Times.

Janet asked me to put all our letters in my computer – wow, it's a job! So I am working on it, typing 1 or 2 letters a day. I type with one finger, you see what a job is that? But it's interesting to reread our letters. For one thing I realize I never sent you an encyclopedia you asked for. Do you still need it? And I never sent you a music tape. Griffin Bay has some, you want me to send some? If so, what kind? Classical, or pop, or jazz, or both?

Weather is beautiful here now, not too hot, just fine. Lucky is improving a lot, he will be a great dog in a few months. And Zizi stopped shitting on the floor! Delights of life. This reminds me of that wonderful Jewish joke – it's in my book, but I tell you again, in case you forgot it: a man goes to the Rabbi, wailing:

"Rabbi, I can't stand it anymore, I live in one room with my wife, my seven children, and my mother-in-law. What can I do about this?"

The Rabbi strokes his beard:

"Do you have some pigs?"

"Yes."

Some chicken?"

"Yes."

"Goats?"

"Yes."

"OK. Go home and put all the animals in the room."

"But Rabbi..."

"Just do what I tell you and come back in a week."

He comes back, pale, crying, wailing. The Rabbi:

"OK,OK. Now put out the animals and come back in a week."

The guy comes back, radiant:

"Oh Rabbi, I'm so happy!"

It's in my book, I tell it my mother, when we get back in our miserable apartment after the ghetto, the siege and the persecution.

In one of your letters I reread you tell me to write more about my life after I left Hungary. Well, I am thinking of it now and started to write down a few things.

End of this funny letter.

Love,

Agi

June 19, 2003

Dear friend,

Be mushy! I loved your loving words in your 6-15 letter which I got today. I put mine in the mailbox and there was yours. And I feel like telling you right now that you touch my heart. Yes, "God is love" and every living soul need it badly. I didn't get enough in my life: my father wasn't at all the kind telling you he loved, although he did love me. My mother's hysterical and too possessive love was disastrous. And my men – let's don't talk about it, it would be volumes. So our pure friendship and unconditional love is very dear to me.

That's all I wanted to say today.

Agi

June 25, 2003

Dear Agi,

Hello my Lady. I got your letter of 6-18, which was the best part of the day, seeing and hearing my name called for mail call.

And, also I got a card from Newsweek magazine telling me a gift subscription from you will arrive shortly; muchas gracias. Note: do not renew Reader's Digest. I can get that (free) from the library – don't forget, OK?

You asked me about getting me an encyclopedia, if I want one? No, no, not now because the library in my pod has a whole set of them and I love that. Did I tell you that a lot of the books you have sent me over the years are in there, too? And the ones that are not in there are out in the general population library being read by inmates all over the whole prison not just on death row. Your kindness has spread over Man.C.I. What a woman!

Yes, there are two tapes I would like very much and if they don't have these don't send anything else until we talk. Look up under Gospel and Christian Music: artist Velasquez, Jaci: title "Heavenly Place". If Griffin Bay N/A , look up Amazon dot com.

Second choice: under Soundtracks title "O Brother Where Art Thou" I would love having those two tapes. If not now, maybe for Christmas. (No hurry.) I feel weird/guilty asking because I promised I would not ask for anything else since you just bought me a new pair of tennis-shoes, which, by the way, I received last week and they feel real good to jog in, better than the state shoes/boots they give us.

Rent this movie/video: "Last of the Mohicans" Good acting (Daniel Day Lewis) good music (film score by Jerry Goldsmith) story: historical fiction. In truth, I have a special affinity for Native Americans. Have you seen Dances with Wolves? If not, rent that one, too.

I saw Howard Dean on Meet the Press last Sunday. Yes, we want him to win!

Ciao, love you Agi,

Rich

PS The rain has stopped and the sun feels great. I'm actually getting a tan. Be happy and enjoy your summer. Be careful swimming in your lake. (Take some pictures of the lake area.) More later.

God bless,

Rich

July 2, 2003

Dear Rich,

These pictures are not yet the ones I made for you, obviously, since the fair booth one was made some years ago (read the T-shirt on the right) but it occurred to me I never sent you a picture of Zizi. The roll I am doing for you is not yet finished I will finish it on Friday at the parade – we are going to march in the parade, carrying an Amnesty banner.

The Newsweek subscription I did before you told me not to. I'm not going to renew Reader's Digest. I will try to get the music tapes – I doubt Griffin Bay has them, they have a limited amount of music tapes. And my skill for computer...well I'll try.

About the movies you recommend: I have seen "Dances with Wolves" and the "Last of the Mohicans" I am afraid of. It bound to have violence in it and I just can't watch those – I have enough nightmares.

I didn't go swimming yet, but will soon – weather is nice. The trouble is Lucky: I can't leave him home because the damn thing is running after my car and I don't want him to get on the road. And at the lake I doubt I can find a parking place in the shadow and, of course, I can't leave him in the car when it's hot. Next month we have the Fair when I will be there the whole day long – I will have to put him in the kennel for the day. I don't know how to get him not to run after the car, hell! He's a goddam nuisance and a pain in the ass – I am telling him all the time but his answer is to look at me with his yellow eyes and lick my hand.

Hey friend, I am so glad you are outside a lot and got a tan! How is your chess and ping-pong going? How is your new friendship(s) going? I bet you will read less now, that you are not locked up all the time. But that's good. I am really, really happy for you.

Love

Agi

PS I almost forgot: give me the name of the paper where the law students' article appeared. Important!

July 5, 2003

Dear Agi,

Well, happy 4th of July! Boom-bam! (prison firework) ha-ha. I watched fireworks on TV last night. Do they have fireworks on your island?

I see you are putting our letters in your computer, one finger at a time, eh? I took two years of typing in high school but I'm sure after all this time, I could only type one finger at a time, too. Anyway, I do like the idea of putting the letters in your computer and on your disk for safekeeping; they are special, to us, anyway, huh? Indeed!

Yes, I do believe and feel you should go on with your story (book) after you left Hungary. <u>Note:</u> another inmate, I have made friends with, read your book and was very touched by it (like I am) and he said the same thing – i.e. he wanted the story to continue. Keep writing.

Heck, I don't know if it's pretentions or ego or what but I've been thinking (again) of writing my little story, too. And then you and Janet can clean it up, edit, rewrite it to make it read better. I think I would love to have my story on a computer disk. I have tried before to start writing it but I think too much and suffer from paralysis of analysis. I could write and/or create better if I had a joint and/or a drink or two…well, in my case, let's say a bottle. Well at least I'm honest and I never said I was a saint. I ordered two pairs of socks and because my future is so bright, I bought a pair of shades (sunglasses & sunscreen too)

Campbell got life in prison and Lewis Williams is on the retardation claim stay. And I'm still alive & well, my Love. Be happy & God bless you Agi.

I love you,
Rich

July 17, 2003
Dear Agi,

Thank you so much! You always come through for me. Sometimes I think you're an angel in disguise. I got your letter of 7-2 with the two pictures of you and Zizi. I must say you didn't look very amused that day; maybe you just needed a coffee or cocktail break and no one was there to help you out, eh? Boy, I could use a cocktail break. I wonder if God will let me have one (or two) when I get to Heaven?

One big thing about being free to visit with other inmates is I hear more about other people's cases and their fears and anxieties that goes with it. I find it tiring and most of the time boring. Not all of them and not always, but some, who I need to learn to avoid inconspicuously, wear or bring me down if I get stuck with'em too long.

Part of my spiritual charity is really try not to offend anyone and hurt no-one's feelings because I am very sensitive myself – always have been, all my life, over sensitive, truth be told. That's one, of many, of my character defects. I am way too sensitive for prison life some days. When I'm tough, I'm only pretending (acting) and I would rather just be myself – i.e. a fun loving musician but I reckon those days are over which in a way makes me too a dead man walking… no, no, no, that's bull sh….

What I was trying to say is: with more free time, which is very good, indeed, I not only get more "feel good" time out of my cell but with it I do also get <u>more</u> negative vibes, too. With the good comes the bad. Man, I'm a terrible writer. But you're smart and I know you'll get the picture.

Zizi sure is a pretty cat – big, too! I was trying to read your videos but I can't see'em, the titles. I would like to see your house if that's OK with you, inside & outside.

We had our first cell inspection last week and mine was OK but the guards are unfriendly, more than usual.

I'm doing A-OK but need to learn how to live in a more opened death row. Jesus said, Behold, I send you out as sheep in the midst of wolves; therefore be shrewd as serpents and innocent as doves.

Well that's all for now, Agi. God bless you, Agi, and thanks for being my best good friend and <u>always</u> being there and here for me. You do live in my heart everyday.

Much Love, Ciao,

Rich

PS Thought I would bring a little levity to the picture today. So here's a joke for ya:

A man was walking down the street when he noticed his grandfather sitting on the porch, in the rocking chair, with nothing on from the waist down.

"Grandpa, what are you doing?" he asked. The old man looked off in the distance without answering.

"Grandpa, what are you doing sitting out here with nothing below the waist?!" he asked again.

The old man slowly looked at him and said, "Well, last week I sat out here with no shirt on and I got a stiff neck. This is your grandma's idea."

(Kind of cute, huh?) I'll be back soon.

Ciao, Rich

July 20, 2003

Hi Agi,

Oops, I forgot. In your last letter of July 2, you asked me at the end for the name of the paper where the law students' article appeared, and I forgot to tell you in my last letter of 7-17. Anyway the paper was/is The Cincinnati Enquirer. (Enclosed.)

I wrote to you last Thursday and Friday I got a letter from Intercommunity Justice Center with a copy of that article, so I am sending it to you and you keep it; I still have my original copy. Also they sent me a questionnaire to fill out (letter enclosed)

That's all for now my Sweetheart; yes, your heart is sweet – I shall call you my Sweetheart.

Ciao. Love

Rich

July 21, 2003

Dear Rich,

I just realize I didn't answer your last letter of July 5, where you ask me about fireworks on the island. (Your letters were all in one stack because of typing and that one came under the stack. Sorry.)

There is a firework in FH, but on the neighbor island, Lopez, it used to be much better. So, Janet wanted to go over there to watch it and asked me to go with her. So we went, with a third person, had a nice dinner and walk with the 2 dogs – she has a very old dog who can hardly walk and we expect him to die any day, but he is hanging on. After dinner we went to watch the firework, we waited a half hour, it was very cold and uncomfortable to sit on the grass. Finally it started and after 3 minutes it stopped: there was something wrong, a fire there. It was about 11.00 pm and our ferry back to FH was scheduled for 1.15 am. We went back to the restaurant where we had dinner, but it was closed, but the terrace was lit and there were tables, so we played cards until it was time to go to the ferry – it was late. By the time I got home it was 3 am. And the next day we heard that the FH firework was better this year.

We, Amnesty, participated in the parade, carrying a banner. I shot some pictures of that, will send it.

Last week-end I was in San Francisco for a chamber music week-end, it was wonderful. You might get our card before this letter. Coming home, as soon I entered the plane, my nose started to run – I had to ask 3 times for kleenexes in the two hours flight, and it still didn't stop running, damn!

Hey, I don't like your excuses not to write your story. To hell with "paralysis of analyses," and that you would need a drink to do that. Just sit down and write! Start any old way – once you have a first draft, you can rewrite it, if needed, several times. And then Janet and I can help you more. For example: first write a sort account of your background, your life story before you got to prison. "I (was born) grew up in a family that never said we loved each other. I think today w 20/20 hindsight that it was truly sad." I am quoting you, right? This would be a good beginning. Then write about your professional life and that at one point you started to drink which caused your downfall. I could quote you a lot, you wrote many times about drinking and what a terrible thing it is – and now you want a drink to be able to write! Shame on you Riccardo! Your mind is clear when you don't drink, right? I would understand that one little drink would help, but you "alkies" can't stop at one drink, am I right? Think about all this, friend.

So, after this lecture I will stop. Hope you don't mind.

Love,

Agi

July 31, 2003

Dear Agi,

Great pictures! Your house looks so warm with all the wood and earth colors, and artistic things hanging around. I always knew you were a hip lady and you are.

I see Lucky is getting tall/big, eh? I love that bookstore, so many books, they are beautiful. Note: When I got the pictures, there was no letter or note with them, which is OK if you didn't put one in, but I'm just checking to make sure the mailroom people here didn't take it out and forgot to put back in, while they are looking for contraband and so on. The tear in the paper you see happens sometimes in the mailroom here when they open letters – no biggie. That's life in prison.

I feel very good today because of your sweet thoughts and work you have and do for me. Your letter of 7-21 and postcard from San Fran. and the beautiful pictures of your smiling friends. I feel part of your group and that you are sharing me with them, Nancy, Janet and your friends in San Fran., too, that makes me feel good that you include me, too. See I told you I was/ am very sentimental, things like that touch my heart – Big Time.

I saw a good movie this week: "Shakespeare in Love." At first I didn't think I would like it, but I got into it and enjoyed it very much. Have you seen it?

I would like to read some Shakespeare. Maybe at Serendipity you can find a <u>used</u> Shakespeare book sometime. Have you read Shakespeare? I would guess yes. I thought Gwyneth Paltrow was very good in the film; definitely a good role and part for an actress to show her talent. Judi Dench is a great actress too, I liked her in this film and, also, in the film "Chocolat." If you haven't seen them rent: "Shakespeare In Love" & "Chocolat." You'll like'em.

Your story about going to the fireworks made me laugh. Rough night, huh, Sweetheart? I would bet next year you'll stay on Friday Harbor to watch fireworks. Question: Is the "old dog" still alive?

<u>Question:</u> Is Nancy going to AA? There is no such thing as a recovered alcoholic – only "recovering alcoholic." There is no cure only a daily reprieve. In the picture, which one is Janet? On the right? Louisa on the left?

Your yard through the kitchen window looks like a dense forest with lots of trees. Beautiful. Quest.: Do you cut your grass? Do you do yardwork?

Gardening? I would guess, no. Correct?? Most musician don't care for yard work. I know I didn't.

God bless Bob Hope, he always made me laugh. And God bless you Sweetheart; you always make me feel good. You give me love and that's the best.

Much love to you, ciao,
Rich

August 5, 2003
Dear Rich,

Got your 7-31 letter. Answers: there was no letter with the 3 pictures, that's correct. – I thought you would recognize Janet, I sent one picture of her before. She is on the right, Nancy in the middle, Louisa on the left.

I will look for Shakespeare in Serendipity. It is not easy to read though, you realize, don't you? Yes, I read all the plays at one time and keep rereading them here and there. I read them in Hungarian. And, of course, I have almost all on videos. There was a performance of "Romeo and Juliet" here the other day. A couple moved here a few years ago, he an actor and she a director and they put up plays – mostly Shakespeare – outside of their house and they are mostly excellent – you know I'm not easy to please, am very critical, but I like what they are doing.

You are right, I don't do much yard work; here and there I get help. I am doing some though, but it's wild, you can't take care of 4 acres easily. I tried to have a vegetable garden, but the soil is very rocky and there's little sun coming through the trees, so it doesn't work. My 4 acres are all tall trees, I love it, but my house is not warm. These days are great summer weather, and it's agreeable, but in the fall and spring I have to heat the house more than others which get more sun.

I am just finishing "The House of the Spirits." It's because of you I got interested in I. Allende and I took it from the library. It's good.

Bless you,

Agi

August 10, 2003

Dear Agi,

Boy! Time sure is going by quickly, eh? I'm getting so much outside time – outdoor & out of my cell period – time is flying by, to me. I just want to savor every day, every cloud, sun-drops and breath of fresh-air.

I've been thinking about you a lot and how sweet and kind you are to me. I feel very close to you, you are always on my mind and in my heart.

Sometimes I'll be watching TV and I'll see or hear something and I'll say to myself: "I wonder if Agi has seen them or knows this" etc. etc. I guess I just want to share things with you, share experiences and feelings and thoughts and things like that.

Question: Do you know who Corrie Ten Boom was? I'm starting a book called "The Hiding Place" and it's about her. Do you know it or have you read it? When I read these stories, you are always on my mind, and when I see documentaries on PBS, and see Nazis – man, oh, man, in truth, I could kill Nazis. I hate them more than any people on the planet. (I don't like to hate anyone, but, sorry, I do hate Nazis.)

OK, Nields, settle down, I'm getting worked up. Question: Have you seen The Pianist? It's about a musician who survived the Holocaust while hiding out in Warsaw. I'm hoping they show it here when it comes out on video.

Last week I saw Gangs of New York. I really like Daniel Day Lewis, a wonderful actor, and he was very good in this, too. But, I was disappointed in the film, too much violence for me. And, I didn't care for Leonardo Di Caprio in this (in Titanic I liked him OK) but in this, he's too much of a pretty boy for the part. (Note: I'm glad I'm not a pretty boy while I'm in prison – they pick on pretty boys here.)

I don't want to talk about it too much but on my mind has been what to do with my body when I die. Should I bury it or cremate it. The State will bury me, I know. You're wise and I know as time goes by you'll help me to decide.

I love you Sweetheart. Be happy – I am

Rich

August 19, 2003

Dear Rich,

Thanks for your sweet letter of 8-10. Answers: I don't know who Carrie Ten Bloom was. I assume she was persecuted by the Nazis. – I didn't see the "Pianist" – I was to rent it, but I don't want to see Warsaw ghetto and stuff like that, you would understand that, I'm sure. I just can't stand that. I told you, I have enough nightmares; I need to see cheerful and uplifting things. I have to avoid any violence; it would follow me up for a long time.

I just finished the Fair; it was, as usual, fun and exhausting. We made over $900, filled 13 sheets of moratorium petitions, and I'm still dealing with it, delivering raffle prizes and stuff. It was even more exhausting than usual, because I had to put Lucky in the kennel for the day – the damn thing is running after my car, I can't let him get on the road. So, I had to drive him first to the kennel, then pick him up in the afternoon, it made me drive over the whole island twice a day. But it was good, people eagerly signed the petition against the death penalty – times are changing.

My friend, don't talk about your death – bury or cremate your body? It doesn't make any difference. But I hope to God you would die a natural death. I am working on your case, I don't want to talk about it any more. Your body is just an object after death but you will live.

Enjoy sunshine, play chess and ping-pong. I sent you some Shakespeare, hope you enjoy it.

Love,

Agi

August 20, 2003

Dear Agi,

What beautiful houses. Your house where you live and the house you played music are both real nice. I enjoy the pictures you're sending.

Yes, alkies are insane as you wrote. But if you clean them up and get 'em sober, usually they are really good people, the booze is making them nuts. It truly is like night and day – for me anyway – while using booze and drugs (pot) I'm pretty much out of reality and I only live for myself, i.e. I 'm living for the next drop and, indeed, that is crazy, huh? Of course it is.

Hey, the mail just came and guess what I got? Four Shakespeare books. How nice. Thank you, Agi. I'm going to read Hamlet first; my friend, David, (he's the one who read your book) he's going to read Othello. I'm glad for the footnotes explaining Shakespeare's vocabulary or I would have a real hard time.

The book Hamlet is 271 pages, I see. The story/play is only 141 pages, so the rest, 130 pages, are notes, very long introduction, an overview, etc, etc. I'm going to take my time and savor his words e.g. "knows not my feeble key of untuned cares" (The Comedy of Errors act v. sc. 3 (?) I love that line which I just opened randomly. I noticed the word key and untuned. In music, if it's not tuned, it's not in key – that's an oxymoron – I think?

I'm glad you're enjoying "The House of the Spirits." I liked that, too. I remember Clara, I liked her. The civil war/political turmoil sure was ugly, eh? Why can't people just live in peace and love? I know you will love Daughter of Fortune by Isabel Allende, read that one too someday. The story starts in Chile but comes to San Francisco and what a picture Isabel paints of early San Fran. She puts you right in Chinatown.

Yes, I can see why you don't have to do yard work; you live in the forest. I love the design of your house with all the windows and angles – you are a true artist in music, thoughts and lifestyle – you're the best, Sweetheart.

Lots of love,

Rich

August 27, 2003

Dearest Agi,

Hello my Lady. And how are you today 😊 peaceful and serene, I do hope.

My week has been up and down for me. Somedays I wish – not too much but a little – it was all over. Living in prison is a real drag. I do like all the new freedom I have here in DR-6, but along with it come a lot more strife, discord amongst the inmates. I hate strife!

Hey Sweetheart, I'm loving my Hamlet. Shakespeare sure was a genius, huh? Yes, to be or not to be, indeed – especially here – is a very good question. Man! I love Act 3. 1. 56-90 in Hamlet. Truly beautiful, and thought stimulating; so deep and…well I lack words for it right now, how about you? What are your feelings and thoughts on Hamlet Act 3. 1. 56-90? Take your time and someday write your thoughts on "to be or not to be."

Maybe talk it over with your friends at the card game, Janet, Nancy & Louisa – that ought to stimulate some chit-chat; though I doubt you guys have any problem with keeping the conversation going. (I wish I could be there.)

I've been going to bible study every other Tuesday. It's the first time I've been to bible study class. In truth: I prefer AA meetings a lot better. Sober drunks are fun and honest and usually can laugh at themselves and life in general. Bible class tends to be drab, and I notice Christians have strife amongst themselves over the interpretations of the Bible. It's all bull-sh…to me and hypocrisy – i. e. arguing over the word of God. Isn't it ironic that all the wars on the planet today, bottom line, is over the God thing? God must think we're pretty nuts down here on earth. War, what are we fighting for? Oil, money, land, power, my God is the one and only true God yada, yada, yada, etc. Hell, I thought God is Love (and he is) but where's the love?

OK, I'm babbling, I know, I'll stop. Oh yeah, that priest (Catholic Priest John Geoghan) that got killed in prison by another inmate, that's nothing but a set-up. Guards lookin' the other way. If they (prison) wants to protect someone from harm, they can easily by putting them into isolation and not nearby neo-Nazis. Well on that upbeat note, I'll close.

Lots of love,
Rich

PS Later Wed. just got your letter of 8-18 w/3 pic. Will respond in my next letter.

Rich

August 29, 2003

Hi Riccardo,

Glad you got the Shakespeare, hope you will like them. I wish I could send you videos; I have Hamlet with Lawrence Olivier, the greatest actor. I have Othello with him, too, but that one I liked a little less – I mean the acting, not the play, the play is great. It's also my favorite opera, by Verdi. It's his next to last opera, he was in his late 70s – he didn't write anything for 15 years and then boom: he did his greatest.

I just came back from a meeting with our democratic congressman, we talked about how to get rid of GWB. Howard Dean seems to be the forerunner now.

I have already some funny pictures for you in my next roll, you will get some good laugh.

<u>Important</u>: did you see or hear from your lawyers since Christmas? I have some misgivings about them: I wrote them a letter asking for an update of your case and they don't deign to answer. And they didn't want to talk to me. I tried to call them several times. If necessary, <u>you can request to have another lawyer</u>. Let's talk about this later. I am working on that.

I hope you enjoy the sunshine, your new friends – how nice that you have a better life now! I am really happy about that.

Love,

Agi

September 4, 2003

Hey friend,

You seem to be a bit depressed (your letter of 8-27). What was your strife? Were you involved? Of course, life is a drag in prison, even in DR-6. But you know, life is not all rose, even if free and having a better life than many. You started your letter saying you hope I am peaceful and serene. Well, I am not. There was a series of unpleasantness in the last few days. It started with a neighbor complaining about Lucky barking a few times early in the morning, called the police. He left a message on my phone – a low kind of man he thought they would put me in prison because of my dog barking. Now I have to lock the pet-door for the night. This seems to be a trifle, but it bothers me. I lived here for almost ten years in peace; that neighbor I have never seen, he is pretty far away. Oh well, it's nothing compared to your misery.

Then one of my best friends here went berserk, got offended by a phone message of mine, intended to be funny. This is a friend I took to a splendid trip to Europe a few years ago, gave her a lot of money – she is poor – and was nice to her always. She sent me an e-mail which probably will cause the end of our friendship.

Another of my best friends here, the actress, is kind of lost too, because of her asshole of husband who is a Bushie.

I still have Janet, I hope it will last.

And yesterday my car broke down, I got it back; it cost me "only" $ 624.

Well, let's get to something less disturbing: just in parenthesis, my canasta game is not always the same people, there is a "canasta club" of several members, Janet and I being kind of steady.

The Hamlet monologue you are talking about is, of course, one of the most famous lines in literature. I don't know what to say about, except there are now people returning from death and telling fantastic stories about how great it is – again I'm referring to the near-death experiences. It must have always existed, but nowadays they can revive people whose hearts stopped beating, who were really dead for a few minutes. There is one case of a man who was "dead" for a week-end; they started autopsy on him when he came back. In his out-of-body state he met his parents he never knew and learned they didn't abandon him, as he was told, but they were killed by the KGB. It was a Russian. Another one, a woman, met a baby over there who claimed he was her brother. She said, I never had a brother, but when she came back it turned out that she did have one who died in infancy. "There are more things in heaven and earth, Horatio, than are dreamt in your philosophy." Hamlet Act 1. Scene 5.

As for your Bible class – dear friend, I really hesitate to disturb your faith, but my conviction is, as I said several times – that religions are man-made. They all claim to have the TRUTH and have all the answers. Have faith! But not necessarily on one religion. There is a God, there is some reason for all our misery. I really believe it, I know it.

Love Agi

P.S. I am reading "Daughter of Fortune". It's very interesting, describing 19. century Chile and China (I am not yet in San Francisco) but I like it less than "The House of the Spirits."

September 14, 2003

Dear Agi,

Well be with you my lady. I know you had some strife with your neighbor and your friend. (I got your letter of 9-4) I do hope all becomes harmonious again; these are little things in life, a dog's barking – I would love to hear a dog's bark today – and a misconstrued phone message.

My strife here (you asked me) is even smaller than that. One problem is over outside rec time. We are only allowed 5 men at a time to go out in the rec yard. Well there's 18 guys on the second tier and we all rec together, so we have to divide outside time fairly, and it becomes a problem when a few of the bigger bullies want to stay out longer than we are suppose to. The C.O.s don't monitor this; they leave it up to us grown men to work it out fairly amongst ourselves. Boy that's a joke! We are suppose to go out for 1:15 (one hour 15 min.) and then come in to let somebody else go out and then later, when nobody else is out, you can go back out. But needless to say, some guys don't do that and it is a small problem. But in prison, small problems can get you beat up pretty good or worse.

Last week, I experienced the smell of tear gas for the first time. Not in DR-6, but next door, in the same building but on the other side of the wall is the HOLE for general population inmates. There was a fight over a dessert and tear gas was needed to break it up. The gas came through the ventilation system over into our pod. Strong stuff.

Please don't lose your actress friend over her husband because he is a Bushie. Friendships are much more important than politics, especially with a fellow artist. Agree to disagree, amicably. Like you and I are on religion. I'm more aware and hip than what you think I am. For the record I am not a right-wing conservative Christian nor a fanatic or zealot (not that you called me that because you didn't, but in case you were wondering if I was). I am very opened-minded to all kinds of religious and spiritual thoughts and philosophies.

When I was living in Southern Cal, February 1971 to August 1983, I went through the process of finding God or myself, and I read lots of books, from L. Ron Hubbard who started the Church of Scientology to E.S.T. an offshoot of Scientology, to Eastern philosophy to the Greek writers, to Emerson and Thoreau and others. Plus, a lot of New Age stuff. And I liked it all and still do. In truth, I didn't retain much as for being specific about any of it, but as I was going through it, I was mostly in agreement.

Agi, when I mention God, Bible or anything religious, I'm <u>just sharing</u> my thoughts. I am not trying to convert you or to change your mind about anything. Sometimes I just feel like talking about God or students of God, which I am. I like Joseph Campbell, who I always listen to when he's on PBS. And I love Kahil Gibran, who wrote The Prophet. I read that book Christmas Eve 1976, while staying with some friends who went to San Francisco to be with family and I was alone in their house, which had a library, and I saw that book and read it. That book changed my life, because I became a reader after that night. I read all of his books and they continued on the road of discovery until my alcoholism took over my life, and when you drink like I did, you can't read because you are either too drunk or too hung over – I was always one or the other after 1980.

But as a drunk or going to AA, I've always been interested in the God thing. Like most men – esp. in here – would rather talk of sports – and I do too once in a while, but I enjoy talking about God too. Not arguing but talking and sharing opinions, and as we say in AA "opinions are like ass holes, we all have one." Kinda crude, huh?

Anyway, I just don't want you to think I'm a prude or dogmatic. I am not. I am a cosmic pilgrim, like all of us just trying to find the road home. But I'm in no hurry to leave earth. I'm having a great time getting to know you, my last best good friend.

So fare well, my lady and remember: Love thy neighbor because you are thy neighbor.

Peace & love ciao,

Rich

September 19, 2003

Dear Rich,

I got your strange letter of 9-14. Why the hell do you think I take you for a religious fanatic or zealot?? I don't think I wrote anything which would suggest that. And that you are trying to convert me, or I you??? All this is very funny – you used to think straight my friend, what's the matter with you? We are both <u>sharing</u> our different views, OK?

Also, you don't answer my important question: did you see or hear from your lawyers since Christmas? Perhaps you didn't get that letter. But there was always a strange silence whenever I tried to help you – I understand you are afraid of having false hopes. Is there any other reason?

So far I alerted a lot of people about your case, lawyers in Ohio, institutions like Eunice at her project, the Innocence Project (telling them you are partly innocent (robbery) and I'm sorry to say nothing very promising happened. Your lawyers don't answer my letter.

Do you want me to stop trying to save your life? According to a prominent lawyer you have about 5 years to go before it becomes crucial. What I did so far can't hurt you, a lot of important people are aware of your unjust sentence. I can continue to try or I can stop and just hope things will change for the better. If GWB loses the election, there is some hope.

You will be glad to hear that I started to work on a script I started a long time ago. I am going to take Janet's class on memoir writing; that will give me a kick I hope. I started my music class again, too.

Cheers, love,

Agi

September 23, 2003

Dear Agi,

How now my Lady? I do hope this letter finds you well and happy. Are you? I am.

Well, I finished Hamlet and, yes, indeed, the story is woeful and wonderful. I loved it and I love Shakespeare. I am a fan.

"If music be the food of love, play on." (I love that!) Yes, I just started "Twelfth Night" and that's the first line.

Hamlet was sad (tragic) at the end; everybody dies except Horatio. I love his line: "Now cracks a noble heart. Good night sweet prince, and flights of angels sing thee to thy rest."

Just color me stupid; I did not know Hamlet would be killed. And Laertes – he wasn't a bad guy – he just lost control because Hamlet killed his father by accident (he was thinking the king, Claudius, was behind the curtain) and then Laertes lost his sister who flipped out; question?? Ophelia's death was suicide, right?

So, Laertes, being emotionally out of control, was easy for the real bad guy, the king, Claudius, to manipulate to fight and kill Hamlet.

Questions: Was the queen in on the murder of her husband? Was she going to bed with Claudius – having an affair – while Hamlet's father was still alive? <u>Opinion, please.</u>

I would love to see Lawrence Olivier play Hamlet. I'm hoping PBS will have some Shakespeare this season.

Note: the book, a signet classic, was put together very well, excellent, in fact. They put unusual words and terms at the bottom of each page explaining clearly what they mean. Whereas "Twelfth Night" the explanations are in the back and it's sort of a drag because you have to look it up etc.

But, after just reading "Hamlet", I can feel and see I'm already getting better at reading Elizabethan…well, better than I was a few weeks ago.

Yes, I know "revenge" good or bad, right or wrong is what the story is all about. Something to think about, eh? Hamlet could have told the ghost to stick it or "Go shake your ears" and lived a long & prosperous life. But he didn't.

Lots of love, my Lady.

Ciao,

Rich

PS Agi, I do enjoy all the pictures you send me. I feel close to you seeing the island, stores, Lucky and our friends.

Coda: Sometime when you are on the ferry, take a shot of your island, ocean, etc…Man, I miss the ocean. I like the ethnic store too – my kind of stuff. I'll be back soon.

September 29, 2003

Dear Agi,

Hello my lady. Be happy. You make me happy.

I'm so sorry I did forget to answer your important questions – really I did forget. Sometimes I just start writing and sharing and, yes, babbling and driveling, too. My train of thought just goes free flow and I neglect the important stuff. (Got your letter of 9-19. I get all your letters)

OK. You asked if I heard from my lawyers. No, I have not. Not since April 29. David Hansen called me to tell me my federal appeal has been filed. There is nothing else for them to do now. That's why it doesn't bother me that they are not in touch. My case is over at this point. We can not add any new evidence, any new anything. Even if I had the best lawyer in the country, he could not add anything new to help me now. (What and when I needed a good lawyer was at the trial.) Too late now.

Believe me, I do appreciate your work and effort to save my life – I love you for that!! Nobody else in the world cares about me except you! I will <u>always</u> love you for that! Pray. Yes, pray is what I do that it's in God's will to make a Federal Judge to see the light and grant me a new lighter sentence. At this point I do not think lawyers can do anything. The ball (my life) is in the judges' court. (Sorry about the pun.) Reading too much Shakespeare, just keeping my sense of humor.

Yes, please, keep up your work. That is your passion, I know, because I know your life story; I have read your book two times. If I was completely innocent I would be mad as hell if I was in here. I did commit murder, I'm guilty, so maybe I do owe God my life. I'm ambivalent and think about: to live in bondage is better than death? Or "to be or not to be." Do I want to spend my life in general pop.? Do I fear death – yes – but once it's over

NO – hell, we all die someday anyway. These are my thoughts and living like this is a drag. That's why I do not write, talk, share about these things but prefer to talk about the aesthetics of life. Plus, being alcoholic, I escape reality somehow: i.e. I try not to think or worry about it. Some guys here are worrying themselves nuts. I want to enjoy the rest of my life as much as possible. I apologize (really.) Don't be mad at me for not answering questions about my perfunctory lawyers, OK? OK.

You keep up your work with AI and others, like you are doing, because if my life is not saved, you will help save someone else down the road, I'm sure.

I love you, Agi, please never leave me, or stop caring about me.

Love,

Rich

Sweetheart, sorry about "strange" letter of 9-14. I was just driveling that day. No, you did not write anything to bring that out. I know you are putting this in your computer so I wanted that on record. Just sharing, like at an AA meeting.

September 29, 2003

Hey friend,

Welcome to the Shakespeare's fans club! I'm delighted you like it that much. Your questions: I' am sure the queen wasn't in for the murder of her husband (see Hamlet-queen dialogue in her bedroom) whether she had an affair with Claudius while her husband was alive, is not clear, you can think either way. Ophelia's death wasn't suicide in my opinion, or wasn't conscious suicide – she was just out of her mind and didn't realize what was happening to her.

Twelfth Night is one of my favorite comedies, the other I love is Much Ado About Nothing – was this among the ones I sent you? I don't remember. Shakespeare's women are lovely, he must have loved women. Ophelia, Viola, and many others are created with much love.

I started to work on the story of my marriage, this beginning I wrote a long time ago, but now I revised it and am continuing the story; but it will be long and difficult work. Up to the wedding was kind of easy. The subtlety as it little by little deteriorates will be difficult. But now I'm for it. Tonight my goddam computer froze, otherwise I would have worked and would have written you later.

I hope you are all right – I expect an honest answer to my last letter.

Love, Agi

October 5, 2003

Dear friend,

I promise I will never get mad at you and I will never stop caring for you. I'm sorry if I was a bit cross in my last letter.

Your letter of 9-29 touched me to the core. I understand that living in bondage is not better than dying – but the cruelty and injustice of your case! It's crying to God – no, you don't owe your life to God for a moment of drunken folly. What they condemn you to is thousand times worse. Patty suffered a short moment of agony – and yes, it's terrible to take a life – but if they kill you it's thousand times worse: an inhuman, cold-blooded, premeditated murder and ten years of agony, living in hell before that, waiting to be killed.

There is something wrong with the human brain, I see it all the time. Maybe we are sent to the Earth for developing our souls, until we are ready to have the eternal bliss. We have to go through agony and suffering to earn that. Well, you did develop, you are a good, wonderful human being now. You took a big step toward God, toward redemption.

But I still want to save your earthly life and will continue trying.

I hope you got my story and will enjoy it. It's pretty amusing, what? Of course, what comes after it's not so great.

Love,

Agi

PS I finished another roll of pictures, you will have some soon.

October 8, 2003

Dear Agi,

I concur. Thanks for responding to my Hamlet questions. The queen was not in the murder plot against her husband, and Ophelia's death was an accident by her own madness.

I got your letter and transcript of your story with Luke. I liked your story about meeting Luke and finally getting married.

Question/request: You were 22 years old when you met Luke for the first time in Paris. Would that be the best time of your life, or later, or now?

Do you have any pictures of yourself while living in Paris? If so, send me one.

You came to America during a time of change, somewhat turbulent times, with the Vietnam War and race issues creating protests in the streets and so on.

My brother, Doug, he was 3 yrs. older than me, went to Vietnam in the Army. He made it back OK, but mentally he was shucked up somewhat.

When I see that movie "Born on the Fourth of July" boy can't I relate to that one. My family (then) was just like that. (I'm the younger brother – same attitude – as the one in the film.)

In truth, I'm against the war mostly because I don't want to go, because I just want to play music which I am just starting to do professionally – well on week-ends – because I'm still in high school until 1969.

I finished "Twelfth Night". Indeed it was very clever. I liked it. Now I'm reading "Othello". I didn't know he was a Moor and he married a white woman, Desdemona. I like her name. More on "Othello" later, I just started.

Last week I also read "Dead Man Walking" by Sister Helen Prejean. Have you read it? It's a lot more than what the movie was. On second thought, you should not read it – it's a downer and very explicit on some of the executions she saw with the electric chair. (In the film, Willie got the needle, but really he got the chair.)

Heard through the grapewine: Dale Ashworth, he's over in my old pod, DR-1; he's waving his appeal and is asking to be executed as soon as possible. He has given up. He has decided not to be. Don't worry, not me; I will never give up. I might get depressed but I won't quit. I promise.

Ciao – love you,

Rich

October 13, 2003

Dearest Agi,

Hello my lady. Thank you for your sweet, kind and compassionate letter of Oct. 5th; I am a lucky man to have you in my life. I wish I could write like Shakespeare, so I could express my touched feelings of my heartstrings. You have tuned them up into perfect harmony or, as in Hamlet, "a hit, a palpable hit." Touche. (or, as they say in Nashville, "you're a damn good woman.")

Check this out: somebody sent me a CD last week – people I don't know. Do you know Frank and Kat Brunner? They live in Bellingham, WA. Is Bellingham an island or a town on an island? Anyway, they sent me Jaci Velasquez's "Heavenly Places," which is one of the tapes I asked you to send me a few weeks back. So, I'm guessing, they are friends of yours. Am I correct in this?

Mansfield is sending the CD back to them. We are <u>not</u> allowed to have CD's. Only cassette tapes allowed, and they have to be new tapes – <u>NO</u> used tapes allowed. Like books, the cassette tapes must be sent <u>directly</u> from the place of purchase w/a receipt. Or use an internet place – e.g. Amazon dot com – they sell cassette tapes. I'm not worried about music tapes and you do enough for me already, so don't worry about that stuff.

I buy, borrow, and barter with other inmates who have an excess of music tapes. We are only allowed 15 tapes so everybody is always trading and loaning them out.

I liked the 4th of July parade pictures. I guess that's downtown Friday Harbor? It looks nice and clean and a safe place to live; I'm glad you are there, where you can live in peace and comfort. I know and, I am very proud of you, that you have indeed come a very long way since your days in a one-room apartment w/your parents and brother, and evil Nazis outside. You are a woman with true grit and moxie – i.e., the ability to face difficulty with spirit; pluck. Yes, you are a moxie woman and, as my friend, the crème de la crème. Oui. I think the world of you Agi.

Love,

Rich

PS Oops, I almost forgot. You asked me if "Much Ado About Nothing" was among the ones you sent me. No it was not. Still reading "Othello"; not as good as "Hamlet" but I 'm enjoying it. Ciao.

October 13, 2003

Dear Rich,

Got your letter of 10-8 – it goes pretty fast these days. Correction: I was 30 when I met Luke – I was 27 when left Hungary. I found these 2 pictures from Paris – send them back please. That's all I have – those days I didn't have a camera and didn't get the bug taking pictures. I actually got the "bug" from Ros, my stepdaughter, that's her passion, and I like it now because it's nice to look up old pictures and remember the moment. Now I have 10 or 12 albums – I wish I could show you all of them.

The picture at the ferry is the first of the new roll, I will send them all.

"Dead Man Walking:" I have both the movie and the book, the latter dedicated by the author whom I met in San Francisco at a death penalty meeting – I was the DP coordinator of the SF Amnesty group. You shouldn't read that, it must be upsetting to you. You know, there's an opera of that, too. Unfortunately my colleagues say the music is not very good. SF Opera premiered it 2 or 3 years ago, but since the New York City Opera put it on. It's good for our cause. Sister Helen Prejean is a big fighter for abolition. The petitions signed at the Fair come from her organization called Moratorium Now. I would prefer Abolition Now, because moratorium is only half of the solution – they believe it would lead to abolition, but it's a conjecture. Once – in '63 -'73 – <u>was</u> a moratorium here, but then they started the killing again.

Till next, love,

Agi

October 19, 2003

Dear friend,

Damn! The CD came from Amazon dot com, not from friends. Maybe you told me that CDs were not allowed, I don't remember. They will get back to me I'm sure and maybe it can be changed to cassette. So, the "somebody" who sent it, was me. A stupid, "moxie" woman.

I will look for "Much Ado About Nothing" next I go to Serendipity. So, you like "Othello" less, what? It's a tale of an elder Moor who is not very bright, who has inferiority complex and is easily persuaded that Desdemona is cheating on him.

Here are some pictures of the San Francisco chamber music weekend. Enjoy! More coming.

On Tuesday the carpet – wall to wall in the whole house, except the kitchen area – will be changed. What a mess it will be! They have to move everything, and I have about 600 books and three hundred videos. But it will be great to have it done, it really bothered me. I like a nice, cosy place to live – maybe because of my early life of squalor.

The "crème de la crème" sends you her best,

Agi

October 23, 2003

Dear Agi,

Hello my lady. I hope all is well with you and your island.

Sweetheart, I love these pictures of you in Paris. Please make copies for me, OK? Don't forget.

I guess the year was 1951, is that right? (I wish you would put more dates in your stories, in your writing. I get lost what period it is. I like to know when, where, how and why.) OK, Nields, cool it. Sorry. I am a little cranky today.

Boy! You're right about "Dead Man Walking" book in that I shouldn't read it. It made me "blue" for a few days but I'm OK now.

This week I'm reading a happy love story. I usually don't read romantic novels but I have always heard this is a great book and, yes, indeed, it is. Have you read it: "The Bridges of Madison County?" I can't really tell if this is a true story or not. Was there really a Robert Kincaid and Francesca Johnson? I do know the bridges are real. I saw the movie back when it came out with Clint Eastwood and Meryl Streep, but I was drinking (half drunk) and I didn't enjoy it then because I could not wait to leave the theater and get back to the bar, of course; story of my life. (Booze sure did mess up my life.)

I'm still reading – well I'm on break now – but I will return to "Othello". It's not as good as "Hamlet". Opinion, please.

Down the road of Serendipity – good name for a bookstore, huh? I would like to read: "Much Ado About Nothing", "Macbeth", and I always wanted to read a book about "Joan of Arc." (just a small paperback, not a thousand pages.)

Helen Keller said it best: "What we once enjoyed and deeply loved we can never lose, for all that we love deeply becomes part of us."

Yes, you are part of me.

Rich

PS Please make copies of pictures and send back when you have time – I love'em. You're very cute my little sweetheart.

November 3, 2003

Dear Agi,

Well be with you my lady. I do hope you are doing better than Desdemona right now. (I'm just starting Act 4.) I hate Iago! He is more than a rogue or scoundrel or a knave, he's pure evil. I can't believe what he is doing to Desdemona and Cassio.

I know Othello will kill his wife and Cassio but I do hope at the end he kills Iago too. I know I said I didn't like this story a few letters back but now I'm into it, big time. It just took longer for it to hook me than Hamlet did. So I no longer can say "Hamlet" is better than "Othello", akin to Mozart is better than Beethoven, they are just different – like apples and oranges – they are both delicious.

Shakespeare is really growing on me, and I do find enjoyment and escapism from here whilst being in the stories. I like him (Shake) more than I thought I would.

Words do paint pictures, don't they? Boy, can I relate when he spoke of booze and alcoholism in (Act 2. 3. 272-292). e.g. Othon invisible spirit of wine...call thee devil! And this... in their mouths to steal away their brains!...transform ourselves into beasts! (Me 3 27-97) i. e.: I became a beast March 27-97.

Shakespeare was not only funny, witty and clever but indeed he had much insight of the human attributes and defects as Hamlet's revenge and Othello's jealousy gone mad. It sure would have been fun to attend AA meetings with this guy or actually just to hang out with him.

Glad to read you got new carpet in. You have 600 books, eh? And 300 videos. Do you have a library in your house? I have seen a little of the front room (I guess?) where you are playing w/your friends – nice pictures, by the way – so, where are all the book shelves? Do you have a basement? Loft? I like the picture above the fireplace. And I love the hat rack and the Indian rug behind the couch. Your house looks real nice, hip, and comfortable. I do not like houses that look like a museum inside. Also, I like earth-colors too.

If I wasn't in prison, I'd come to visit for a long time.

Coda: Don't worry they are never going to let me out. You're my Angel, Agi, thanks for the dates and the wonderful pictures of you playing. You are the crème de la crème.

Ciao,

Rich

PS Question: the woman in pink, across from you with picture, she is playing a viola, correct? You and the puppet, very cute indeed. It's nice to see you smile and feeling joyful.

Love!

Rich

October 27, 2003

Dear Rich,

OK pal, here are my dates: I was born January 5 1929; the Germans invaded Hungary March 19 1944. War ended in Europe 1945 May. Revolution started on October 23 1956, I left the country in November. Lived in Paris between December '56 to January '62 – so those pictures were taken between my age of 28 and 33. Between '62 January and '66 July I lived in Germany, so I was 37 when came to the US. One year I was in Indiana, 4 years in Texas, I year in Georgia, and 6 years in Ithaca. I remet Luke in 1974 – met him in Paris in '59 – a year and a half later, on New Year's Eve of 1975, we were married, so I was almost 47 – he was a year younger. In 1980 I went to San Francisco – before, between '78 and '80 we lived in New York. I left Luke in '92 – I was 63 – and retired from SF at the very end of '93, and came here to FH. So, I will celebrate my 10th anniversary on the island on Dec. 16: Beethoven's birthday. Does this satisfy you?

I really can't tell whether Hamlet is better than Othello. I think they are about the same level – sorry if you don't enjoy Othello that much.

Joan of Arc: if you don't know her story, here it is in nutshell: she was a common peasant girl, who started to hear voices about her task to liberate France from the British oppression – England occupied most of France for 150 years. It started with the battle of Agincourt, and the whole war started because of some tennis balls! It's true. The French king sent Henry 5. tennis balls for a present, and this was naturally a great offence for a king. So they invaded France (Shakespeare has a play "Henry 5" and it irritates me to hell: a whole country's misery and many thousand deaths because of some tennis balls, oh human shit! And of course Shakespeare looks at it from the English point of view. He thinks it was glorious.)

But back to Joan of Arc – it was really miraculous: a young peasant girl – a girl! – became head of the French army and was victorious. It would be too long to tell the whole story – I will look for a book for you. Then the British captured her and burnt her on the stake as a witch. She was 19 at her death. She was declared a saint 500 years later – the whole story happened in the 13. or 14. century, I'm not sure which.

Well, I enjoy my "new" house: the carpets were changed and now it's clean and nice. But what a mess it was!

This is the end of the page, so I have to stop.

Love

Agi

November 7, 2003

Hi friend,

I'm glad you started to like Othello. You probably know by now that he doesn't kill Cassio or Iago, but himself.

You Quatschkopf (German for "nonsense-head") those pictures were taken in San Francisco in Vicky's house. Baa! Here I send you my study where most of my books are. There is one more big book-case in my bedroom. Here you can see all my movies and Shakespeares, and in the living-room are all the operas and CDs, about 200.

Janet's class on memoir writing is very nice and I became kind of a star in it. I read excerpts of my new writings and they liked it very much. I'm really in it now, but it will be a long process.

Love to you – you Quatschkopf!

Agi

November 11, 2003

Dear Agi,

Hello sweetheart. Thank you so much for the pictures and letter of 11-7. I do appreciate all you do for me. Without you in my life this situation would be much much harder. Your love and friendship and support give me strength, the ability to endure this dire place of anguish – it sucks. OK I'll admit it, I'm a tad down this week. Why? I don't know. It's just the way it is. I'll get back up though as fast as I can.

I miss my family. Mom and Dad and my brothers, Doug and Bryan. I miss playing music. I miss being around other musicians. Note: I really don't have much in common with the other inmates in here, but I do try (and I am) fitting in okay.

There's no problem but I just feel lonely inside. I can handle and in fact I enjoy sometimes being alone, but being lonely inside is different, as you know, I'm sure.

Boy, I sound like I'm on a pity-pot, huh? Sorry Sweetheart, I'll get back up. Heck, I'm already feeling better just writing this head-garbage out.

I've been watching PBS the last three nights doing a 40 year anniversary on the Kennedy assassination. Watching that takes me back to 1963, when my family was still together and everybody was fine.

Note: I'm not feeling sorry for myself, really I'm not. I'm just sharing like at an AA meeting. (Just kind of melancholy.)

Sort of funny I always say that; i.e. "sharing like an AA meeting" like that is the only place I ever shared but, of course, that is not true. But, in retrospect, maybe it's the one place where I learned to be completely honest with myself and others.

That's what I mean when I write that; i.e. I'm sharing 100% honestly with you. Man, oh, man, I am driveling today.

I love the picture w/your books & things. You have a lot of trees around your beautiful house. I like that.

I love you Agi. Back soon.

Ciao,

Rich

November 13, 2003

Dear Agi,

Hello Sweetheart, and how are you today?

Back here right now is snowing very hard, and it is very pretty today to watch the green earth turn white Well I finished Othello. Man what a dumb ass Othello was. To believe an ensign, Iago, over his wife. Was glad Emilia told the truth at the end but saddened that Iago killed her, too.

I enjoyed reading it very much. Do like Shakespeare. Thank you, Agi, for tuning me on to this.

I learned something: the story was actually written 40 years before Shakespeare wrote it into a play. It was written in 1565 by Giovanni Battista Gizaldi Cinthio. His ending is different than the Bard's. In his version Othello is arrested and taken back to Venice where he goes to prison. Condemned to perpetual exile and there he is killed by Desdemona's relatives. And Iago too is arrested and tortured and dies a miserable death. Great Story.

I wrote down all your dates so I'll know where you're at in your stories.

Question: In 1966 you left Paris to go live in Germany, why? Love? Music? I have many more questions but I'll ask a little at a time.

You sure did move around a lot in your life, huh? I did too but not as much as you or as far a distance. All my moves are in one country but 4 different states.

Howard Dean is looking pretty good, huh? I can't stand Bush. I hate that people are dying in Iraq and this war is truly in a quagmire, but hopefully people will wake up and see the light that we do not belong there and Bush does not belong in the White House.

It will be very interesting indeed next year what happens. I don't think we will or can win in Iraq. It's becoming like Vietnam did. They are willing to die for their cause (the Iraqi people) but in America if soldiers are dying, the people sooner or later will rise up and say enough, like they did in the '60s. Hopefully it won't take as long as it did back then.

So fare you well my Lady.

Ciao, love,
Rich

November 18, 2003
Dear Rich,

So, you think Othello was a dumb-ass. Well, he wasn't very bright, but don't forget, he was black: inferiority complex. Also much older than Desdemona.

I didn't know about the other Othello story, where did you find that? It's interesting – Shakespeare rarely created a completely original story, he needed inspiration from stories he read. Almost every one of his plays were based upon some other stories – but then he made it so much better that the other ones were forgotten. Isn't it much better that Othello kills himself on the spot? Going to prison, that doesn't fit Othello's character and dramatically it's infinitely better.

Quatschkopf! You still mess up my dates. I went to Germany in '62 – the reason was I couldn't get a job in France, being an alien – and came to the US in '66.

So you have many more questions, but you'll ask a little at a time. Clever! So I will have to tell you things in every letter. Go ahead and ask, pal.

Our Christmas sale is coming up the 6 of December. Another, bigger event is planned in January: the 10th birthday of my group. It will be a two-days event. Two high standing officials of Amnesty are coming from San Francisco. They will go around schools for a day and the second day will be a public event with them talking and there will be an excerpt of the play based on our correspondence!! The best actor here will be you and his wife, the director will be me. I told her, brace yourself, you have to drink gin-and-tonic, smoke, and swear! And imitate my Hungarian accent.

Well, it's not written yet but I bug Janet to do it. It is planned for only half an hour; the play hopefully will be longer, if ever Janet will move her ass. If not, I will try to do it.

There will be also display of the history of the group; flyers, newspaper articles, photos, letters, etc. My group is all inflamed to do that. We will have the place decorated, there will be a big cake with 10 Amnesty candles – you know the logo of Amnesty? Candle with barbed wire. I have a stamp, here it is:

That's the flame of hope for prisoners.

This will be January 31st. Everybody will think of you.

Ciao

Agi

(Several letters from Rich are missing here.)

December 7, 2003

Dear Rich,

I can't find your letter, it got lost in the mess of "Bizarre." But I remember you asked what I was doing in Bloomington Ind. It was my first job in the US, I was assistant to a famous violin teacher. Bloomington is the biggest and best university music school in the country. It had a great faculty of many famous musicians. I am writing about it in my new project, you will hear about it.

The "Bizarre" was a stupendous success; we made 1,763. Yesterday was a busy, exausting and happy day, and we finished it with a game of canasta.

And today we had a meeting discussing the January event. Janet is working on the script, finally!

I sent you three more Shakespeares: Much Ado, King Lear, and Measure for Measure. That's probably enough by now, you might get shakespearitis. If you want other things let me know.

How is everything in DR 6? I know you were disappointed with some of your new friends there. Is there anybody you can call friend?

Till next, love

Agi

December 16, 2003

Dear Rich,

Today I celebrate the 10th anniversary of being on the island. It is also Beethoven's birthday. Yes, he wrote a "Triple Concerto" for violin, cello and piano. It's not very often performed, not his best piece.

I hope to God Dean will be nominated and I'm confident he can beat Bush. Well, Bush didn't win the last election! And now there are so many who are furious with him – some Republicans hate him, too. One of them here said he is not a Republican, he is a Fascist!

The capture of Saddam will help him for a moment, but there's so much against him that it will be forgotten by the time of the next election. You are not well informed, because you see only the media which is controlled by him, by the corporations. There are other articles, some uncontrolled press, Molly Yvins (you know her?) etc. which you have no access to There is a very strong opposition. If Gore won by half a million votes, it should be much better this time. And Dean is not a wishy-washy, like Gore was. He has such an incredible list of Bush's wrongdoings that even a Bushist media will have a hard time when it comes to a debate.

So, chin up friend.

Love

Agi

January 4 2004

Dear Rich,

The North Pole descended onto Friday Harbor! It is unprecedented cold, wind howling and snow and ice on the ground! I am snowed in for 2 days, driving conditions are bad – we postponed the Amnesty meeting and won't have any fun on my birthday. My property is littered with fallen branches and my poor dog doesn't have a walk. Misery!

I did have some fun for X-mas and New Year's. There was a New Year's Eve party at the home of the actor and actress-director – the ones who will be you and me on Jan. 31. It was nice.

Thanks for your nice birthday-card and letter. You asked why I care for you. Well, let's see. Firstly and mostly because you are a nice guy. I do enjoy receiving your letters and I like writing to you. Somehow I feel telling you what I do and what I feel. Secondly, of course, my heart aches for you and am outraged about your wrong conviction. Is that a satisfactory answer?

How is your chess and ping-pong? Reading? Cross-word puzzles? Did you have some celebrations for X-mas, New Year's?

Till next, love

Agi

January 11, 2004

Dearest Agi,

Hello my lady and how are you today? Happy New Year to you Sweetheart.

I'm feeling better today. All last week I was dealing with flu and cold symptoms again. Living in a pod like this with 36 other inmates when one or two guys get sick (cold) it seems to just move from cell to cell.

Remember that book you sent me about Joan of Arc? Well I read it last week and it was great. I love Joan of Arc and by the end I was and am so disappointed in the Church I'm glad I don't belong to any church; a bunch of bs hypocrites. And Charles VII what a bum. He wouldn't help her after all she did for him. Duplicity and mendacity, that's what happened to Joan – just like what's going on today in our country especially with Bush in the White House. He and his cronies are liars. OK, I'll get off my soapbox – you know a lot more than me anyway. You know, in my book, and my heart, you are a great lady. I think the world of you, Agi.

I put my photo album together with lots of your pictures, the ones you took. Note: I still want the one of you sitting at the table drinking coffee in Paris.

Anyway I really was touched by Joan of Arc. (kind of fell in love with her   ha-ha. I think I could use a hug – I miss music, playing music a lot but I sure miss the touch of a woman. Well, at least you know I'm not turning gay – not that there's anything wrong with that.

Boy, I'm babbling today.

Question: Have you played Bluebeard's Castle a one act play (opera?) by Bela Bartok? Did you know that Joan of Arc & Bluebeard knew each other for a short time? Yeah, they met each other at Charles VII's coronation.

Rent this movie: "The Life of David Gale" with Kevin Spacey. A college professor ends up on death row in Texas.

I got a feeling that Dean might win in November.

We have 3 executions coming up. One next week.

I love you Agi – <u>a lot!</u>

Rich

January 16, 2004

Dear Rich'

I thought you were sick, I got no letters for 2 weeks. Did you get mine? You were so full of Joan of Arc that you didn't reflect on it. Well, it's quite legitimate to be taken by her story she is really a miraculous figure in history. I have a <u>great</u> movie about her, a silent one by a Danish director: nothing but her trial and burning, using the official text of the trial. It is probably the greatest movie ever made – for me anyway. What a stupid, infuriating thing that I can't do things like that for you! Meaning to send that movie.

We are getting close to the big event on Jan. 31st. It will be filmed! Mostly the letter-reading. If it happens I will try to find a way to send it to you.

This morning I got a bad news: a member of my group, very active, a nice man, had a heart-attack last night. He is in hospital on the mainland. I hope he will recover.

This is all for today.

Love

Agi

P.S.   I didn't play "Bluebeard's Castle," but of course I know it, have two videos of it. It's beautiful. I didn't know about Bluebeard and Joan of Arc, how on earth did you find that? Bartok's opera is kind of a psychological metaphor, nothing much to do with the real Bluebeard.

January 25, 2004

Dear Agi,

Hello Sweetheart. How are you today? I'm sure you're excited like I am about this coming Saturday.

If you can take some pictures or if you're too busy maybe one of your friends will take pictures for you.

So, they are going to put it on film, huh? That's great. Sadly, I don't have a video machine so I won't be able to see it. I would though like to read the script if I could get a copy.

Yes, I got your letter(s) of 1-4 & 1-16. Sorry, I know it bothers you when I forget to reflect on them and take off my own Joan of Arc.

You asked me how I knew of Bartok's opera "Bluebeard's Castle" it was in the book you sent me – the writer, Mary Gordon, mentioned it.

Sorry to read about your friend having a heart-attack, and I hope he recovers.

You asked me if I have friends. Yes I do. But I don't have much in common with them. Yeah, chess & ping-pong I do that but that's not much of a conversation piece of topic.

All my life I hung out with musicians and/or drunks – sober going to AA or drinking like bar flies – like me. It probably sounds funny to you but I do miss my alcoholic friends the most – the ones I knew in AA. They're the best.

Thanks Agi for the picture of you at the Paris café – I love that one.

They executed Lewis Williams on the 15th and I heard he went screaming and kicking and fighting, and it took 9 guards to get him up on the table. Sad, huh?

Is Dean in trouble? He may be, huh? 🎗️ Please, don't get too upset if that happens.

I'm taking a break from Shakespeare for awhile; keeping the books in my cell and will get to them. I'm in the mood and need to read another book by Kent Haruf. You sent me a Haruf book, "Plainsong" back in 2001 and I loved it. I would like to read another by him. No hurry – I know you are busy this week!

I love you, Agi.

Rich

January 27, 2004

Dear Riccardo,

Thanks for your nice letter – you give me a great feeling when you say I make a difference.

Excitement is mounting for the week-end. It's not only the Saturday event – did you get the flyer? – it starts Thursday when two persons arrive from San Francisco – high officials of AI. We have a pot-luck dinner that night for them and for school principals, because they, the AI people will go around in schools on Friday to talk about human rights and AI. That day another guy arrives from an island who will be my house guest. And we might have a smaller, casual party in my house, for just them and members of my group. And then Saturday, the big event. The hall will be decorated with art works and display of the history of the group: flyers, articles, photos, etc. You can get a feeling from the flyer.

Sunday night the two actors – you and me – and Janet were here for dinner and they read through the letters – it's only a selection of course – there are about 200 hundred letters by now, do you realize? They love it. We made some pictures of that party, you will get it soon.

And, it will be filmed! Now, there's a problem: I want you to see that. How can we do this? I am thinking of sending it to your prison authorities asking them to show it on your movie time if they don't want to give it to you. What is your opinion, would that work? If yes, it might even do you some good there, unless they are really mean and resent it. It's possible, knowing the extent of human shit. Well, tell me what you think.

Cheers friend

Agi

Hey, I got your 1-25 letter today, before I mailed this one. Answers: my friend who had a heart-attack is up and fine, thank God! He will be there at tomorrow's dinner.

Yes, Dean is not doing great and I am sorry, but not very upset. It was just two primaries and he still has a chance. But if not, I'll vote ABB: Anybody But Bush! ☺

I heard today that a life-long friend of mine died. She was 90, so it's natural.

Love

Agi

February 5, 2004

Dear Agi,

Hello Sweetheart. Good to hear from you; I got your letter of 1-27. OK, let me answer your questions.

Yes, I got the flyer and I love it. I realize you want me to see it and I would like to see it but that is not my decision. You will have to deal with warden, the administration.

Question: I would be satisfied to read the script, is that possible?

Truth be told: I don't feel real good about having our letters read here while I'm still here. Prison is a cold-hearted place and we write with a warm heart and I'm sensitive about what's being shared. I really don't mind sharing our private letters with Jan and your friends and the people at AI, schools and places like that, where people are compassionate, sane, caring, loving, warm hearted and so on, but here? I'm not feeling too good about having that showed on our prison TV, in fact, I wish you wouldn't do it – PLEASE.

I'm a private man (esp. here!) and I want to protect my anonymity and do not wish to have any attention directed towards me. Out there in the real world that's fine, and if I was there with you, I would help spread the word 'Truth Be Told.' But, in here, - a cold world, the less people, i.e. inmates & personnel, pay attention to me, the better I like it.

I don't know what's being read, and it might be innocuous and I'm over reacting – I usually do – that's the alcoholic way, just ask Louisa.

Agi, you can show that film, "Truth Be Told" any place you wish – I'm fine with that. But, if the film is shown here, I wish to remain anonymous. OK, Sweetheart? OK.

We had another execution, Tues 3rd, John Roe. Next month (I think?) we're having another one.

Sorry to read about your life-long friend dying. Happy to read the heart-attack guy is up and fine.   ☺

Love you. Ciao,
Rich

February 1, 2004
Dear Rich,

Yesterday's event was the most beautiful we ever had, and the main attraction was the letter reading done with those two wonderful, professional persons. People were touched to tears, as you can see. There were all kinds of ideas, to send the tape to Amnesty for distribution, to publish it, etc. It should be seen and heard, everybody thought – it would help to abolish the death penalty, and, it might help <u>you.</u> You might become famous, hey, what do you think of that?

The hall, which is otherwise rather unattractive, was beautifully decorated, there were about 70 people, and everything went well, the speeches, music, the birthday cake, etc. And, as a total surprise to me, my group presented me with a plaque with a text: Agnes Vadas, Devotion, Determination, and Accomplishment. Tenth Anniversary 1994-2004 San Juan Island Chapter 607 Amnesty International.

It was a heart-warming, great event.

Love,

Agi

Janet's note:

Dear Rich,

You were with us in spirit. Your letters – and Agi's – gave everyone a deep personal insight into your very human plight and Agi's very human heart. Truth be Told – and it will be!

All blessings to you,

Janet

February 10, 2004

Dear Agi,

Wow! What can I say. I'm lost for words but I'm full of emotions. I got your wonderful letter of Feb. 2nd with Janet's note at the bottom. Also, I received the green poster with all the beautifully written best wishes and 'thank you' notes. I am truly deeply touched – it's the best feeling I have experienced in a long, long time. I'm talking about all the messages on the green poster.

Hey, Sweetheart, you and I did touch some people's heart, huh? Of course, I realize Janet did the orchestration, you and I gave her the notes, maybe the melody, harmony, but she put it together into a sweet song, metaphorically speaking. <u>Thanks</u> to Janet for her talent and creativity; I know she must have worked very hard on this – definitely a group effort. Tell Janet I appreciate what she did, OK.

Congratulations Agi on your plaque; I am very, very proud of you. You do inspire people – I know that. You are devoted and loyal to the cause. I have never known such a wonderful, kind woman as you.

If it wasn't for you, Truth Be Told would not have happened – that's for sure.

Hopefully AI can use the play as it wants to help end the death penalty. That would be wonderful. And maybe a few drunks (alcoholics) might see it, hear it, and stop drinking so they don't do something nuts like I did and end up in prison.

Anyway that's all for now. I want to get this in the mail before it leaves the pod in a few minutes.

Your letter & Janet's note was great. And the poster really touched my heart. You know, truth be told, some days my life here on death row just seems silly or pointless. But yesterday when your letter and poster got to my cell, it was as if your finger touched my heart and said "wake up."

Thanks Agi for being in my life – you make me smile.

Love,

Rich

February 11, 2004

Dear Rich,

I am so sorry I can't send you the video, but I understand fully well, I should have known how you feel about it. And I also forgot to take pictures while they were reading it – but somebody did take pictures, maybe I can have them. But instead, here are pictures, when they, a few days before the event, came to dinner and read it through. So here is "you and me" and Janet – I have more pictures taken that night, will send them. And I just called them, will have the script tomorrow and send it.

Well, my friend, you might not realize, how great your letters are.

I went to the Democratic caucus here, it was unbelievable, the turnout was unprecedented. It was jam-packed, several hundred people. And apparently it like this all over. We will get rid of horse's ass in the White House!

I know you were depressed, because of an execution there – not from DR 6 I hope?

Love

Agi

February 16, 2004

Hi friend,

I just got your letter of 2-10 – I am so glad you hade a nice moment reading that poster. Did you notice it was on a drawing by children? Part of the decoration in the hall was children's drawings representing the 30 points of the Universal Declaration of Human Rights. If you don't know about it: on December 10, 1948 the UN signed that document, which is kind of a guide to Amnesty. Someone had the glorious idea of using point: right to life to write to you on.

Since I can't send the video, I will tell you a little about the reading. Before that, Janet said a few words about the letters, then, before starting Helen – the "me" – said there was a daunting thing to imitate Agnes – you can't imitate her. Then Dan – the "you" – said: "Just say a couple of goddams." Laughter.

There were more laughters during the readings, about my outbursts of shit and goddam, about your saying: "baby, I'm impressed," and so on.

I already sent the tape to the regional office of Amnesty and tomorrow I mail it to the central office, to the Director of AIUSA, see what they can do with it. So we are off to fight the death penalty! There are plans to perform it other places, too. We'll see.

Before this letter you will receive the script and pictures of the reading. Enjoy!

Love,

Agi

February 21, 2004

Dear Agi,

Hello my lady. How are you today? I got your letter with pictures of actors and Jan. (Feb. 11)

Yes, I am looking forward to reading the script; actually I'm excited about it.

Yes, I got the poster all the nice people signed. And, yes, it did move me.

I remember in AA we say "acceptance is the key to serenity." True, huh? So, on death row, I have to accept what I am able to do and what I am not able to do. Somedays I just fight that inside my head – I want to be able to do more than I can…I want to go home, be free from prison. One way and one day I will die in prison, period. I know that.

Sometimes I get depressed because I do know that, but instead of accepting that, I resist it.

It's hard for me to explain why I get depressed but, truth be told, I don't stay down long in the blues of E flat…hell, baby, you know me. I always bounce back up to a happy tune of the key of A, A for acceptance and acceptance is the key of serenity. Boy, am I getting corny or what (ha-

ha). Well, anyway, you always make me happy, just by talking to you and knowing that you are always there for me.

You have taught me many things, Agi. I see how you get meaning into your life by devoting yourself to others, being as human as you can be, sharing with your heart.

"All you need is love," John Lennon sang. And baby you got that – coming out and right back to ya.

Ciao, my lady,
Rich

February 28, 2004
Dear Rich,

You must have gotten the script and photos by now, hope you like it. I like Dan and Helen a lot, he is a good actor and she is a great director. She is British, he is American. She does an incredible job of putting up Shakespeare plays on their lawn, working with mostly amateurs, but making them do well.

It is "hard to explain why I get depressed" – you are funny, my friend. It's not hard at all – it's quite natural, and you are great not to be depressed all the time.

My computer had to be shipped for repair, it's very frustrating. I'm working on my book and now I'm stuck.

And my fucking neighbor called the police again: one night I was writing away and I forgot to close the pet-door, and Lucky got out and barked for about 3 minutes at 10.20 – sure enough that bastard called me, saying "your damned dog" etc. I hung up. The police called me a minute later, and 2 days ago I got a paper: they fined me for $25. That's not a lot, but I got outraged. I spent $110 for a spray collar and I do my best to keep him from barking. He doesn't bark that much, here and there a few minutes. This low bastard makes my life miserable here – oh well. I am afraid he would kill the dog – this is the kind of guy who would do that.

All I need is love – how true! But how frustrating and miserable to get this shitty people, quite the contrary of love! You don't have peace in this world until dying.

Love,

Agi

P.S. A better note: spring is coming! I've seen the first blooming tree today! My camellia is budding and I have a few little daffodils out.

March 1, 2004

Dear Agi,

Hello sweetheart. I got the script; I have read it three times and baby we sure have come a long way together, eh? I didn't realize how much music talk – real and metaphorical – was in our letters. Also, you can see and feel our special bond, friendship and love growing through the years of dialogue. It's beautiful.

I really like it and I could or can talk more about it but it would sound egotistical.

I do want to say though that one (of many) thoughts that came to me is, that when this is over, you will have something nice and special to remember me by. That is, death ends a life but our relationship will live through this work that you and Jan put together. That thought makes me feel good. That I will be remembered by you and others on your island.

Also, yes, I got the three pictures of the actors, they look like nice people.

Well spring is in the air back here. The temperature got up to 60 over the week-end and melted the snow and ice off the track in the rec yard.

I enjoy my fast walk/slow jog around the yard. Ten laps is equal to a mile. Last summer I was doing a ten minute mile for five miles which is good enough for me. I'm not a fanatic. I became a pretty serious jogger back in 1978 when I lived in Huntington Beach. (I rented a small house behind a house.) Of course, I had my regular course I did and 3 miles was running right on the beach. It was so wonderful. Some days the wind (esp. Santa Anna's) would blow all the smog away and I could see the mountains from the beach – so beautiful.

I knew then (1978) I had a drinking problem and that I was an alcoholic. Sometimes when I'm out on the prison track I think back to running on the beach and going to my first AA meeting on that same beach. More later.

I love you, Agi.

Ciao,

Rich

March 11, 2004

Dear Agi,

Well be with you my lady. Yeah, I'm reading Shakespeare again, "Romeo and Juliet." Of course I know the story from movie versions but books are always best. What are you reading these days?

Yes, I got your letter of 2-28 with pictures of actor – what is his name? What is the actress' name? (oops, Dan, that's it) Forgot.

So beautiful the picture out your window of all the snowy trees and forest; I think your island is a wonderful place to live – so beautiful. Also, the picture of Zizi is great, what a cool cat, eh? I noticed a few pictures back how big Lucky has gotten. Labs are good dogs, loving dogs and I'm so glad him and Zizi get along okay.

Well I saw one of my lawyers Monday the 8th. Dave Hanson came over to say hello. He came up Man CI to visit new clients and came over to DR6 to say hi to me. There is no news on my case. Which is good. At this point we are done on this end. Now we wait, hopefully for years, until a Fed judge takes a look at my case. I asked him (Dave) how long before that happens and he could not tell me because he just doesn't know.

Dave was real impressed with DR6 pod. It was the first time he was in here. He noticed how clean, quiet and big the pod is and how well behaved the inmates are.

Man, you sure have a cranky neighbor. I could understand if Lucky was out barking for hours – that would bother anybody – but a few minutes, come on! Give the dog a break and you, too. Somebody needs to kick that guy off island, like they do on Survivor. (Yeah, I watch Survivor and I enjoy it, but it's the only reality show I like.)

Don't renew "Newsweek." I can get that here via library via other inmates. You do enough for me already, and Agi, God bless you, I really appreciate it, yes, I do.

You're the greatest, baby.

Ciao. Love,

Rich

March 15, 2004

Dear Rich,

I got two letters, thanks pal. Glad you enjoyed the script. Now it should be developed into a play or book, and I wonder if Janet will do it soon. She is poor, has to make a living and has other writing jobs and classes to teach – well, I'll kick her to do it. The actors' name is Dan – Daniel Mayes and Helen Machin-Smith. If you still have the flyer I sent you, it's there. By the way, they are doing "Much Ado" this summer!

New development on Lucky's "case": I got a notice for a fine. I got outraged and went to see the Sheriff, who I know. He read me a report saying that the dog barks all night! I said it was an outrageous lie; he advised me to talk to the Judge – but you can't just talk to such a great man; they gave me a date in April, and since I contested the fine, it will be a <u>trial</u>, they said. I don't know if they will have those charming neighbors there, or I just can talk to him.

Hey, you gave me a nightmare by telling about "when this is all over." If I fail to save your life it will be my biggest failure. Enough of this now…

I sent you 3 books: 2 Hemingways and 1 K. Haruf, that's all I could find.

Love,

Agi

March 21, 2004

Dear Agi,

Hello sweetheart. Is everything OK? I do hope so. The last letter you wrote was February 28th and today is March 21st so it's been awhile. I'm a tad worried.

Well the weather is crazy back here. Earlier in the week it was snowing (6 inches) and cold, overcast and windy. Today it's sunny and warm – up to 50, and the snow is already melted, which is good, of course, but the track is really soggy and muddy.

As I'm writing this letter, I'm listening to Ted Kennedy on "Meet the Press." Now there's a guy who can articulate the Democratic position and, in my humble opinion, the truth. Man, anybody but Bush in November.

I'm curious so I have a question: Who would you like to see Kerry have as a Vice President candidate?

Check this out. I read in the paper that two thirds of Americans would actually pay, i.e. sign up for pay per view, to watch executions on TV of state death row inmates. That doesn't say much about our society, in a good way, huh? People have become desensitize to death, violence, and injury to other people.

To me, I thought it was silly the whole country got upset at Janet Jackson showing her breast at the Super Bowl but, yet, TV in general has so much violence is more detrimental to a young mind than sex is – come on – wake up.

You wrote "you don't have peace in this life until you die." Come on my sweet lady don't become cynical or pessimistic or cranky. Peace, happiness and joy come from within and I know that you know that, too. Sometimes we have to take action to find those things. The culture we have does not make people feel good about them selves. And we have to be strong enough to say if the culture doesn't work, don't buy it. I find peace, joy and happiness writing to you, Agi. You're my Lady.

Love,

Rich

March 26, 2004

Richissimo,

I just came back seeing a rather bad play with Janet, and afterwards we had a drink. Today is cold and windy; I decided, this will be the last cold day. The hummingbirds are back! I love those tiny creatures and always put out sugar-water for them. In the high season they are just swarming around and I have to change their food two or three times a day.

I have not the slightest idea who would be the Vice-President, and I'm not even worrying about it too much. I hope Kerry will be smart enough to choose a good one.

Let's don't even talk about paying to watch executions; it's disgraceful and disgusting.

And you say I'm cynical or pessimistic when saying you don't have peace until you die – it's the truth my friend. See, the above is enough to disturb your peace, right? Or a fucking neighbor, or a tooth-ache, or whatever is your daily life. I do have inner peace, but am outraged about what's going on in this country, and disturbed by little or bigger things. The proof that I have inner peace is that I believe you have peace when you die; you see what I mean? When you can forget about Bush and executions, you have peace.

I'm working on my book and it slowly takes shape. If you want I can send pages to see what it will be like.

You must have gotten the books by now.

Ciao, Richissimo,

Agi

March 31, 2004

Dear Agi,

Hi sweetheart. I got your letter of March 15th. Also, I got the 3 books – 2 Hemingway and 1 K. H. I will enjoy all three, I'm sure. I just read chapter one of Hemingway's To Have and Have Not and I'm already hooked on it. Note: (Reading Hemingway's book and your book I noticed or felt you write – your style, feeling and so on is like his in some ways) 😊 that's a compliment. I saw the movie "To Have and Have Not" on PBS a few years ago. Humphrey Bogart Lauren Bacall and Walter Brennan were the main actors. I love them all. Are you a fan of H. Bogart and his films? I am. Film noir they call it: dark moods, gloomy, cynical; black and white movies from 1940s and '50s e. g. "The Maltese Falcon," "To Have and Have Not," etc... I enjoy watching those. Did you know that Bogart and Bacall got married here in Mansfield, Ohio? Yeah, there's a famous writer Louis Bromfield from here who was friends w/Bogart, so he (Bogart) and Bacall came to Mansfield to Brunswick's (sic) farm which today is a state park called Malabar Farms, not too far from the prison.

We had another execution yesterday. William Wickline was his name. I didn't know him but that doesn't make it any easier. Since I have been here,

Ohio has killed eleven people. I am hoping that in the next election Ohio will elect a Democratic Governor and maybe he'll end this killing.

Monday we had a 2.4 inspection (2.4 is the size of the cardboard box we have to fit all our belongings into) i.e. everything I own has to fit in <u>one</u> box! Thank God I'm not materialistic really; I have never owned a new car or house – not that I wouldn't like to have those things, I'm not an idiot, but I always tried to live without a bunch of monthly bills. Being a club musician I never made a lot of money. One time, I ended up homeless and believe me, that's very hard to deal with. In some ways, being homeless is harder than being on death row. More later. Be happy.

Love,
Rich

April 4, 2004
Dear Rich,

Did you like "Romeo and Juliet?" Did you ever get to "Much Ado?" I love that play. As I told you, Dan and Helen – "you and me" – will put it on this summer.

I see what you mean about my style a bit like Hemingway's – it's simple and direct. Of course, my style is like that because English is not my native language. But thanks for the compliment anyway.

Talking about movies – it seems to me you don't know much about foreign movies. Humphrey Bogart – yes, he is OK, but I'm not a fan of his. There is a wealth of great French and Italian movies which you don't seem to know. How great would be I could show you some of mine! For example there was a French actor whom I wouldn't exchange for any Cary Grant or

Humphrey Bogart. His name was Gerard Philip, a dashing, handsome man and a great actor. He starred in many of Rene Clair's movies – a director I love. And there is the great Danish one: Theodor Dreyer, who made only 3 great movies, but they are masterpieces. One of them is "The Passion of Joan of Arc," of that I told you before. There are some great British movies, too, and others, Russian, Czech, Hungarian ones. Too bad you have no access to these treasures.

Of course, there are some great American ones, too. I have in my collection "12 Angry Men" which is a masterpiece in my opinion. I have also three British "humor noir" ones with Alec Guinness. And, if there is a favorite actor of mine, it's Laurence Olivier, the great Shakespearian actor. Want to laugh? I have had rarely erotic dreams, but once I dreamt I went to bed with him. Ha-ha! But afterwards I thought, hey, I don't have bad taste!

OK, enough babbling for today.

Love,

Agi

April 11, 2004

Dear Agi,

Hello Sweetheart. And how are you today? Aren't you glad spring is here? I know I am.

I got two letters from you since I have written: March 26th and April 4th.

I'm glad to hear you are working on your book. And, yes, I enjoy reading what you are writing, so when you want send a few pages to me.

We are having another execution this month, April 27th, Greg Lott.

Isn't it a bad situation in Iraq? Now they are starting to kidnap people. Man, anybody but Bush in November.

Truth is, most people here in Ohio and in the prison, the employees and most inmates are for Bush and the war and so on. I hear them talking but I stay quiet because I really don't like to talk/argue politics. It's not a subject I know about or even care for. I really lost interest – not that I was ever really interested in the first place – after the Watergate mess. I find most people don't really know the issues, or the party's position, platform, etc., etc.; they mostly choose (vote) on the personality of the candidate.

I'm taking a break from Shakespeare. I didn't finish "Romeo and Juliet" or "Much Ado" but I will. Truth be told, when I started "Romeo & Juliet" I got mad at the families for hating each other and I thought Romeo was somewhat a sissy. But, I think it was, and is, my mood I'm in. I'm down.

March 27th was 7 years since the day I killed Patty and lately I've been hating myself and God and life, everybody and everything in general.

You're the best!

Love,

Rich

PS Thanks, Sweetheart for putting up with my mood swings. I must sound like an out-of-tune violin to you sometimes, where you want to scream "goddam shit" eh? Man, this place works, plays on my psyche, my soul and I get out of tune.

April 18, 2004

Dear Agi,

Hello Sweetie. So you went to bed with Lawrence Olivier in your dreams, eh? Well at least you have good taste. (I rec. your April 4th letter.)

Yes, you are right, I am not hip to foreign films; I have only seen a handful. I used to go to a lot of "Arthouse" films years ago up in Long Beach, California, and I wasn't paying much attention to the names of the directors or actors. I was usually high/stone on pot and mostly I just got into the story and the music.

Music in foreign films as I recall, usually had a jazzy flavor to it. Agree? One movie I especially liked was A Man and a Woman". I liked the movie but fell in love with the tune "A Man and a Woman".

I played that tune every nite during my dinner gigs 90-95. Man! I miss my keyboard.

In my opinion, I do believe European people are more hip (I know I need a better word) to music, films, books, plays, clothes, and so on because Europe is more humanistic than America is and I like that.

I finished "To Have and Have Not". It was OK but not his best, of course. I'm done with him now. I have read 8 Hemingways. I feel bad for Ernest blowing his brains out with a shotgun. You know why, don't you? Another alcoholic sick and tired of being sick and tired. I like Ernest Hemingway. He knew how to live a full life w/adventure and travel – he was a man's man – not that I'm gay – though there's nothing wrong with that; just keeping the record/story straight, you know. Most men I admire are musicians, of course, but Ernest I think he was a cool cat except for the suicide part.

You are a wonderful (God sent!) loyal, kind-hearted friend.

Last week one of our videos was the film "Amadeus". I know, I don't take the story seriously or literally, it's just entertainment, somewhat amusing. The clothes they wore, high society, with the wigs and all – men and women – kind of strange, huh?

Till next week, Ciao.

Love,

Rich

April 18, 2004

Dear Rich,

Yes, I am glad spring is here. The weather is mostly glorious, sunshine, trees blooming: beautiful.

About politics: in general, in normal times, I don't care too much either. But politics can get into your life as it did into mine, and it can be crucial and devastating, as it did to me. And now it's getting similar here. Do you realize that if GWB is reelected, we have a good chance to have a nuclear war? And our civil liberties destroyed? So I do care now and do anything I can to send back the idiot bastard to Texas.

It's no wonder you crave a "big ol' drink" my friend. If you would live a normal life I'm sure you could be strong enough to fight your alcoholism. But living the way you do – of course you would need a drink – my God, I would become an alcoholic if I would be in such an awful place. And don't hate God and yourself and life. At least don't hate three things: God, yourself, and me. OK?

Love,

Agi

April 25, 2004

Dear Agi,

Hello, sweetheart. Are you feeling good today 😊 I hope so.

Myself? Man I got blue during the week reading this downer of a book called '1984' by George Orwell. Last year I read "Animal Farm" by him and I really enjoyed it. The theme was the animals take over the farm, and slowly and insidiously the pigs take control (they become tyrants, dictators of all the other animals) on the farm. It was a clever and witty and satiric story of bad government(s) etc. If you haven't, you should read "Animal Farm" by Orwell. I'm sure you would like that one.

Because I enjoyed reading "Animal Farm" I figured I would like Orwell's '1984.' But man was I wrong on that! I made myself finish it but it sure was a horrible picture he had of the future, i.e. war is peace, ignorance is strength, freedom is slavery, is their slogan. Big Brother is watching and listening via the telescreen (TVs). If you control the present, you control the past. And if you control the past, you control the future. They (big bro) control reality. (Kinda like Bush is trying to do in Iraq.) Big Brother controls the past by

destroying books and rewriting their own history. No Shakespeare. 😊 They even have "thought police" i.e. you can be arrested for your thoughts or facial expressions. The world is ruled by three countries: USA, Russia and China. Truth be told: it was a dark picture of humanity – maybe warning – I'm glad I read it even though it was somewhat depressing. Bush is like Orwell's big brother in Iraq. I can't stand that guy!

Orwell wrote it in 1949. Have you read it? Have you read "Animal Farm?"

On a happy note – if there is one – everything is the same here for me. The execution set for Tuesday has been called off. Greg Lott got a stay. Why? I haven't heard. I wish him luck.

What are you doing? Yardwork? Working on your book? What happened w/your case? The 'Lucky' case? I hope you ad your cranky neighbor can work it out.

Write soon. I miss you.

Ciao,

Rich

\April 26, 2004

Dear Rich,

To continue on movies: in Paris I went 2 or 3 times a week to so-called "art-cinemas." It was my escape from my problems. So I have seen many great ones. "A Man and a Woman" is a pretty good one, not the greatest. Music can be different, some has classical. My "lover," Laurence Olivier used music for his Shakespeare films by William Walton, one of the well-known modern composers.

If you finished Hemingway and took a break from Shakespeare, you might want some other books, do you? Shall I go to Serendipity and look around for you? The trouble is, I am not "hip" on anything but kind of classical. (Do you think I am a snob?) Anyway tell me what you want, otherwise I would pick randomly and it might not please you.

I am a bit sad now. Last night, at our usual canasta game, Janet got mad at me and left, yelling at me. It was the second time, once before it was even worse. (Not at canasta that time.) It means I am losing my three best friends here. The artist, who offended me before, is OK, we made it up, but I never see her, she is too busy. And so is my actress friend, she calls sometimes but I didn't see her for months, except I ran into her once in the grocery store. Her husband, the "Bushie", wrote an idiotic letter in the local paper – it was so outrageous that I answered it. It was a good letter; a lot of people congratulated me for it. But in spite of this his wife is still friendly. But all three are now halfway out, you know what I mean?

And my peace here is disturbed by that goddam son-of-a-bitch of neighbor. There was a hearing about Lucky barking, and I didn't take it seriously, I went alone without a lawyer. That guy came with his girl-friend and a lawyer and made a testimony, lying shamelessly, stating that the dog barked for hours in the night. And they stated it went on for 2 ½ years! Lucky is 1 ½ now. I thought I got them on that. I told the judge this – and they just ignored it! Can you believe? And they fined me. We have a great justice system here, do we? I was very upset.

Oh hell, I know all this is nothing against your plight, but I can't help to be upset. Maybe I should move – but I love my house.

Well, enough complaining.

Love,

Agi

PS I'm working away on my book, there is 90 pages now. I wanted to send you a few pages about my student years, but this time my printer was not working. The joys of life…

May 1, 2004

Dear Rich,

Here is our fifth anniversary. Ours is a beautiful friendship, and I cherish it – I know you do, too.

I read both of Orwell's, "The Animal Farm" and "1984." No need to get depressed pal: he was wrong! Both is a satire on Communism, during the cold war. But it collapsed on its own failure. Only China remains and I'm sure it will collapse, too. That doesn't mean, unfortunately, that all totalitarian dictatorship died. They are well and alive, and even here we experience some of it. (Go back to Texas, Georgie-boy!)

There is a very strong movement to send him back – you can't be aware of it, and can't see how many people feel like you and I. We will see it in November!

Yes, I'm doing some yard-work, burnt a huge pile of fallen branches. And I'm writing away, have now over 90 pages. I have the idea of putting the two together: "Tales from Hungary" and this, which will be a complete account – well, kind of complete – of my life before Friday Harbor. And I have a title of my new book: "Memoirs of a Stupid Woman." Don't protest my friend, it's a good title, and it's true in certain sense. I'm not stupid, but everybody can be both stupid and intelligent. I did a few very stupid things in my life. You too, huh?

Well, I wish we could celebrate our anniversary together.

All my best, Richissimo,

Agi

Well, I succeded to print out these pages. Hope you will enjoy it.

May 2 2004

Dear Agi,

Hello my lady, my lady with a sweet heart, kind heart, a heart full of gold in perfect pitch and as steady as a metronome. Sorry, Agi, I know that's corny, my sad attempt at wit. I should rewrite it but I'll leave it maybe I'll get a smile or small chuckle.

I got your letter of 4-18. I do feel better and I am not hating God, life, or anything or anybody now. But I am greatly disappointed in myself needless to say, I'm sure. Being a failure at life just leaves a bad taste in my mouth.

Last Sunday on TV Hallmark Cards presented the movie "Plainsong" by the writer Kent Haruf. I read the book back in 2001 and loved it. (You sent it to me.) The movie wasn't very good because it's a story you have to read to feel it, some stories just can't be movies except in your own mind. I loved the book. I have the Kent Haruf book you sent me last month "The Tie That Binds" on my top bunk. I'm saving it for the right time, right mood.

After I read Orwell's "1984", I needed to lighten up so this week I'm reading a cowboy book hee-haw!   but man I am enjoying it; I've been on the trail this week taking cows and horses from Mexico up to Montana – boy! It's a rough job. Larry McMurtry – I like his writing style – wrote it: "Lonesome Dove". Wonderful story. Getting away from the darkness of '1984' to the wide open spaces of Texas has been good for my soul. I'm not a cowboy type; I'm city and nocturnal but I do enjoy a Western movie. One of my favorites is "The Magnificent Seven" – I love the film score too by Elmer Bernstein and OK I admit it I do enjoy those old spaghetti Westerns w/Clint Eastwood. He's cool and the music was hip I thought. I love the way the composer used a man whistling for the main melody. You don't hear that too much.

I never could whistle, can you? Do you whistle as you work, Agi? I'm in a silly mood. Be happy.

Love,

Rich

May 5, 2004

Dear Rich,

First one good news: we made it up, Janet and I. We agreed that it was stupid to ruin our friendship about nothing. I guess she has other troubles, and it wasn't me she was mad at: she has a son and there was some trouble with him, she didn't want to talk about.

What do you think about the prison pictures from Iraq? You have probably seen it on your TV. Now the US has a nice image to the world, right? God, if this doesn't undo GW I will have no hope for this world.

The trouble is, I don't like Kerry – naturally I will vote ABB, and I'm supporting him, contributing to his campaign and do everything I can to get out of this nightmare – and I believe the fate of the whole world depends on the next election.

Oh well, let's talk about something else, something nicer:

Love,

Agi (the metronome)

P.S. Yes, I can whistle.

May 10, 2004

Dearest Agi,

Hello my love. How are you today? I got your letter of 4-26 and I see you have been going through some strife.   🌹   man, life can be a bitch sometimes.

I shall respond as best I can. You asked me "do you think I'm a snob?" No, no, I do not think you are the least snobbish. I know your heart is sweet and kind and that you are a lady with compassion, sympathy and consideration for others; like me, a man on death row whom you have never met, did not know at all but yet support with great friendship, loyalty and real concern about me from the very first or second letter, i.e. "do you need anything, what can I send to help you," you wrote. A snob would not do that. I have known snobs and you are not a snob.

It does sadden me to read you and Janet are out of harmony; man I hate hearing that. I know words can be very hurtful and to forgive and forget is hard to do. Hell, I still have resentments that go back to the 60s. We all fall short and we all have character defects.

When I saw "Amadeus" a few weeks ago, I also thought of you being a child prodigy and, in truth, that makes you somewhat different than a common person. You are way ahead of the class in many ways. Most people are probably going to bore you – hell a lot of 'em bore me. After I read your book, I was reluctant to write to you; in fact, I quit writing to you because I felt I would be boring to you and you were somewhat intimidating for me. Not anymore. I love you dearly because you let me be myself. I'm just a bar-fly, club musician and that's okay with you. And I'm happy it is.

In AA we say "the higher our expectations the lower our serenity" and sometimes our friends won't meet our expectations. (Maybe we don't meet theirs.)

Anyway, sweetheart, I do really, really hope everything comes into harmony again with you and your friends on your island. You live on a small island, I live in a pod; we are kinda in the same type of boat where we have to work on our relationships and give and take a little.

I love you.

Rich

May 16, 2004

Dear Agi,

Hello my lady. And how are you today?

No, no, no, you cannot name your book, "Memoirs of a Stupid Woman" – come on, now, that don't fly. I got four pages, 20-23, you sent. Question: where are pages 1 thru 20? You didn't send 'em, did ya?

So the Music Academy was named after Franz Liszt, huh? Probably the greatest piano player who has ever lived on planet earth.

When I read about the "Eastern five-tone scale," I must admit I do not know that, unless you were speaking about the Pentatonic Scales?)

Of course the Pentatonic can be played in any key and they are very popular for improv. Esp. in jazz music. So teach me – write one out – what is an Eastern 5-tone scale. I love music theory but the course I studied was for jazz players. But music is music and I well understand if I see one that you draw. There are two (I don't think I told you this) guys in my pod w/guitars and I have been writing out and teaching them all the basic scales and chords and now I'm starting them on the modes: Ionian, Dorian, Phrygian, Lydian, Mixolydian, Aeolian, Locrian, i.e. I=is maj, ii minor, iii=minor, iv is major, v= dominant vi is minor, vii is half diminished. I have heard music by Kodaly and I remember I liked it a lot. I sure do miss my piano and playing music. I miss that more than anything. Even though I became a drunk, an alcoholic, I did take my music and my playing seriously, at least thru the '70s,'80s and early '90s. Of course, after a time, the booze took me seriously. "First a man takes a drink, then the drink takes a drink and then the drink takes the man." Touche. Now that is stupid. You're a wonderful friend, you're my Lady.

Love,

Rich

P.S. Happy 5 year Anniversary, Agi. I'm hoping we can get 5 more. You're the best. Much love, Rich

May 22, 2004

Dear Rich,

Your 5-10 letter was especially nice, thanks friend. Well, everything is fine now with Janet, we just finished a canasta party and things were fine. I didn't tell you before, Janet had a terrible childhood. They abused her terribly. No wonder she is nuts sometimes, it's even a miracle she is normal and a nice person.

Answer to your 5-16 letter: of course I was talking about pentatonic scales. Now, you're a bit confused about that: there's no such thing as pentatonic major and minor. Your first example is wrong, the second is right. The pattern of pentatonic is: minor 3rd, whole step, whole step, min. 3rd, whole step. You mentioned the modal scales accurately, but the Ionian is the major scale, and I don't quite see what you mean about major and minor there. Of course there are <u>major-like</u> and <u>minor-like</u> ones, according to the major or minor 3rd, like Dorian is minor-like, Mixolidian is major-like, etc. The best way to figure it out is to imagine playing scales on only the white keys of the piano. Starting on C you get the Ionian-major, starting on D the Dorian, and so on. Aeolian is the natural minor. Of course, you know that, but you shouldn't call any of those major or minor. There is D Dorian, A pentatonic, and so on.

Well, enough of this lecture. I knew you would protest about the title of my book. It's a good title, and when you read it you will see the reason. I wrote over 100 pages, I sent you those about my student years knowing that it would interest you. Maybe I will send you other pages, or the whole thing, but it's not ready, I'm still working on it.

Love,

Agi

OK, here is a pentatonic scale

P.S. It's great you are teaching music there. How about trying to play the guitar? That would be a bit of a replacement for the piano you miss so much.

May 23, 2004

Dear Agi,

Hello sweetheart, my little angel. I am so happy – very happy 😊 – (to read you and Janet are in harmony again, that's wonderful news. (I got your letter of 5-12).

So you can whistle, huh? I never could but that's OK. But, on the other hand, I do wish God had given me the talent, vocal chords, so I could have been a decent singer. I can't sing worth a crap! Never could. How about you? Can you carry a tune? Well, I can carry it but I'm spilling it all over. Maybe in my next life I can be a singer and player. But maybe too in my next life because my Karma is so bad from this one I might be a low animal of some kind, eh?

I was thinking about us the other day, why we met and you became my friend and a person I love, maybe we knew each other in a past life. I know the concept of karma and reincarnation is something like salvation is reached by canceling the effects of past evil deeds by virtuous actions in one's present life. So what I was thinking was: "Agi will be rewarded for her benevolence to me and others (AI) ...well I could be in deep sh... my next time around."

😟 (oh, man!) if reincarnation/karma is true...Lord have mercy on me. These were some of my thoughts the past week. Maybe I have too much time on my hands, eh? Ha-ha.

Someday (later) down the road I want to read "Siddhartha" by Hermann Hesse. Right now I'm still in my cowboy mode. I'm reading a prequel(?) to "Lonesome Dove" called "Comanche Moon" by Larry McMurtry. In truth, I have a special affinity for the American Indian. We - us white people from

Europe -sure did do them wrong. Kinda like we are doing today in Iraq. Take their land, their oil, kill'em, rape'em and take pictures! Man-oh-man how inhumane we can be.

Agi, you're my earth-angel.

Love you. Ciao,
Rich

May 29, 2004
Richissimo, you silly guy,

Your karma is <u>fine</u>, I guarantee it! You did a bad thing, but you are not a bad person – your words. You did a bad thing when you were not yourself, a moment of madness, and you deeply regret it, and you are cruelly punished, for years and years, for that one crazy moment. And you are now a much better person than before. That's what counts. So, no more talk about bad karma. I know you're OK.

Are you into Buddhism that you talk about karma and reincarnation? That reincarnation business, I don't quite believe it. I told you, I think my brother and Zoli are watching me – they are dead for 50 years, no, more, so why didn't they reincarnate? Also, people meet relatives and friends over there (near-death experience) it's against what Buddhists say that you come back in 47 days. I think it's silly. So, chase those thoughts from your head. You are not in deep sh…I tell you.

Yes, I can sing and carry a tune, not great, but recognizable.

I was honored today at the Soroptimists – a large group here. Got a bunch of flowers and a "title" of "woman of distinction" or something like that. Janet came with me. And the lady who did my honoring mentioned our letters. Since we (my AI-group) are doing a campaign for women, the Soroptimists is a good thing; they might help us writing letters.

I just wanted to say this today.

Love,

Agi

P.S. Here are a few more pages of my book, which might interest you. I chose the form of my husband questioning me about my life's "adventures" - to understand better why he is there.

May 30, 2004

Dear Agi,

Hello sweetheart. Well it's a holiday week-end, Memorial Day on Monday. I wish you and I could go on a picnic together. Wouldn't that be fun?

Actually, truth be told, I never cared that much for picnics because of the ants and small bugs etc. Kind of a hassle too; I prefer nice hotels or restaurants or a nice boat on a river or lake or the ocean. I prefer room service rather than setting up camps. (I quit camping when I quit the Boy Scouts.)

My dad was an outdoor man, i.e. he enjoyed hunting and fishing and camping but myself once I reached the age of 13-14 I enjoyed the most being in my basement with my piano and drums and my albums.

You know, in many ways, I was a lucky guy in life. I got to experience the joy of music. And the joy of having a dream, a goal and an earnest purpose to live for. Of course, I know not as serious as you at 16 going to the Academy – now, that is serious!! – but my love and dreams were probably as strong.

Heck, in my head and soul, one week I was going to be the next Buddy Rich (jazz drummer) or Ringo Starr (rock drummer) and then after hearing "Take Five" I was going to be the next Dave Brubeck. (Jazz piano player.)

But I kept it real, too. I did practice what my teachers told me to practice and I went through many music books over the years I enjoyed it, too. Practicing on fundamentals was never a drag to me.

I can't believe the price of gas, unreal!! In Fullerton, Calif. (Orange County) I read it is over $4 dollars a gallon. What is the price of gas on your island? These new hybrid cars are going to be popular, huh? It's a great idea gas & battery together, and when it's running on gas power it is recharging the battery.

I watched on PBS a documentary on the building of the WWII memorial in Wash. DC. I think it's beautiful and I like where it is on the mall. I hate war. I wish we could just live in peace on earth.

You're my angel Agi.

Ciao. Love,

Rich

June 6, 2004 (D-day)

Dear Agi,

Hello my lady. I got your 5-22 letter and I am happy all is well again with you and Janet. You are playing Canasta again, I see, jolly good.

I would like to clarify what I meant about the maj. and minor modes. I'm sure I didn't explain myself too clearly so I wrote a few out on some manuscript paper. Yes you are right on the modal scales, yes, they are major and minor like as you wrote. What I meant about I & IV being major, etc. was chords built from the major scales.

I have thought about maybe getting a guitar but my mind says no. Heck by the time I'm any good my time will be up so what's the point. I know it's negative thinking but real too. Truth be told, back in the early 80s I was teaching at a music store part-time and I used to play around on the guitar a little bit. I really didn't have the aptitude for it nor the desire to learn.

Living on death row has dimmed my enthusiasm somewhat – I don't like to admit that because it's like saying this place has beaten me – but in some ways it has.

Ronald Reagan died yesterday. I can't say I was a fan 'cause I wasn't. I remember him as governor of Cal. And I didn't like him then. What is your opinion of Reagan? I'm curious. Who is your favorite American president? I bet I can guess…Kennedy, right? He's mine too, along with Lincoln, Jefferson and Washington, and Clinton.

Next month Stephen Vrabel will be executed I heard. He dropped all his appeals and asked to be executed. I hate that.

Agi, thanks for being in my life. You are a wonderful friend, and our friendship has been a real power for me to stay the course.

Ciao Sweetheart. Love

Rich

June 10, 2004

Dear Rich,

These last days I was typing the remaining letters – our letters – now I finished and am going to work on it. Janet won't do a thing, she is too busy. What I have in mind is to catch the essence of our letters, rather than selecting a few. I want to compose letters, our words of course, but putting a few together. It will be hard work. The material is overwhelming, more than 200.

I took a break from my book. Now I have something like a first draft, but I am not satisfied. Did you get my story?

Troubles never end: now I have car and video trouble: the windows of my car don't work, one is covered with plastic, another is halfway open and can't move it. Rain is falling in…And one after other videos are going wrong, the sub-titles are cut off, and on an on…I don't know if it is the television or the VCR, I will have to look into it. Money, money – it will cost me a lot, both of these troubles.

Weather is funny these days: one day is full summer; the next is cold and rainy.

And I was diagnosed having some degeneration of my eyes, having cataracts on both – not yet bad – and a <u>mole</u> in one eye! Hell, I didn't know things like this was possible. Well, it seems that the degeneration is a slow process. I certainly hope to die before I go blind. Getting old is not a nice thing.

I got your 5-30 letter; thanks. I also wish we could live in peace, but right now there's anything but peace here. Sorry about all this not very enjoyable news, but we are sharing right?

To finish something funny: it looks like GW is really going berserk. I read a report, he is talking about God and the next minute calling somebody a "fucking bastard" and he goes back and forth like that. He should be in the mad-house. Wow, we do have a president, we are blessed...

OK, enough of this now. Next time I write a more cheerful letter.

Love,

Agi

PS To cheer you up after this kind of black letter, here is the story of how I got the SF job.

June 13, 2004

Dear Agi,

Hello sweetheart. Are you enjoying your summer? Back here lots of rain, but the temperature is starting to get hot which I like for outside rec.

I got your letter of 5-26 with chapter 6 of your story. Thank you my Lady.

We had an execution last week that I didn't even know about until I saw it on the news after it was over. William Zuern was his name. I didn't know him. We have had twelve executions since I've been here. And I can tell ya that quite few of the guys in my pod, DR 6 are getting anxious. Five or six of'em on the upper tier where I am, - we rec together – have been here 18 to 20 years, so they know their time is very short.

You asked me if I was into Buddhism. No not really. Jesus is my Lord and Savior. But I do find the philosophy, theory interesting, and I also know about the peace and serenity I find when I meditate and do the breathing and stretching exercises of hatha yoga.

So you received a title of "woman of distinction" eh? I concur and congratulations my Love. To me you are a woman with spunk and panache. Otto Klemperer saw it and, by the way, I'm so happy you played well for him and yourself while playing the Bach Concerto for three violins. As I read your story this quote comes to mind: "For all sad words of tongue or pen the saddest are these: It might have been." (Whittier) Sometimes life is just unfair. Of course, we don't want to get on the pity pot, do we? No. But I do realize your frustration - i.e. not being able to do more concerts when you were young.

Note: Agi on page 26 you call it Bach Concerto for two violins and on page 29 you call it three violins. Need to correct?

Love

Rich

June 14, 2004

Hi friend,

I got your D-day letter – it was that time a great news to us. We have seen the light at the end of the tunnel.

My opinion of Reagan? I call him to myself a wooden dog – there is a saying in Hungarian "he smiles like a wooden dog," meaning he smiles unchanged, about anything. That was Reagan all right. He became president because of his goddam smile.

And you didn't guess right: my favorite president was Jimmy Carter, of course. He was the one with a human heart, with integrity, with honesty. The

Republican press killed him: whatever he said or did, they jumped on him. And that wooden-dog-ass beat him. Now he – Carter – is doing a beautiful thing: building houses for homeless people around the whole world in the underdeveloped countries. And he is speaking up sometimes, supporting the right causes – he made a statement about the death penalty, did you know that? A great guy.

See my answers to our musical argument at the enclosed pages.

How is everything on DR6? Let me know if you want books.

Love,

Agi

Hi friend,

I got your D-day letter – it was that time a great news to us. We have seen the light at the end of the tunnel.

My opinion of Reagan? I call him to myself a wooden dog – there is a saying in Hungarian he smiles "like a wooden dog," meaning he smiles unchanged, about anything. That was Reagan all right. He was a bad president. He became president because of his goddam smile.

June 21, 2004 (The longest day of the year.)

Dear Rich,

Weather is great here. For several days it was so warm that I was thinking to go swimming. I didn't yet, but I will.

Quatschkopf! You didn't get the joke in my story. The Bach Concerto in question is, of course, for <u>2</u> violins – Wanda {Wilkomirska}and I played it. When we got to the Opera to rehearse there was a third violinist, so the manager, to ease the tension, was saying it looks like you are going to play the concerto for 3 violins. Baa! You used to be brighter than that, pal.

This Saturday I will play a little bit: just in the ensemble in Andy's concert. (Remember: Andy Senior, the violinist, father of the cellist who died. He has chamber music concerts here regularly. I didn't play with him for a long time, but now I will.)

Other than that there is not much news. I contemplate to quit smoking – that's cruel, but the eye-doctor said it would slow the process of degeneration of my eyes. I have a few more packs of cigarettes and I didn't order another batch. (I buy cigarettes from Indians who sell it much cheaper than the store.)

To cheer you up, here is another part of my book.

Love,

Agi

W.D.S.P.

(woman of distinction, spunk and panache)

June 21, 2004

Dear Agi,

Hello my sweet lady. I got your letter of 6-10 w/short story of getting San Fran. Opera job.

I hate reading that your eyes are having problems. Hopefully the doctors can do something about that. It seems to me that doctors can remove cataracts and replace with artificial lens if need be. But let's hope you won't have to go through that. Please keep me informed on that. I hope I won't have to learn to write in Braille (ha-ha) sick joke, huh? Sorry baby. You know I love ya – just goin' for a laugh. Yeah, touché, getting older is a drag when it comes to the physical body. Things just start breaking down and sometimes they will need to be repaired.

I do want to say this though, for the record, I want to die before you die. I <u>do not</u> want to be here without you being there. No way!!! Now you probably think that's a weird thing for me to say but I can't help it I feel that way. I can't explain how lonely and empty I would be inside if you were gone from the outside. I don't love you because I need you; I need you because I love you. As John the Beatle said, "All you need is love" (right?) therefore I need to love you because I like loving somebody. You are the last woman I will love. Boy, I'm getting heavy & mushy and lost. Sorry.

Let's don't talk about death & dying, OK? Let's just live and be happy and enjoy each other.

Are you planning on reading Clinton's book? I watched his interview on "60 Minutes" last Sunday. I like him. I wish he could run again.

I read a long article in Newsweek on stem cell research and I think, yes, we should be allowed to do it. Nancy Reagan will be good for that cause. Your opinion please.

We are having two executions next month. Both guys dropped their appeals, i.e. they have given up. Not me. I'm goin' to keep on keeping on and the state of Ohio can kiss my ass! (ha-ha) You're the best Agi – you're my lady. Ciao.

Love,

Rich

June 29, 2004

Dear Agi,

Hello sweetie. And how are you today?   I got your letter of June 17 yesterday and today is June 29. The workers here at Mansfield are way behind in the mailroom, I see.

Jimmy Carter, yes, I like him too. And you are right he is and has been doing wonderful work for the downtrodden peoples of the world. Mr. Carter is a honest, caring, intelligent human being. A good Christian man. He still teaches bible classes in Plains, GA when he's in town. He's very humble. I like that in a person, humility.

In your letter you asked if I want any books. Yes I would like to read Jimmy Carter's latest book: "The Hornet's Nest" about the Revolutionary War. And, I would like to read: "Siddhartha" by Hermann Hesse.

Now Agi, I know you have had extra money problems lately – i.e. your car windows, VCR and/or TV and eye doctor, so if the book store doesn't have used copies please don't buy new ones – just wait until Serendipity gets used ones OK?. OK.

Everything in DR 6 is fine. Last week Man. C.I. changed the outside rec rule to where 8-guys at a time can go out it was 5-guys only at a time. Eight is better.

I think we are having 2 executions in July. Both guys dropped their appeals. Also, I heard, another guy in DR 1, my old pod, is dropping his appeal.

Did I tell you that last month I walked and jogged 80 miles on the track? That's the best I've done since I've been over here in DR 6. Note: Not doing so well this month, my legs are tired. And at night I'm getting muscle cramps in my calf which is very painful. I guess I need to drink more water.

I read R. Bach's "Livingston Seagull" & "Illusions" back in the late '70s. I enjoyed 'em. Have you read them? I even had the album by Neil Diamond doing the story of Jonathan w/music. It was pretty cool. Rent the movie "The Last Samurai". You'll like it (I did). It's well done.

Hey, has anybody told you they love you today? Well they have now.

I love you

Rich

July 4, 2004

Dear Agi,

Hello my lady. Happy 4th of July. I love summer holidays – always have.

Yeah, just color me stupid, I didn't get the joke of 2 violins vs. 3 violins in your story. Sorry sweetie.

I got your letter of 6 – 21 w/story of getting job at I. U.   You make me laugh when you write "hell, why do they play music in a rest-room?"

"In Europe it's called what it is, toilet." Ha-ha. For some reason I found that funny. What a journey you went through. The gossip was you were the lover of a gay man, or you were lesbian. Ha-ha. Not funny then, I'm sure, but now it is. When you were 37 you were Assistant Professor w/an Artist Diploma from Liszt Academy, which is equivalent to a Master's degree. Hey, I'm impressed, no doubt. Plus, coming to a foreign country while having a very hard time w/English, man oh man, that took spunk – you are something else. I am very proud of you Agi. You're one in a million.

When you took a bus from the Cinc. airport to Bloomington, you went through my hometown via US 50 which goes thru Aurora, Ind. (Aurora is about 30 miles from the Airport.)

Have you been practicing? Keeping your 'chops' up as the jazzers say. How did it go w'Andy Saturday? What music did you play?

Good luck on the smoking thing. I know that will be hard for you – very hard.

Rent this video: "Cold Mountain." I enjoyed it. I'm hoping I get to see Michael Moore's "Fahrenheit 9/11" when it comes out on video. Have you seen it?

I remember last year you and Jan went to another island to see their fireworks but the trip ended up weird or something. You said that this year you will stay on your island to watch Friday Harbor's fireworks. Well, how was it? I hope you & Jan et al had fun over the weekend.

Did you get your car windows fixed? How about your VCR and/or TV - did you get that fixed? How's Lucky doin'?

I think your fair is coming pretty soon isn't it? Aug. or Sept.? Be well and happy my lady. Ciao.

Love,

Rich

July 4, 2004

Dear Rich,

I am just finishing watching "To Have or Have Not." I realize I've seen it before and I don't care too much. I also re-watched "Gone with the Wind" – and I got annoyed. Hell, they are lamenting to destroy a "civilization" which is based on slavery – a fine civilization! And they portray the blacks as treated just fine by their masters. They are like members of the family and there's no indication to ever have suffered of mistreatment. And this is an American classic! Downright disgusting.

I guess I'm angry mostly because this is the second day of not smoking. It's hard. But I'm too scared of my eyes. Actually, one doesn't become blind by this disease, "only" you lose your central view, so you can't read and can't drive. Well, thanks a lot!! The cataracts are no problem; nowadays they can remove them easily with laser. That's the degeneration which worries me.

We had a nice parade, people cheered us very nicely.

Love,

Agi

July 12, 2004

Dear Rich,

Well, I did it: it's the 10th day of not smoking. Shit!! It's a goddam nuisance.

My car-windows are still not fixed, apparently it's difficult to get parts for a Mercedes – it was a mistake to buy it. My TV is not fixed either. I was waiting for a guy who promised to come over. Of course, he didn't, so today I went to another place, found out that's the TV, not the VCR – which is more expensive, and more trouble, of course. The guy is coming over tomorrow and I'll see if I have to go to "America," the mainland, to buy another TV or it can be repaired.

Lucky's no-bark collar doesn't work either. I know you would be happy to have all this trouble and be free. But it's annoying, and my mood is sour and depressed, mostly because of not smoking. Hell!

Congratulations on your 80 miles; pretty damned good.

I will get you "Siddharta" very soon. The new Carter book, since it's new, won't be available yet at Serendipity, I'm sure.

Good news about the Kerry-Edwards bill, right? It's a good choice: he is a Southerner – that will help in the South, and he's "cute." One stupid woman at the caucus here voted for him for this reason – and I'm sure there are enough stupid people to vote for him because of that. But there are an incredible amount of stupid people who are still for Bush. It's really incomprehensible to me, after all he did. Oh stupidity, it will undue this world…

The Fair will be August 18-21. Soon I will have to go begging and organize everything.

Oh, I played only in the ensemble in Andy's concert, played in 3 pieces, not a big deal. But at this point it was good for me. I started to practice a bit, after a long time I did almost nothing.

This year I missed the fire-works of 4th of July, nobody asked me to go with – I'm sure I didn't miss a great deal.

Years ago I was in Vancouver for only one day – from there I went to an Alaska cruise where I played quartets on the boat – and they just had an international competition of fireworks. It was great. I love fireworks when really good. Do you?

Enough babbling?

Love,

Agi

July 12, 2004

Hello, my lady. And how are you today? I received your July 4 letter and I shall respond.

Yeah, I know how hard it is to quit smoking but I know you can do it. Have you ever tried those nicotine patches? Try those. I've known two people who went that route and both ended up quitting smoking after a few months. I imagine certain times of the day are harder than other times. After eating or while having a drink, I'm sure are tough times, when the craving is strong. Buy some nicotine gum, see if that works.

Smoking is a habit and, of course, the nicotine is the addictive drug. The gum and the patches are made to wear you off the habit and the drug a little at a time. Don't beat yourself up if you have a bad day and smoke a lot of cigarettes; Just start again the next day if that happens. There is an old saying: sow a thought, reap an action; sow an action, reap a habit; sow a habit, reap a lifestyle; sow a lifestyle, reap a destiny.

Yeah   I can hear you now – I know what you are thinking, Agi. "Too bad Rich you didn't implement that old saying, huh?" Touché my lady, touché – ouch –   a wry smile. Ha-ha.

Twiddly diddly dee, Gone with the Wind. I used to play the theme from that movie. I liked the melody. And, you're right, Hollywood esp. back in the early years did not speak/ show the truth about downtrodden people; i.e. the blacks and the American Indian.

You and Janet maybe need a small break from each other. I do that here. If a guy is getting on my nerves for no reason, I don't hang with him for a few days, and then it just seems to work out by itself. Sometimes people just nit-pick, unjustified criticism, and they don't even know why themselves.

Baby we all have character defects, and we all fall short. You hang in there and keep on keeping on and remember: Ti amo.

Ciao,

Rich

July19, 2004

Dear Rich,

I got a good laugh reading your 7-12 letter advising me how to quit smoking. You think I would torture myself for several months…no pal, no nicotine patches and all that crap. I just quit and suffer for a few days. It's still bad, but essentially I'm over the trouble. Now I have to be careful not to gain a lot of weight.

My TV is still in the shop, my car-windows are still not fixed, and Lucky's collar is not working – other than that I'm fine.

I sent you 2 books – they didn't have Siddharta, but they promised to call me when they get it. Hope you enjoy those two.

I have here an amusing paper called, "President Bush: Flip-Flopper-in-Chief." 1. Bush opposes the Dept. of Homeland Security…Bush supports the Dept. of homeland Security – quotes from his speeches. 2. Bush supports free trade…Bush supports restrictions on trade… and so on, and so forth.

This is becoming very tense and improbable – what is improbable that there is even one person still supporting him. Maybe I will hurt your patriotic pride, but we pledged to be honest with each other, right? Well, I think a big percentage of American people are stupid. I can't believe there's still a high percentage supports that fascist idiot in the White House. Even though Kerry is winning, there's something like 40-45% for Bush. You are probably not quite aware of the monstrosity of this fact, because a high percentage of the media is corrupt, owned by the big corporations, buddies of Bush. What he is doing is unprecedented. But there is a strong opposition. I work for them, signing petitions, donating as much I can, spreading the word. We have to win in November, otherwise there's <u>big</u> trouble, for this country and for the whole world.

All the best.

Love,

Agi

July 21, 2004

Dear Agi,

I'm so proud of you going 10 days (longer by now) of not smoking. Hang in there, my lady, it will get easier as the days go by. I can understand your mood, being sour and you are depressed and I'm sure a tad cranky too. (I got your 7-12 letter.)

Also, thank you Agi for the two books by John Irving. I have never read a book by Irving, so I'm looking forward to that. I see he wrote "The Cider House Rules." I saw that movie and truly enjoyed it. I like stories like that. And, of course, the books are always a lot better than the movies.

I saw the movie "Cold Mountain" last week and it was okay but the book by Charles Frazier was excellent. I also saw (videos) "The Hours" and "Gosford Park". Both of these were good and I think you would like 'em. I can't tell with you and films –i.e. what you like and don't like. You are very European, and I know Hollywood is disappointing to you, and it is to me also. They make movies 98% of them for kids not for adults.

I was wondering how Lucky was doing. I didn't know they made collars to stop dogs from barking. Maybe they should make collars for people to get 'em to stop talking, huh? Ha-ha. Especially in prison where some inmates never stop talking even if they have nothing to say; it's like their mouth is working overtime but their brain is on vacation. OK, Nields, cut it out. Who am I to be judging anyone? Well, I can't help it – some people just bug me. Hey who is writing this letter, anyway? Hell, I don't know; I got a three-way conversation going on in my head – a group meeting, ha-ha. This place is crazy.

Yes, I like Edwards too. He'll probably be president some day down the road.

I like it when you are playing music. Stay in Andy's band and keep on playing.

Ti amo.

Ciao,
Rich

July 27, 2004
Dear Agi,

Hello my lady. I got your letter of 7-19 – I shall respond.

Yes I received the two John Irving books. I just started "The Hotel New Hampshire" and it's very good. I find myself laughing almost to tears on some of the passages, it's so funny. I like Irving's sense of humor. Have you read these books?

I'm so pleased to read you are not smoking. Keep it up baby, you can do it – even without patches and gum, I see. Don't worry about your weight; just do more walking or some kind of exercise; that will make you feel better.

These are just_friendly_ suggestions sweetheart. I know that you know what to do. I'm just trying to give you some support and inspiration. That's what friends are for, eh? You bet.

I'm watching the democratic Convention on PBS 8 until 11PM. The networks are only covering it 10-11 PM. Last night (Monday) was great. Mr. Gore, Carter and both Clintons were right on. I like all of them but my favorite person is President Carter. I love his sincere compassion for his fellow man. Human rights are his passion – like you. Most people are too damn selfish to help people in need of help. Not you, though. You are an amazing woman Agi, a beautiful human being.

You know, I do believe Hillary Clinton could be president someday. I would vote for her, wouldn't you?

Sweetheart, you do not hurt my patriotic pride when you write "American people are stupid." My pride is more about the early history – the founding fathers – than what is going on today. Most of the world (sadly) today don't like America or Americans. I do believe we come across as offensively exaggerating our own importance and power – like Rome did.

I hope you got your TV back in time to watch the Convention. Did you?

I like Teresa Kerry, she reminds me of you. She speaks her mind. Stay happy.

Ti amo.

Ciao,

Rich

July 27, 2004

Dear Rich,

I watched the Democratic Convention last night – did you? There were good speeches by Clinton, Al Gore, and my idol, Jimmy Carter. Tonight and tomorrow I won't watch it; I can't bother my friend every night. But I want to hear Kerry's speech Thursday, so I will bother again Tony, my "frenchie" friend. I don't think I told you about her: she is a nice old lady – ten years older than I am – used to be a college teacher of French. We get together regularly once a week to speak French, not to forget it. We usually have dinner in my house and after dinner we watch one of my videos. Thursday I'll go over to her house to watch Kerry. And Friday there is a special about the death penalty I want to see. So we will have dinner in her house, watch the show and then go to see "Much Ado," which is opening now.

I can't stay in Andy's "band," for many reasons: there's no such thing, Andy assembles musicians, different for every concert. The stupid thing is that the theatre doesn't pay local musicians, the idiots! There are a couple of locals who play sometimes, they are not professionals – but I am! And I think it's not right to play for nothing when everybody else gets paid. So, there's not much chance I'd do this very often.

It's very warm these days, quite unusual, I went to swim only once so far.

Ciao,

Agi

PS I'm reading Carter's book, it's interesting.

August 3, 2004

Dear Agi,

How are you today my lady? I hope you are feeling good and enjoying your summer days. I'm doin' okay myself.

I like this book "The Hotel New Hampshire" by J. Irving. This guy is different than anyone I have ever read. Have you read this story? It's hip. It makes you laugh and it makes you sad. Yesterday the mother (Mary) and the youngest son Egg died in a plane crash. This is a very strange family, indeed, but a good family and they are fun, too: one son is gay or 'queer' as they called it back in the 50s; one daughter, a vivacious girl – I like her a lot, she has grit – sadly though she was raped, but she recovered and is still in love with one of the football players who raped her. John, who is telling the story, is 15 years old and he is having sex with the maid and also, this was funny, learned to kiss with a black girl, 30 years old, who took her teeth out see if kissing was better with or without her false teeth in her mouth; they both agreed it was better without the teeth. Ha-ha. And the youngest daughter Lillie is a dwarf. I love stories and people like this. I root for them to win in the game of life. Don't you? I know you do.

Well, are you still smoke free? I hope it is getting easier for you now. But, I'm sure there are times when the urge is strong to have a cigarette. Hang in there Agi, I know you can do it.

Did you get your TV fixed so you could watch the Democratic Convention? I watched all of it and I thought Kerry was great in his speech Thursday night. (Note; I won't write on the issues – too complex – and I know that you know 'em better than I do anyway.)

I am surprised though that Kerry & Edwards didn't get more of a 'bounce' or 'bump' in the polls; even though I don't put much validity in polls. John Edwards is a good speaker, huh? He's better than Kerry but not as good as Pres. Clinton. Clinton is the best.

I'll be back soon. Be happy.

Love,

Rich

August 6, 2004

Dear Rich,

I got two letters, thank you pal. Glad you enjoy "Hotel New Hampshire." No, I didn't read it.

Don't believe in polls and the media's coverage of the Democratic Convention. It's all the work of the corrupted media. Once again, you don't get the whole picture – you miss the strong opposition. Polls are favoring Kerry, not overwhelmingly, but he's definitely got the edge.

Here is Fair-fever once again. On Wednesday I had my whole group in my house for a potluck, and we had a nice visitor, a French lady, who just retired from being the Director of the Western Region for Amnesty. A delightful lady, about my size, petite; I like her. I drove her around the island on Monday, we had a good time.

I got back my TV, and my car-windows are fixed, too, hallelujah! And I got a DVD player, but I don't have DVDs yet.

Yes, I'm keeping up not smoking. It's done now. I did watch the Convention in my friend Toni's house. Remember, I don't have a TV but for videos. I watched the first and the last day of the Convention, so I didn't see Edwards and Teresa Kerry.

Ciao,

Agi

August 11, 2004

Dear Agi,

Hello sweetheart. I do love the French language. I think it is a mellifluous language, don't you? It's nice you have a friend like Tony? To speak French with. Is that her name, Tony?

Hey, believe me I understand; I don't and wouldn't play for free. I mean the mechanic isn't going to fix my car for free. The painter won't paint my house for free. The bartender won't give me free drinks, so why should I play music for free? I don't.

Now if you have a cause you are behind that's different. But I never had a "cause." My 'cause' was money to pay the rent and the bartender and the mechanic and to buy food and pot, and pleasure. Lots of pleasure. I was hedonistic and I do not apologize for that, but, truth to be told, today I do realize I should have been prudent – hell I had no prudence – drunks don't think ahead, we live one day at a time.

Being a professional musician in the music business I was good at the music but I was lousy at the business.

I'm glad you got to see the Democratic Convention. Come on, Kerry!! Man, I hate Bush. He is the dumbest president America has ever had, and I hate his arrogance. Bush give Christians a bad name, whereas Jimmy Carter is the 'real' thing. I'm glad you like Carter. I do too. What book are you reading by him? What's the title?

Man, this John Irving book has gotten weird. The family has just got taken hostage by the radicals who want to blow up the Opera House and the hotel. But the real weird part, to me, is Johnny the young boy telling the story, wants to have sex with Franny his sister. They are in love/lust with each other. Plus, there's an ugly girl, who wears a bear outfit, having sex w/Franny, too. Crazy story but I like it. I don't want it to end.

Voila, mademoiselle, you are the crème de la crème. Be happy.

Love,

Rich

PS I used every French word I know in this letter. It was fun. Touché.

August 17, 2004

Bonjour Rich,

Ton français est bon, mais je suis madame, pas mademoiselle. Et je suis la crème de la crème if you say so.

My "frenchie" friend's name is Antoinette, Tony for short. She is American but used to teach French in college.

It looks like I will play again with Andy on the 28th, and I will be paid.

Tomorrow the Fair starts, I already worked a lot setting up the booth and begging, which wasn't too bad – we had a lot of things left from the Christmas sale, so we didn't need much. We still have 25 raffle prizes which is pretty damn good. Tons of T-shirts and jewelry too.

I'm reading Jimmy Carter's new book, "The Hornet's Nest," what you wanted to have. As soon as it goes to Serendipity I'll get it for you. It's a novel at the time of the revolution. It's good, but at the end I got tired of too many details, too much names and repetitions. I'm sure it's well researched and all true but I kind of lost interest. There's also a love story which is a bit meager as a love-story – my opinion. I actually finished the book, but I confess I was skipping a bit in the second half.

Bush is not only dumb and arrogant, he can lead this country to a complete disaster. I hope to God it won't happen. The opposition is very strong and Kerry is leading in the polls. There will be preliminary voting in September, I'll see what it does.

Ciao,

Agi

August 21, 2004

Dear Agi,

Hello sweetheart. How are you today? I bet you're a little in need of some relaxation and maybe some recreation, like swimming or walking or maybe some dancing.

I know how hard you work at Fair week and I do hope it was a success for you and your island group.

Sounds like you enjoyed the French lady, Director of the Western Region for Amnesty, while she visited your island.

I love all of your pictures but truth be told my favorite is the one of you sitting and having coffee at the Paris café – it's just so chic and cool. Oui.

Maybe you should rent – can you rent DVDs? (just curious) or do you have to buy those? Anyway, I never saw it but it's supposed to be very good: "Moulin Rouge" w/Nicole Kidman. She's a good actress. I like her.

I have never seen a movie on DVD. Can you really tell a difference between video and DVD? I would imagine it would be brighter and/or cleaner, akin to a CD as opposed to a cassette tape.

By the way, Manci is changing the rules and I hear we are going to be allowed to buy CD players and CDs starting in Sept. I finished "Hotel New

Hampshire. I enjoyed it but it was weird. Now I'm reading "The Tie That Binds" by Kent Haruf. You sent me that book back in March and I have been saving it; I try to make things last in here. Anyway, I love this writer and this story is very touching, poignant.

This week one of our videos was the movie "Frida" w/Selma Hayek. Frida Kahlo was a painter in Mexico (c. 1900-'50). You should rent this one I think you would enjoy the story. I did. Question: Have you ever visited Mexico? Opinion please.

A man I play chess with, John Spirko, his last appeal was turned down Friday 20th. He'll be getting his date very soon and probably will be killed by Ohio later this year. He's two cells down from me so I will see him leave too like I did Dick Fox. Man! That's weird.

Love you, Agi,
Rich

August 29, 2004
Dear Agi,

Hello my lady. And how are you today? I hope you are feeling good and that last night your gig was fun and enjoyable for you – was it?

Isn't playing music the most wonderful feeling? Learning to play an instrument is serious hard work and it takes years to be good at it. But after you know what you are doing, you're accomplished, music is fun. Life is serious but music is fun. I sure miss playing my gigs. I even miss practicing and learning new tunes. Damn I hate being in prison – prison sucks! Oh well, nothing I can do about it except accept it. "Happy is the man who forgets what he cannot change" as I used to hear at AA meetings.

It's funny but I miss being around drunks – the ones at AA and, of course, I miss being around musicians.

I finished "The Tie That Binds" By Kent Haruf. I like his stories a lot. Now I'm reading the second John Irving book you sent me: "A Widow for One Year." I like this guy a lot too – he's hip. Just started so more on this later.

John Spirko, who is waiting to get his date, is a nervous wreck, but that's understandable, eh? He's spending all of his rec time on the phone saying good-by to his loved ones. He told me a few months back he is innocent, he didn't kill anyone, and at the time of this murder happened he was with his sister. I do believe Ohio is going to kill an innocent man this time.

It's hard sitting here just waiting for a date so Ohio can kill you. I go through a lot of different emotions each week. I get mad (at myself) and then denial – can't believe I'm here – then I make bargain w/God – ha-ha – I can't help it (I hope God has a sense of humor) then I get depressed, and on good days acceptance kicks in. Man that's a big bag of emotions. No wonder some days I <u>really</u>!! need a drink. I always had a hard time dealing w/life's terms on the outside so I drank. Now I'm here, dealing with all that crap – which is far worse – and I'm sober. I think God does have a sense of humor. Agi, I am grateful <u>every day</u> that I have you, and that makes me happy.

Love always,

Rich

August 30, 2004

Dear Rich,

The Fair was better than ever, we made almost $1,100! It was also good outreach work. And the week after I played a concert with Andy: lots of rehearsal and lots of waiting, because it was so badly organized. And the day after: yesterday, I went over to Lopez Island to an anti-Bush event, where they asked me to have an Amnesty table. I bet you don't hear about these kind of events, do you?

About your questions of DVD: I did buy one player and rented some movies to see. It was clear and good, but I didn't see essential difference between VCR and DVD. But now one after the other of my VCRs go wrong and I'm looking to replace them with DVDs.

Good news you allowed to have CD player – do you need money to buy one? If so, how much? You know, that's great. I will be able to send you some of my recordings through one of the bookstores here; I'm sure you would like that, what?

I never went to Mexico I'm sorry to say. I would like to go everywhere, but don't have enough money to do so.

I better don't reflect on the man who will be probably killed. I have no words for that. And I vividly imagine how you feel about it. We live in a bad, stupid world my friend.

Love,

Agi

September 5, 2004

Dear Agi,

Hello my lady and how are you today? You must be thinking about me lately. I can feel the vibes and last night you were in my dreams. I don't remember what the dream was about; I just know you were there with me. Thanks for being there. You are always there for me.

The vibes in DR6 are palpable. Everybody is feeling aware of their own inevitable execution coming down the road. When a man in your own pod is just waiting to hear his date, and he knows it's coming, and everybody else does too, it really does change the attitude of the whole pod. It's a weird place to be and nobody knows what to say or they are afraid that they will say the wrong thing that could make 'em lose their tough-guy image or persona. I don't know though, maybe people really just don't know what to say or do. I know I'm lost for words.

Bush and Kerry both have been campaigning hard in Ohio the last week. There's a lot of people out of work in the state so hopefully they will vote for Kerry. Ohio usually goes to the republicans, and history shows that no republican has won the White House without winning the State of Ohio. So needless to say it's a very important state for both candidates to win. Come on Kerry!! Kick his ass!

I enjoyed my books by J. Irving. Truth be told, my friends in books are so much more fun to be around than my so called friends in my pod. I guess I enjoy living in fiction more than reality anymore. Fiction is fun; reality on death row is a drag!

Agi, you are wonderful, an angel in my reality.

Much love & peace. Ciao,

Rich

September 5, 2004

Dear friend,

John Spirko won't be the first, and most probably not the last one to be killed in the most inhuman way, being innocent. Tell him he would go to a better world... tell him I send my love... what can I say?

And I completely understand your emotions. I feel it deeply – that's why I'm fighting to abolish this sorry remnant of the Dark Ages: the death penalty.

I feel so powerless to help when I would love to.

Well, here is something else: I volunteered to be a helper to prevent the Bushi-bastards to cheat at the election. It was the only thing worried me: the goddam shits would cheat, as they did in 2000. I volunteered to go to one of the key-states to prevent cheating – and guess what state I chose – Ohio, of course. I will probably go on election day to Columbus – but once I'm there I might go to Mansfield to visit you. How do you feel about this? I feel very mixed: to see you through a plexi-glass won't be great. Listen, if you don't want that, I'd <u>absolutely</u> understand. If you want, I might see you the 3rd of Nov.

Love,

Agi

September 12, 2004

Dear Agi,

Hello my lady and how are you today? Full of love and serenity, I hope.

I got the 3 books by Hermann Hesse. Thank you, Agi. I will start them soon and I'm looking forward to it.

About the CD player, yes, I will need money to buy it. The catalogues haven't come back yet to our pod so I don't know how much they are.

I'm looking forward to hearing you play someday. Don't send any CDs till I tell you because we can't have them until our unit manager says it's okay. (Note: In a bureaucratic system like this prison, whenever they pass a new rule it has to travel down through the ranks, so to speak. For example, last week an inmate in my pod got 2 CDs in and the sergeant made him send them back because the unit manager hasn't signed the necessary paper work. Stupid, huh? I'll let you know when we are allowed to order CD players and when we are allowed to receive CDs. When you do send a CD, do it like you do the books. It has to come from the place of purchase with a receipt, and it has to be <u>new</u> and unwrapped in clear plastic – like they come when you buy them. Don't open the CD, because if it's been unwrapped Man CI <u>will</u> <u>not</u> accept it and they will charge me to send it back. <u>No used</u> CDs allowed either.

Dave Hanson, my lawyer, is coming up to see me Tues.14th. I need to sign papers to move my case into the Court of Appeals down in Cincinnati. My case was turned down by the District Court in Dayton.

After I see him and talk to him and learn the details, I will write and let you know what he said and what's going on. It sure seems like, to me, my case is moving through the system quickly.

Anyway, I'll be back soon. Be happy.

Love,

Rich

September 14, 2004

Dear Agi,

I got your 9-5 letter and I say, yes, let's visit. Are you sure you can handle coming to prison? Oh, hell, if you can deal with the Nazis you can handle visiting death row.

OK. <u>First</u> thing we have to do is get you on my "visiting list" – you have to be approved before you can come to Man C.I. I will kite my case manager, Mr. M. and he or somebody from the office will send you a Visitor Application to fill. I don't know for sure but this might take 30 days? Why? Bureaucratic bullsh…

If we don't make it by Nov.3ʳᵈ (but we might-- I really don't know) but anyway, once you're on the list you can come visit anytime you want. Let me know beforehand so I'll be ready. Before you can visit you have to write and/or call Man C.I. to set a visiting day and time; i.e. you can't just drive in and come visit, you must first make a scheduled date, day, time, etc…I'm sure they will explain all the visiting rules to you – i.e. what to wear and don't wear, what to bring and don't bring, etc etc.

Don't you have a friend who lives in Mansfield? Maybe you can stay with them? Be real nice if they would pick you up at the airport. I hate and I will worry about you traveling – esp. driving – alone. I think Mansfield from Columbus is 1 ½ hr. drive? (Don't know for sure)

Visiting days Mon. Wed. Thur. Fri. don't come too early I'm not a morning person. I'm excited about meeting you. It will be fun. I'll get the paperwork started.

Much love, ciao,

Rich

September 17, 2004

Dear Rich,

I got two letters – 9-12, 9-14 – so you want to see me. Fine, but there is a complication. Janet is coming with me and naturally would like to see you. Is it all right to bring a friend of mine, after filling out the questionnaire the way you said? Or she has to fill one, too? If it's too difficult she just would have to wait outside for me, but that would be very unpleasant. How long can we talk? Answer all these questions soon, will you?

Quatschkopf! You forgot I'm coming to Columbus – we are – so I can't possibly stay with friends – who are not in Mansfield anyway, only close by. It's only the widow of my cellist friend who died of cancer, and I'm not in touch with her. Janet and I will most probably fly back from Columbus that night or next morning. We would drive over – rent a car – from Columbus, so there is no danger we would come too early in the morning. Say early afternoon Wednesday the 3rd Nov. We have to do it that day; I can't stay in Ohio longer.

Ciao now, write soon!

Agi

September 19, 2004

Dear Agi,

Well be with you, my lady. And how are you today?

I sent my paper work in Wednesday the 15th to my case manager's office. So, hopefully, any day now you should be receiving a visitor, approved friend application. Send it back ASAP so they can make a visit date and time for Nov.

3rd. Also, because you are out of state, Man CI will give you <u>special privilege</u> to visit more than one day for the week you are in town. For example, you can visit Wd. Thur. and Fri. if you want, because you are out of state visitor. Also, visits are from 8.30 am until 2 pm. 9 am to 12 would be good for me. I can't go any longer than that on a phone.

I sure hope you're a talker – <u>please</u> be a talker – my keeping a conversation going skills I know have diminished so you play the lead (melody) and I'll back you up (chords).

My lawyer hasn't come yet but I talked to him on the phone. Hell, I'm a dead man walking now. I got the worse judge I could get as a head judge for my 3-judge panel 6th Circuit of Appeal. Judge Boggs, a right wing, conservative, pro-death penalty "kill'em all and let God sort it out" type of judge 😐 ouch!

Man! If I didn't have bad luck I wouldn't have no luck at all (blues tune in B flat). I wish I could get a bottle and some pills and just do it myself (ha-ha). Nah! I will keep it spiritual and not go out a fool – I've been foolish enough for one wasted lifetime.

Still haven't received the CD player's catalog; will let you know.

Much love. Ciao,

Rich

PS Agi, if for any reason you don't or can't come to Ohio in Nov., do the paperwork anyway so you become an "approved friend." That way you can visit whenever you want.

September 21, 2004

Dear Agi,

Hey the mail is moving fast which is good. I just got your 17 letter and I will answer your questions.

Can Janet come? No. Not without filling out an approved friend application. Maybe she can drop you off at the prison and then go to a coffee shop, read a book for a few hours and pick you up. Or you drop her off at coffee shop, drive to prison etc.

You can schedule a visit at 8 to 11 am or 12 to 3 pm., whatever you want. Mansfield is 60 some miles from Columbus. Are you sure you want to make that drive? It's a long way to come for a couple of hours visit.

Remember, if you don't come, fill out the paperwork so you will be an approved friend. I'm thinking maybe this will be too rushed and somewhat emotional to do all this; i.e. work the election which might be all night and then drive 60 miles to come to death row. If you don't come it will be alright with me. I understand. Truth be told, it makes me nervous, too. I have mixed emotions also. Hell, I'm embarrassed on top of everything else. Crap, I'm handcuffed to a chain around my waist, and I'm shackled too, like a wild beast, and we have to talk on a phone through a window. It's not pleasant or comfortable either.

I'll leave it up to you. Whatever you decide is A-OK with me.

I can't believe Bush is still ahead in the polls in OHIO. Goddamn shit!!

Ciao, my lady,

Rich

September 25, 2004

Dear Rich,

I thought the visit would be normal, oh hell! Well, I want to see you anyway – I'll come unless you don't want it. There's maybe a small chance to do it differently: in Columbus I hope to meet Mr.K, death penalty coordinator of Amnesty. If he would come with me, we could <u>maybe</u> see you in the lawyer's room.

Right now I am completely involved in politics, attending meetings, receiving tons of e-mails, trainings for being an election monitor, and so on.

So, Janet comes with me, which is very nice, and she said we shouldn't feel too bad about she can't visit you.

I have a new car – well, new to me – I got so frustrated with the Mercedes. The last drop was that I went on the mainland, and driving on a highway with 70 mile speed-limit, the damned thing didn't go faster than 50-55. I went off to a garage, where they told me to just release the pedal and it will go. So, I continued – it worked for 10 minutes, then it got slower and slower. Finally I turned around – I was afraid it would stop – and had a painful 50 miles to drive on the right lane much too slow for the traffic – I was glad I could come back home at least. But that was it – now I have a little Chevrolet, hopefully a good buy.

Ciao friend,

Agi

October 3, 2004

Dear Agi,

Well I got your papers, your visiting approved-friend application and I sent them to Mr. M. How long it takes for them to process them I don't know. Let me know when you hear from them.

About the lady who wants to help: I am very grateful, but there's nothing anyone can do, besides maybe a great lawyer. And even that is probably too late. It is in the hands of God. If God wants me to live, God will enlighten the Federal judges to give me life.

I'm nervous about our visit. I'm hoping we don't talk on this subject too much. I want to talk on your life, music, and light topics. I'm worried your mood will be sour if Bush wins, too. When I write "I could use a big ol' drink" that's a country song verse and I'm being facetious; I'm just trying to keep a sense of humor; I hope you will too. Please. To coda: It's easy to become frustrated by the power of evil in the world, and to become embittered. Let's make sure we don't do that. Ciao my lady.

Love,

Rich

PS I'm a little on edge this week. ManCI is doing 2.4 inspection; all my stuff is packed in my box which is a drag. I'll be glad when they get to my cell so I can unpack. I'll be back soon.

October 8, 2004

Dear Rich,

Is your case at the last stage? Answer this; otherwise I will have to talk about it at the visit.

If you are nervous – and I would completely understand, as I said so – and really don't want it at all, say so. But I don't know if we ever would have the chance to meet otherwise. I don't like the fact to talk on the phone through a window. Listen, I don't think I can do that for several hours. Let's do it for an hour or so, agree? And I hope I won't be upset because I think Bush will lose and go to hell back to Texas where he belongs. By the way the only paper in his hometown endorsed Kerry! And the town's legislature asked for the abolition of the death penalty – what do you say to that?

I couldn't get in touch with Mr. K. yet, but will try to get him coming with me. Maybe it would make a difference? I don't know.

I just watched the second Kerry-Bush debate – unbelievable! Bush had the guts to boast of his successes regarding the environment!! My God, I get tons of letters, petitions to sign from environmental organizations, saying what a catastrophe the Bush administration is. Let's see what the polls will say – so far the first two debates were won by Kerry and Edwards. The commentators first said after the Cheney-Edwards debate that they were even, but afterwards people more clever detected <u>twelve</u> lies of Cheney.

I wish the election would be tomorrow, I hardly can stand this tension. I was never so involved in politics, surely not in this country before, but I know it's enormously important. And a lot of people feel the same way.

Ciao,

Agi

October 9, 2004

Dear Agi,

Well, hello my lady. How are you today? Aren't the presidential debates fun to watch? I think Kerry is kicking Bush's ass.

Have you seen "Fahrenheit 9/11"? They showed it here last week. (By the way, Man CI now has a DVD player, so we now see our movies on DVDs. I don't see that much difference.) But it's nice. They now are showing us 4 movies a week around the clock one after another. Anyway, I really like Michael Moore and really loved his documentary Fahrenheit 9/11. Bush is a liar and downright evil. I despise him. I know you do.

I can order a CD player now. They cost $ 49 plus shipping. I'll need $55 when and if you want. If you want or need to wait, because I realize you are spending a lot of money coming to Ohio next month, that's okay. I'm in no hurry.

Have you heard from Man CI yet? Probably not, I would guess. Things move slowly here. I haven't seen Mr. M, my case manager in weeks; I heard he's been down in Columbus Ohio testifying on some case.

Also, Mr. K. would have to make a reservation too. I don't think you can call here (a lawyer maybe?) but I heard you have to write to the visiting office 2 weeks in advance to schedule a visit. Did they send you a rule book/visiting rules how to go about making a reservation? We should have done all this paperwork earlier but I didn't know or think you'd come to Ohio. I'm glad you are coming and I'm looking forward to meeting you but we sure are cutting this close, huh?

This past week I've been down and just haven't felt like writing. Plus, all my stuff was packed into a box for Shakedown 2.4 inspection. They finally got to my cell yesterday and I just finished unpacking. I hate these things.

Did I tell you the story of my father? He lived up on the Columbia River and you could see Mount St. Helens from his house. I was there a few weeks after St. Helen blew in 1980.

Note: you might want to make a list of things you want to ask me when you are here. By the way, I shave my head a la Rod Steiger.

Ciao, love,

Rich

October 17, 2004

Dear Agi,

Hello my lady. I hope all is well with you.

In your letter you asked me if "my case was at the last stage?" Yes, this is the last appeal court in the whole process. I'm under this new law of '96 and it looks like they are speeding me through the system.

Have you heard from Man CI yet? I wonder if they even let you know if and when you are approved for a visit? I haven't heard anything yet either. I sent a kit in asking about you but I haven't heard back. You should write to the <u>visiting office</u> – not to me – and set your date Nov. 3 and your time (?) anyway. Or call Mr. M. and talk to him. He is death row's case manager. Be nice ☺ cause it doesn't pay to get these people mad at you or me. You might try calling the visiting office if you can't get hold of Mr. M. Explain the situation that you are coming from Washington State, 2000 miles away, and they should work with you on this, hopefully.

Is Mr. K. a lawyer? If so maybe he can get in with you and then we might be able to meet in the lawyer visiting room. But I don't know if they would allow you in being you're not a lawyer; i.e. if they would check that I don't know.

I've heard there is a web site for the Sixth Circuit Court of appeal where you can see where someone's case is. I'll look into that.

OK. Yes, an hour or two on the phone at your visit is plenty. Make a list of things to talk about/ask me etc. or if you are like me, you will forget. And then on your way home you'll be going "damn I wish I'd asked him" yada, yada, yada ☺ sometimes I get out of bed and forget what I got up for. Oh, well. Ciao

Peace & Love,
Rich

October 18, 2004
Dear Rich,

I watched all the debates, including the vice-presidential one. It's unbelievable how GW and Dick have a big mouth and lie all the time. There's a bumper-sticker here: "Pull the Cheney and flush Bush." How do you like that? The New York Times endorsed Kerry, other papers too.

I have seen "Fahrenheit 9/11." I'm glad they show it there, too. It's good, but it could have been even better: I thought a few things were unimportant and I wished he would have shown Bush "flip-flopping," like saying one thing and then saying the contrary. Unbelievable: Bush accused Kerry of flip-flopping; he had the guts of bragging about his incredibly dismal environmental record. I'm getting every other day letters from environmental organizations complaining about the murderous record of the Bush administration. Man oh man! And there is a concern of them cheating in the election. I hope to God the Democrats won't let him get away with that – I hope I can help it a bit.

Well, we – Janet and I – will fly to Columbus on the 30th. On the 31st and 1st we can do some work – I don't know what kind yet – and have a training on the first. I asked D. Hanson to give me an appointment on Monday the first. I will also meet Mr.K. hopefully. He won't be able to come with me to see you but some other Amnesty guys will drive me over to Mansfield. By the way I didn't hear from Man. C.I. yet, I hope I will before going.

Maybe it's a good idea of making a list to talk about. It will be such a goddam thing to see you in that awful situation that we both could be so embarrassed that we won't be able to talk. By the way, so you shave your head "a la Rod Steiger"? Who the hell is he and how does he shave his head? But I see you are afraid you won't be handsome enough, huh? Well, I will see a bald man and you will see an old woman. Let's try to make the best of it, OK? By the way will I be allowed to take pictures?

Ciao,

Agi

P.S. Yes, let's wait a bit with the CD player – I had lots of expenses and the trip costs me a few hundred of course. One guy here donated $100 to help us, isn't it nice?

October 23, 2004

Dear Agi,

Well the next time I talked to you it will be here in the visiting room. I am happy and very excited about meeting you.

I got your letter of 10-18 and I see you have not heard back from Man CI. I haven't either. You do realize you must and I emphasize must schedule day and time of visit; they won't let you in if they don't have paperwork on you – you must be scheduled for a visit. I can't do it from this side. Hell I can't even get Mr. M. to respond to my kites and I have sent two with no reply back.

Also, if you talk to someone on the phone, M. or visiting office, I would be reluctant about mentioning Amnesty International – that you're a member – prisons, esp. the employees of prisons, don't like groups like A.I. and A.C.L.U. etc. They fear their jobs or reprimands from such groups. You might think that's silly but it's true. No way will they let you bring a camera in here.

Also, no big deal, just want to remind you that our visit, talking on the phone, will be recorded. All phone calls here to someone's home and the visiting room phones are taped.

Rod Steiger? Who is he you asked? He's an actor who won an Oscar for the movie "In the Heat of the Night" (c. '66 or '67) also was in the Brando movie "On the Waterfront." Of course he had hair then.

A lot of guys in prison shave their heads. I hated it at first but I like it now. It's clean and easy to take care of, plus you don't have to buy shampoo. When I came to Man CI from the county jail we stopped at Prison receiving Center where they give you shots, a physical, and shave everybody's head for hygiene reasons etc. Well after that I just kept it shaved. No big deal. I'm not vain anymore. (Well maybe a little – all musicians have vanity)

I'm glad you're meeting w/D. Hanson. Find out all you can about where I'm at. Am I in the 6th Circuit already? I never know what to ask lawyers anymore. I don't trust them and hate most of 'em. They just tell you things to make you feel better – what you want to hear.

Isn't it weird that all the inmates on death row had public defenders? People w/money don't come to death row, only poor people and musicians.

Well, Agi, I'll see you on the 3rd. I sure hope they let you in. I do know you have to be approved and you must schedule a visit. Let's think positive though and I'll see you on the 3rd, the day after John Kerry is elected.

Love, ciao,

Rich

October 26, 2004

Dear Rich,

I talked to Mr. M. today – first he said there's no Richard Nields there! Then, after giving him your numbers he said: "Oh yes, that's the guy with no trouble." That was rather nice. He told me to call him tomorrow morning at 8 o'clock – I said: "Oh dear, that's 5 o'clock to me, then he graciously changed it to 10, which is still 7 to me, but I didn't want to argue further. So, I hope the visit will be all right.

What to talk about? I will certainly have a lot to talk about the election, our work there, the whole adventure. It's very possible that the result of the election will be delayed like last time – I don't think the moron will win straight – the bushies will try hard, but I think the opposition is <u>very</u> strong. You know there are more than 10,000 volunteers to monitor? Plus hundreds coming from all over the world. This election is very, very important, not only for the US but for the whole world. The stake is to allow or stop <u>fascism.</u>

So, that's already a lot to talk about. Also, you can make a list, too, huh? I will be overwhelmed with my experiences there, so I let you talk about music or whatever you like.

Yes, I wrote on behalf of Karla Fay Tucker, you know to whom? GW, then Governor of Texas, who answered me – I sent you his letter long time ago, remember? He said he will seek advice by prayer – the goddam fucking hypocrite. Of course, God told him to go ahead and kill her. In my next letter to Texas Pardons and Parole Board I told them I know the Governor will pray and God will tell him to execute the guy. Ever since, I hated GW's guts.

Well, next I hopefully see you, friend.

Ciao,

Agi

27 morning: I just tried to call Mr. M. and he wasn't there. A woman's voice told me to try tomorrow at 9 – that's 6 to me – damn!

November 6, 2004

Dear Rich,

What a good thing it was to see you! I hope you liked it, too, to see your old friend.

Well, we talked to David Hanson – we all three went to see him – and were pleasantly surprised to hear that he also worked for Kerry and was depressed about the outcome of the election.

Where you stand? You are not yet at the Sixth Circuit, he said. He will have to get you there some time – I don't know how soon.

But Mr. K. wants to do a clemency petition – he said the Governor turns those down arguing that the guys didn't have remorse, therefore they are still dangerous. Well, he won't be able to say that of you. We have the letters and in one of them you say that the remorse is so profound, that you can't express it with words – and you would change places with Patty without a doubt. Mr. K. will give a tape of the letters to Hanson. (He has 3 of them.)

He wants to see you - for the clemency petition it would be necessary to contact both your sisters, maybe your daughter, and the family of the victim. I don't know how would that be possible, but you might have the idea. Anyway he wants to visit you and as an Amnesty high-position person it might be possible, right? I hope so.

Right after seeing Hanson we got into a demonstration – people protesting the outcome of the election. There were speeches, anti-Bush signs – and cars and buses going by were honking and cheering us. There were a few policemen watching, I talked to one of them – he was kind of smiling, looked like enjoying it. I told him I was sure he voted for Kerry. He said no, he voted for Bush. I said: "If you did you deserve it. But I don't believe you."

After that we went out for dinner with a couple of Amnesty people whom Mr. K. invited. I got very friendly with him – he is very nice, very intelligent. He now really wants to do something for you.

Tomorrow, after the Amnesty meeting we will have a little gathering in my house to talk about our experiences in Ohio. We will talk about my visit to you, too.

Cheers, my friend,

Agi

P.S. Also, I have the idea: you could call me maybe once a month, probably on Sundays, otherwise it's pretty expensive, I think. Maybe we could agree on a certain time – what do you think?

November 7, 2004

Dear Agi,

Wow! What can I say? You really blew me away with our wonderful visit. I really, truly, enjoyed meeting you, Agi. You are indeed a woman with the highest kind of quality. I have been on a high ever since you have left; I'm glad you came.

I bet you were tired when you got home, eh? Even though you seem to have a lot of energy, I'm sure after those six intense days, physically and emotionally, you were running on empty.

I hope you got to meet with Dave Hanson. Did you? What did he say?

I can't believe this country re-elected that dumb-ass president. Truly unbelievable. I thought Ohio would go to Kerry that Tuesday afternoon because so many people were out voting. But I was wrong. You would think with all the unemployed people here in this state, they would have voted for Kerry but, no, these hillbillies of Ohio are more concerned with the gay marriage issue than the economy.

I hope you feel good about our visit. I realize it was a lot of work for you to get here, and I'm sure a tad stressful for ya. I enjoyed meeting you a lot. I do hope our visit augmented our friendship and in no way diminished your expectations. Truth be told, you far exceeded my expectations with your charm and energy and European flair – I like that.

You are one in a million, Agi. Thank you from the bottom of my heart for being my friend. For sharing and caring and for all your support. Living on death row is a real drag – it's a bitch – and I really hate being here just waiting for Ohio to kill me. Oh well, I won't worry about that today.

I'll be back soon.

Lots of love. Ciao,

Rich

November 14, 2004

Dear Rich,

What a nice letter I got! So you were "high" seeing me. Well, that's awfully nice, pal.

But I am nevertheless very depressed. <u>The election was stolen!</u> You probably don't hear anything about it. People were voting for Kerry and he should have gotten Ohio, but the bushies were cheating all over, but mostly in Ohio and Florida. Lawyers monitoring the election found incredible things: one county in Ohio counted 97 thousand more votes than voters. Another counted 4 thousand some for Bush where there were about 600 voters. The voting machines were tempered with: when people were voting for Kerry it registered for Bush – and so on, and so forth. Unbelievable. And the media is silent! And, what depresses me the most, people just accept it – there's nothing to be done. So, now we live in a fascist country and devastation will come. And all the tremendous efforts of the democrats were wasted. Why didn't they do something about those machines? This is more than I can swallow – thinking of moving back to Europe.

Oh well, at my age to start all over again…hell.

Sorry to depress or worry you, but I am disgusted to hell. It's worse than people voting for Bush, it's awful to take this outrage and see people saying "oh well, that's it" and take 4 more years of the demented fascist who will devastate everything of value of this country, and once a beacon of freedom and democracy, it turns into a fascist dictatorship. And there might be a nuclear war...OK, I stop.

Ciao,

Agi

November 21, 2004

Dear Agi,

Hello sweetie-pie. And how are you today my lady? I'm feeling okay, myself. I still think of our visit and that brings a smile to my face. You really touched my heartstrings that day: I will never forget it.

I got your "hug-time" card – the cat and the dog hugging and, yes, I got the $35 m.o. too. Thank you Agi, you are very kind.

Question: What is the name of the lady (her character) played by Olivia de Haviland (sic?) in the movie "Gone With the Wind"? She married Ashley and she dies in the movie. She was Scarlett's friend, even though Scarlett was hot for Ashley too. What was her name in the movie?

Speaking of Scarlett O'Hara, who was played by Vivien Leigh, of course, I read the play, "A Streetcar Named Desire" this past week. V. Leigh played Blanche du Bois in the film version with M. Brando. I like the stories of Tennessee Williams. I'm reading "The Glass Menagerie" right now – I'm in Scene vii – more on this later.

In "Streetcar," I sure felt sorry for Blanche, and Stanley was awful to her (eg: for her birthday Stanley gives her a one-way bus ticket, funny but sad). Poor Blanche, at the end she thinks she is going on a cruise with a rich man from Texas, but of course they have come to take her away to an insane asylum.

Yes, I saw the movie a long time ago and Brando is absolutely great as Stanley. But I didn't remember Stanley taking Blanche to bed while Stella was in the hospital.

Note: The original title was, "The Poker Night," but that was before Tennessee changed the focus of attention from Stanley to Blanche. Regular TV is bad anymore I do have a hard time finding programs I actually enjoy watching. I hate all those stupid reality shows.

I wrote Rochelle last week – no fun there. My sisters don't really care about me; they're just waiting for me to die. My family never had much love or compassion for each other. Oh well.

Happy Thanksgiving, Agi. I love you.

Ciao,

Rich

November 29, 2004

Hey Richissimo,

Thanks for your letter and the cat-dog Thanksgiving card. Did you get my letter before that? Where I tell you about the visit with D. Hanson? Did I tell you that he also worked for the Democrats? That was nice.

I had a nice Thanksgiving, was invited by the friends who always get me for Thanksgiving and for Christmas day, a nice couple – he is the one member of the AI group who had a heart-attack a few months ago, remember? He is fine and his wife is a lawyer – both retired. She is now doing service for people who can't afford to pay a lawyer. What a nice thing to do! They have a nice house with view of the sea, and their house is full of ethnic things they get when they travel – they travel a lot, to many remote and exotic places. Last time they went to Ethiopia, spending a month there. Good people!

The name is Melanie – Olivia de Havilland's role in "Gone with the Wind". So you like Tennessee Williams – funny, I just watched the <u>opera</u> "Streetcar Named Desire," which SF Opera premiered a year or two ago. Don't you find TW's plays depressing? I do like him, but they are depressing all right. Well, I'm glad you like to read – quite right, it certainly helps you there. If you need a book, don't hesitate to ask!

Janet and Thrinley, my Buddhist friend, flew today to India. Did I tell you I went there 15 years ago? If you didn't hear about it I could send you the chapter I wrote about it in my new book.

Well, that's enough for today.

Love,

Agi

November 29, 2004

Dear Agi,

Hello sweetie-pie. And how are you today? What did you do for Thanksgiving? Did you cook or go out for dinner. Do you eat turkey? Here we got a small Thanksgiving dinner of turkey, dressing, cranberries, and a piece of pumpkin pie; it tasted good to me.

I received the 3 pictures you sent. (Note: there was no letter in the envelope, just the 3 pictures – is that correct?)

I think your trip to Ohio – even though John Kerry lost – was a success for you (and me, for sure) but also in meeting and making a new friend with Mr. K., too. Oh, yeah, plus my lawyer Mr. Hanson too. Job well done, Agi.

Well, I finished reading, "The Glass Menagerie." Not near as good as, "A Streetcar Named Desire", in my humble opinion.

Now I'm starting "The Fourth Hand" by John Irving. I like his stories. You sent me two by him: "A Widow for One Year" and "The Hotel New Hampshire" and I truly enjoyed 'em. This one –"The Fourth Hand" – someone put in the library. I still have the 3 Hermann Hesse books you sent me to read and I will get to them.

We had a little snow last week for the first time this winter. Winters are long in Ohio. I don't care for the mid-west. Sure wish I would have stayed in California. The other night they played the movie "Dirty Harry" (DVD) on our video/movie channel. It was fun for me to watch it just to see the beauty of San Francisco. I think that's the prettiest city in America.

Ciao my lady.

Love,

Rich

December 3, 2004

Dear Rich,

Meanwhile you must have gotten my letter where I describe my Thanksgiving. No, I don't eat turkey – remember, I am halfway vegetarian – no meat, but I eat fish. I don't eat sugar at all, and anyway I hate pumpkin pie.

But I'm glad you got a tolerable dinner at Thanksgiving. Well, being European – and I never become an American, only on the paper – Thanksgiving doesn't mean much to me anyway. Christmas is different, it means something. But here it became so commercial. Oh well, I don't make much of Christmas either: I send a package to Ros, my stepdaughter, and here I send you a little extra to have some sweets, or anything you want.

I like "Glass Menagerie." Depressing, but very deep-looking. It's apparently autobiographical, about his sister and mother.

I'm again up to my neck with the upcoming Bizarre. Right now I am making necklaces, because the ones I had I sent to Hawaii – hey, somebody was interested in them, how about that?

Weather is getting more wintery and it's very dark, which is not very nice, but in a few weeks it will start clearing.

I am still devastated by the election. It was stolen, there's no doubt about it. I just heard that Bush was ahead by 3.7 million!! Well, the day after the election it was undecided because they were so close. So, where did the 3.7 million came from? This is so dirty and devastating that I can't find the words to tell you what I feel.

OK, I don't start again.

Ciao,

Agi

December 11, 2004

Dear Agi,

Hello my lady. Good to hear from you. I got two letters (11-29 & 12-3) and three more pictures. I especially like the one of you and Janet having dinner, nice. I see you are sitting in the no smoking section too. I am so proud of the way you could give it up…well, anyway, you made it look easy. And also thanks for the $50 too. I will save as much as I can toward shoes and a CD player. I'm in no hurry.

I am happy to read you have some hip friends that invite you over for the holidays. Sorry. I knew you didn't eat meat but some people still will eat chicken, fish but not beef or pork. I knew people in Calif. who always said "I don't eat anything with a face" I think that's pretty cool if one can do it.

Yes, send me your chapter(s) on your trip to India. I would like to hear what you have to say about it. Janet and her friend just went there, eh? That must be real exciting for her. I enjoy hearing sitar music for awhile; it's peaceful. India's music (sitar music w/tabla) tends to hang on to one chord forever and the drums go thru rhythmic changes very fast, finger drumming. I have seen Indian music – now you might not believe this but it's true – the time signature was 3 ½ (i.e. 3 and ½ beats per measure) very odd indeed. It was music by Ravi Shankar.

I'm not real hip to Gandhi but I like what he said "an eye for an eye will create a world of blind people" (one-eye face, ha-ha) I'm being silly.

You must have friends in Hawaii re: sending your necklaces there, eh? Now that's a place I would like to go visit right now. I've been there, back when I was playing on Princess Cruises. The music I was playing was corny and I hated it – I was only 23 then – but the places I went to and got to see and experience were quite beautiful.

Thanks for answering Gone w/Wind, i.e. Melanie. That's it. Twiddly diddly dee that's all from me, oui, oui love you.

Ciao,

Rich

December 21, 2004

Dear Rich,

The shortest day of the year. That's nice, because from now on it will get longer. It's very dark now, at 4.00 it's kind of twilight.

The "Bizarre" was great; we made over 1,200 – every year a little better! Also, we had a "writathon": we got lots of letters and post-cards from Amnesty and people wrote prisoners and to authorities to release them. We did 132 letters!

And the same night I played – only one piece – with Andy. It was certainly a long, exciting day – and the day before, having had two rehearsals and arranging the hall for the Bizarre. I can say with satisfaction that I have lots of energy – I didn't even feel tired after those two days. It's something to be grateful for in my age.

I also had good news about my eye-problem: I went for a check-up to the eye doctor – it looks like I don't have to worry about going blind. I am taking lots of vitamins, and quitting smoking probably helped too. He said the process – which they can't reverse – stopped progressing, the degeneration I mean. That's also because of that Indian herb-doctor who gave me stuff to take.

The holidays don't look like much fun: those friends who used to invite me for Thanksgiving and Christmas day, go visit their daughter this time. Toni, my "frenchie" friend, also a lone old woman, will come over for Christmas Eve, that's all. For New Year's Eve I will be with my actor friends – the you and me of the letters, but it will be quieter than usual. I guess the political atmosphere makes everybody subdued. By the way, the trials are still going on – latest some people testified under oath that they were <u>paid</u>

to tamper with the voting machines. And nothing, nothing appears in the media! This is awful. It smells to me Fascism!!

Sorry to get back to that. But it makes me desperate to see that people – including you! – just shrug this outrage off.

Janet and my Buddhist friend, Thrinley, are in Dharamsala, the town in India where the Dalai Lama and lots of Tibetan refugees live. Janet sends me reports – e-mails – every few days, that's nice.

OK, here is the account of my trip to Nepal and India – it was in 1989.

Ciao,

Agi

PS It's not complete, as you see.

January 1, 2005

Well be with you, Agi, and Happy New Year!

I got your letter of 12-21 with your trip to India. So horrible what's happened there with the Tsunami. I don't have a good map of India so I don't know where Dharamsala is. Is Janet by the coast? Hopefully not. Let me know.

That Bush has no compassion, i.e. he only wanted to send $35 million but because of the "World's" criticism he is sending $350 million. I don't like that guy but I won't hate him because hate is no good – the emotion of hate.

In your letter you wrote and quote "it makes me desperate to see that people – including you (me) just shrug this outrage off."

At this point in my life, which will be ending in a few years anyway, I don't and I can't see the purpose of getting all worked up over politics. Being on death row there's nothing I can do about it anyway, my credibility...well I don't have any.

My sister Rochelle didn't write this year. Usually she would send a card and $50 but nothing this year. Debbie never writes. I guess they think I'm not worth much. Oh well.

We got about 18" of snow last week. But now the temp. is warming up so it is all melting pretty fast.

I've had a cold now for five days. I've been staying in bed reading a lot and sleeping.

A lot of guys in my pod are fearful knowing they are going to get their date real soon now. John Spirko is a nervous wreck. He makes me nervous – this place sucks.

The waiting, not knowing when the black shirts are going to come and tell you to pack your stuff you're going to the hole – you spend your last 30 days in prison in the hole – then they kill you. Anyway, the waiting is hardest I think.

Sorry, not an "up" letter but I'm in a down mood myself. I'll get up soon.

Ciao,

Rich

January 3, 2005

Dear Rich,

Thanks so much for your Christmas – and Birthday cards, the latter I just received today. I didn't have much fun for these holidays: Christmas Eve, Toni came over for our usual "frenching" and that was all. The actor friends didn't have a New Year's Eve party this time – I guess everybody is subdued and depressed, not anticipating a "Happy New Year." That's exactly how I feel. Anyway I was just sitting alone on New Year's Eve, but I got two nice, long phone calls, one from my stepdaughter, Ros, and another from a friend, a former student of mine from Ithaca. My birthday won't be any better. Janet and Thrinley, my Buddhist friend, are coming back on the 6th from India. I got quite a few e-mails from Janet, so I have a pretty good idea what it was like. It will still be interesting to hear more about it. I got a Christmas card from Janet through e-mail – it's amazing what they can do: the card was moving, it was a dog coming out from a house in the snow and he, another dog, a cat and a bird made a snow-man, and all this was accompanied by a Chopin waltz. Really nice and amusing (technology, hey!)

In two weeks I will start another music appreciation class, four will attend – it looks like – this time it will be about chamber music, mostly string quartets. The literature for string quartets is absolutely phenomenal, it is a great ensemble and most of the great composers wrote many master-pieces for it. It will be fun. I had to order another piece of furniture, because I got more CDs and there's no more room on my CD-tower.

I enjoy my new car, it works well – I had nothing but trouble with my "classy" Mercedes, to hell with it!

Happy New Year to you my nice friend.

Lots of love,

Agi

January 8, 2005

Dear Rich,

I am typing up your letters which came after "Truth Be Told." The last one dealt with the fears, awaiting to be killed, and your 1-1-05 letter is similar. My dear friend, believe me, I _feel_ and know what it is like being on death row. And by the way, I have to apologize: it was downright stupid of me to make you feel bad about "shrugging off" the outrages of Bush. Of course, you are kind of outside of it, you don't feel and know a lot of things going on.

Janet is back from India (so she was not hit by the "tsunami") I haven't seen her yet – she is having the jet-lag and sleeping for 2 days. And for 2 days I sat in my house, because there is snow and I hate to drive in snow. It's rare to have it several days; it usually melts in a day or a few hours. Hopefully tomorrow will be better – I have an Amnesty meeting.

So, Rochelle didn't write this time. How awful – what an unfeeling family you have, my poor guy. So, I'm the only one who cares. Well, I won't abandon you.

Did you hear from Mr.K.? He is a weird one; he said to try to get a clemency petition. I sent him a Christmas card and a CD of my playing and I don't hear from him. But I know he is a good person, weird he might be, and I hope he will do something.

I hope you are over your cold.

Love,

Agi

1-9 And I am still sitting here stranded. The snow didn't melt. Most unusual. The AI meeting was postponed.

January 12, 2005

Dear Agi,

Hi sweetie-pie. And how are you today? In your last letter I was happy to read that your eyes are going to be okay. That's real good news.

Also, I see the Bizarre was a big success, huh? Every year a little better, probably because of all the work you do on your island and elsewhere. I'll say one thing about you, and that is, you're a woman who doesn't give up, you stick with it.

Did you go over to Dan's and Helen's place for New Year's Eve? How are they doing? What did you guys do all evening?

Have you heard from Janet? When is she coming home? I do hope she is safe.

The other day we had a surprise impromptu shakedown. Man, I hate those. Sometimes I just feel like telling some of these guards to kiss my butt. But I know better and I would never do that.

Well sweetie-pie, write soon. I miss you.

Lots of love,
Rich

January 16, 2005
Dear Rich,

Real winter descended unto Friday Harbor. For about 10 days it was real cold, freezing and the snow not melting. I was stranded, AI meeting canceled. For a couple of days it was alright to drive, it was cold but dry. Now, for yesterday I was to have a nice party, diner, card-game, and Janet's pictures and stories from India – well, sure enough, it started to snow in the afternoon, and it was canceled. I was working hard to have an elaborate dinner, and I was left alone. And today the AI meeting had to be cancelled for the third time, because it was snowing again.

The thing is, since it is unusual here, they don't clear the roads right away like in a city where it's happening all the time. And I'm dreading driving in snow since I went through snow-storms a couple of times – I'm afraid of my new nice little car, too. And other people are the same. So, my days are rather lonely and frustrated – and my poor doggie doesn't get good exercise. Well, hopefully it will get better soon. It's unusual.

I am just finishing typing all our letters and I wonder if Janet will do anything about it.

Ciao, friend,

Agi

January 23, 2005

Dear Agi,

Hello sweetie pie. So good to hear from you. I received two letters you wrote 1-3 and 1-8. The mail is moving kind of slow because I didn't get 'em until 1-13 and 1-19; also the $40 money order is here but I didn't get it – yet.

I can't believe this crap. They sent me a pink slip "unauthorized item received" saying you are not an approved friend. Someone messed up, but not us. I sent Mr. M. a kite telling him you filled out the paperwork, sent it in last Oct. Also, you came to visit last Nov. and that you sent $50 last month with no problem. So they – at the mailroom? – say you are not an approved friend I can only guess that M hasn't done his job properly and didn't do the computer program right – or something. Hopefully M will get it straightened out this week. I won't know until Thursday, 27th when I get my commissary order slips which shows my balance.

I mean, come on, we have been trying to get you on my approved friend's list, i.e. visiting list, since last October!! Shouldn't take that long, eh? I don't like people who don't do their jobs.

As soon as I find out I'll let you know.

Sorry, Agi (really). I know I turned my usual chit chat into a tirade. This place and a lot of the employees just bug me.

Ros is Luke's daughter? It's nice she called. I remember you and her were going on a trip (Grand Canyon?) last year but her husband got sick.

You must be starting your teaching classes this week, huh? That's good, and boy, are those students lucky to have you there on that small island to inspire them to the beauty of music. Thanks for being my wonderful friend.

Lots of love, ciao,
Rich

January 30, 2005
Dear Agi,

Hello my lady. I hope all is better, not much snow, that is, on your island. To be stranded for 10 days is indeed a long time. I got your (1-16) letter.

I know you told me but I forgot. What kind of "new nice little car" did you get?

I feel sort of stranded myself but your letter of (1-8-05) made me feel better just with your four words "I won't abandon you". I believe you, and believe me your letters and words, your voice on paper, always brings comfort.

You asked me if I heard from Mr. K. No, I have not.

I still haven't received a reply from Mr. M. You are not on my visiting list nor did I get the $40 you sent me Jan. 13th. I sent another kite to M., Thur. 27th. Don't worry about the money order, they cannot destroy funds. In fact, I have the pink slip here and I could send it in with an envelope and the mailroom would send your money order back. I'm waiting to see if I can get M. to do his job and put you in the computer; added to my list and add that $ 40 to my account, like he should do.

I haven't been to the store in two weeks now. We will get this money; we will not let Man C I rip us of. Man, I hate crap like this; people who don't do their jobs. If M. doesn't do it this week, I will file a complaint.

I'm low on everything including my spirit. Ah hell, I'm on the pity pot. Sorry.

Love,

Rich

January 30, 2005

Dear Rich,

I hope you got the money. Red tape is everywhere, not only in your prison.

Yes, I did start my class, already had two sessions and tomorrow the third one. We are doing string quartets this time – request of one of them. Of course, the string quartets literature is absolutely glorious, so many masterpieces written. This kind of ensemble inspired all the great composers. It's fun. Of course I played all the best ones – not necessarily performed, but read them. The greatest pleasure for me is to play quartets with good musicians.

Yes, of course Ros is the daughter of Luke. When I left him, Ros called me saying she loved me and I was a great influence in her life. Ever since we are very close. Luke has another daughter, too, Meredith – but she is a cold fish and we are not in touch. She has completely severed her relationship with Luke. He is not allowed to see his grandchildren, Meredith's three kids. A few years ago I have seen her when an Amnesty meeting was held in New Orleans. She was OK, we were friendly, but when I sent her a nice present next Christmas, she never answered. By the way, Meredith is a lawyer and married a lawyer, and Ros is PHD in clinical psychology. Her husband is a retired policeman (homicide brigade!) He is much older, and ever since he got sick 2 years ago, he is not in good health.

Weather is back to normal, which means in the 40s or 50s. Rains a lot, but that's better than cold and snow.

Love,

Agi

Beethoven's 5th

February 7, 2005

Dear Agi,

Hello sweetheart. And how are you today? I hope you are not stranded by the weather anymore this winter; it's just nice to be able to get out, huh?

It's been crazy here the last few days. Everything is all shook-up. Last Thursday, two death row inmates tried to escape so now we <u>all</u> pay. These two guys over in DR 4 were outside on rec, in the rec-cage, and they built a mount out of the snow and ice high enough for them to get to the chain-linked fence roof and squeeze out. They made it out onto the compound but they had two more fences with razor wire to get through and by then the guards had them surrounded. Did you know about this? It was on the news here in Ohio and I am sure on the internet but I don't think it made national news.

So, anyway, of course, we had a big shakedown by the black shirts – "the riot squad" <u>all day</u> Saturday. They tore the hell out of my cell and everybody else's too. They even dumped food, coffee, sugar out on the floor! Can you believe that goddamshit?! Man, prison is tough and at times like that scary.

Lots of rumors going round now, of course, that maybe DR 6 might shut down, that all of death row will be moved to another prison in Youngstown (I don't believe that will happen.) They put on administrative leave two sergeants, one major, and our unit manager, and some brown shirts (regular COs)

I'm going to send the pink slip w/a self addressed envelope to the mail room and have them send that 40 dollar money order back to you. You should get it next week. Let me know, OK? OK. Why M. won't make you an approved friend, I don't know??? If you want call him and ask him why. Be nice, please. ☺ A gentle answer turns away wrath; a harsh word stirs up anger (King Solomon Proverb 15:1) And right now there's a lot of anger here at Man CI.

Write soon.

Love,

Rich

February 13, 2005

Dear Agi,

Well I finally got to talk to Mr. M. Last Wednesday 9th he came over to DR 6 to help with ID check. Anyway, he said you <u>are approved</u> now so you can send money orders. I sent the mailroom a self-addressed envelope to send back your money order to you – the $40 m.o. you sent me in Jan. You should have it by now. Do you?? If so, M. told me to tell you to send it back and it will now be processed. Hopefully he will remember to type your name into the computer. I actually sent him another kite Thursday as a "friendly reminder" to do so.

Remember when I told you things here move real slow and it's a very dysfunctional bureaucratic place? Well now you know I spoke the truth. Unbelievable, huh? I actually didn't see your money order; I never do, they take'em out in the mailroom. Anyway, on my copy (pink slip) they have your first name as Opes. I don't know if the person in the mailroom just wrote it wrong or he/she couldn't read your writing.

Friendly reminder to write m.o.s <u>clearly and completely</u> or Man CI will not process them.

We are still locked in from outside rec, until further notice. Man CI is still investigating how and what went wrong with those two guys being able to get out. I heard things will stay the same in DR 6 except for maybe outside rec. I've heard probably a guard will be placed in the rec yard with us, which is cool with me.

I had a few dollars on my book, trying to save up for a CD player, so I used that and borrowed to get me though the last month. All my things are breaking down that I bought back in 1998; getting old like me, I guess. I feel tired and frustrated at all of this crap. Like the bible says "you come in this world with nothing and you go out with nothing," or something like that. Everything I own fits into one box. Things are broken and my clothes have holes. I haven't bought new clothes since I've been here. (1998)

Sorry, on the pity pot again. Write soon.

Love,
Rich

February 19, 2005
Dear Rich,

I got two letters. I'm very glad the problem is solved. I mailed the money order last night and will mail the Feb-March order first thing Monday.

How come you are so low on clothes? I thought the prison provides you with some.

An awful thing happened: that scum-of-earth son-of-a-bitch neighbor shot Lucky in the face with a shot-gun. It happened a week ago, around 9 o'clock in the evening. Lucky was barking over there for about 2 minutes – I tried to recall him – when I heard the shot and the dog ran back with a bloody face. He had pellets all over his head and one penetrated an eye. It is still uncertain they can save that eye. Otherwise he is a toughy, behaves normally and barks.

I was thinking of moving, but it would be a long and very expensive thing to do. Besides, I love my house. So, the solution is to build a fence. This is happening already, right now people working outside. It will cost me close to $3,000, and the vet bill so far was $341. And the fence will be ugly; it might reduce the value of my property.

I called the police of course, and the Sheriff, who is a nice guy, said they would charge the guy – but yesterday the prosecutor called me saying they can't charge him, because there is a ridiculous leash law. Now, can you imagine going out with the dog every time he has to pee? Of course, nobody does it, including the goddam neighbor, whose dog comes to my property.

People call Friday Harbor a paradise – I have the misfortune to encounter evil here, too. There is no paradise on earth.

Last Thursday we had an Amnesty event, "Gay Rights are Human Rights." The Director of Outfront, which is AI's section for gays, lesbians, etc. came from New York and did the lecture. Very nice guy. It was enjoyable.

I am sorry you have no rec now. I hope by the time spring will come, you will be able to go outside.

Ciao, love,

Agi

February 24, 2005
Dear Agi,

Hi sweetheart. I got you letter of 2-19 and the $40 money order too. Thank you so much; I was out of everything.

I'm so mad and sad about you and little Lucky having to put up with your evil neighbor. I can't believe he shot Lucky for barking, come on! This guy needs therapy that's for sure. You have to be very sick to shoot a dog for something that is natural for Lucky…barking. Are you putting up a chain-linked (sic) fence? Will it go all the way around your house? I guess Lucky will know how I feel now when I get to go outside – fenced in damn, if only I could get to the neighbor's yard to take a crap… Lucky thinks. Ha-ha.

We do have inside rec now. I hear they are putting up extra cameras outside on our rec yard. Plus, probably a C.O. will be outside with us too. I'm sure by spring we will be allowed outside again.

Clothes? Yes the prison gives us two pairs of pants, two smocks, boots, underwear, socks & white T-shirts. The pants & smocks are uncomfortable to wear. We all wear sweatpants, sweatshirts, sweatshorts and tennis shoes. Those are the clothes I was talking about being worn out, threadbare. It's no big deal. I just keep sewing & patching them up. Really though, I'm not here to impress anybody; it's just some days I get on the pity-pot – feel sorry for myself – and I really don't like myself when I'm that way.

I see Beethoven's 5th is a major 3rd and not a fourth (like I wrote) and in E flat and I think I put it in B flat. Oh, well, I was guessing anyway.

Have you ever heard of a "minor large" chord? Believe it or not it's a minor chord with a major 7th. Very seldom used: odd sounding, huh? It was in a jazz tune but I can't remember which one.

I'll be back soon. Give Lucky a hug for me.

Ciao, lots of love,

Rich

March 3, 2005

Dear Agi,

Hi sweetie pie. And how are you today? I got your card w/the $80 money order. Thank you so much. You are so kind and good to me. What a wonderful friend you are, Agi. A wonderful person filled with unconditional love and compassion.

I am so glad to hear you have the fence up already. Now Lucky will be safe from the evil neighbor and you won't have to worry about that anymore. Peace and serenity to your house, yeah, that's the key – the key of 'B' for beautiful 😊 life can be beautiful.

Note: I never enjoyed playing tunes in the key of B. B flat is cool, it lays nice on the piano; C is easy of course but B w/five sharps was tricky, a little, for me when I had to improvise. When I played my dinner gigs by myself, I would just transpose any tune that was written in B either up or down a half step. But whenever I worked with a guitar player, and guitar players love the key of B (and E, A, D, G), a lot of tunes he/she knew would be in the unpleasant B key.

Correct my memory if I'm wrong on this: when I was learning Beethoven's Moonlight Sonata, back in the 70s, it was written in C sharp? Or was it F sharp? Or was it B? Now I can't remember for sure, but I do remember saying to myself "Hey Ludwig, why didn't you write this a half step up or down?" ha-ha. (Note: I think Ludwig is a cool name, even for today.)

How are things at the College? Do you enjoy your class? Is teaching still a passion for you? I would say yes it probably is. I hope so anyway.

A few letters back, you said playing with a quartet w/good musicians is your favorite pleasure. Yeah, I can understand that. More intimate and a lot less hassle in getting it together.

They're still working on getting it together here. They're still investigating the escape attempt. Also, check this out, someone wrote a letter to the local Mansfield Journal newspaper saying death row inmates in Pod DR 6 have it too easy or something to that effect. I'm hoping they don't shut down DR 6. Man, I don't want to go back to DR 1. We'll know in a couple of weeks what's going to happen if anything.

I hope Lucky is feeling better.

Love you Agi. Ciao,

Rich

March 6, 2005

Dear Rich,

Got your 2-24 letter – glad you got the money. Meanwhile you must have gotten the Feb/March check. Now you are rich, Rich. If you need more money for clothes, I will send some extra (although I'm pretty low right now, because of the fence and vet bill.)

Yes, the fence is up, so I don't have to be nervous when Lucky goes out. It's not all over the house, but the dog has some room to run and I have access to my wood-shed and storage-shack (the latter I had to have for all the Amnesty stuff I couldn't manage in the house.)

On Tuesday, March 8 – international women's day – we have another event: a one-woman show called "Meet Eleanor Roosevelt" with an actress coming, who happens to be the sister of one of the members of the group.

Next day, I am invited for a lunch of the Soroptimists – women's rights group – as a "Notable Woman."

In April I'll go to Austin Texas for AI's annual General Meeting. If you remember, I lived there 1967-71, teaching at the Univ., so it will be interesting.

Just today there was a bad news: the wife of my friend the violinist died. Poor guy, a year ago his son, now his wife.

Well, I hope you can go out soon. Here it is blooming and budding!

Love,

Agi

P.S.   Beethoven's 5th is in c minor, you Quatschkopf!

March 8, 2005

Dear Agi,

Hello my lady. Man I could use a hug ☺ I am so worried about what's goin' on here, i.e. all this talk about moving death row to a supermax prison. It sounds horrible and truth be told a tad scary.

It hasn't been 100 % confirmed yet, but even most of the C. O.s here are thinking it's going to take place. Damn!! A supermax prison is the hardest place to do time. It's for the worst of the worst, most dangerous criminals.

Some of the guys here have been talking about Youngstown and how bad it is. There are a few death row inmates over in Youngstown now that write some guys here sharing how tough and bad the place is. Believe me, DR-6 sounds like a vacation Holiday Inn compared to that place – a living hell. What I have heard so far is that the place was/is made to break you down physically and psychologically, as if I need to be broken more than I am already. At Youngstown there is no outside rec, only 1 hour by yourself inside a cage with no human contact – no more chess, ping-pong etc. etc. You are locked in 23 hours by yourself. No more movies either only 3 stations on the TV. No library, no bible study, no ice etc., really not much of anything.

Thank God, I HAVE YOU! Just knowing I can still write to you and receive your letters makes me feel better. Please stay with me until the end. I probably have a couple of more years and I will be gone mixed emotions. Hell, if we do go to supermax, death might be a good ticket out of there. I heard the guards are real mean and love to beat inmates for any little reason. (At this point I used to write (joke) "man, I could use a drink" but I know you don't like that so "man, I could use a hug" ☺ yeah, that's the ticket.

Well, sweetheart, let's hope and pray this move doesn't happen. I really don't want to spend the last years in a supermax prison. I'm keeping the faith. I'll be back soon.

Lots of love, Agi. Ciao,
Rich

March 13, 2005
Dear Rich,

Hey you Quatschkopf, you seem forgetting that there are <u>minor </u>keys! The Moonlight Sonata is in c sharp minor if I remember right. It is minor for sure; don't you remember the very first chords?

My music appreciation class is not at the college, I do it at my house privately. Only three ladies attend, and there's trouble now: one of them went berserk. That's a bit of a story: she attended fervently all my classes and became a music-crazy, read a lot and bought tons of CDs and videos. She was also my fan, liking my playing very much. And now, the last few classes she behaved very unpleasantly, arguing with me, knowing better what to do. Finally I got tired of this, called her up and asked what was the matter. She said something amazing: she said she blamed me for what happened to Lucky!!? I was speechless, and she continued blaming me about my previous dog, Kali, remember? She was abused and neglected when I took her and was always nervous – dogs never forget. She snapped at some of my guests and actually bit this lady once a little bit. Well, she thought all this was my fault. And when I said something that she was obnoxious, she said that's it, and hung up. So now I'm stuck with two, and one of them is out of town now, so there is a few weeks pause.

Something more positive: we had two very successful events of Amnesty: a lecture about gay rights and the Eleanor Roosevelt-show. It was especially successful, the hall jam-packed, people standing. It was very enjoyable.

I hope your trouble will be resolved and you will enjoy spring outside a lot. Here it's beautiful, sunny, trees blooming.

Ciao,

Agi

March 15, 2005

Dear Agi,

Hello my lady, my "<u>notable</u> lady" indeed. I'm so proud of you.

So, how was the show "Meet Eleanor Roosevelt?" Was it good? (I got your letter of March 6.)

How was the lunch the next day being invited as a "Notable Woman" eh? I am so glad that some people see the hard work you put in trying to make

Earth a better place to live. I know I'm a <u>fruit</u> of your works and compassion. I may be a big lemon but this big lemon has grown sweeter over the years by being part of your life.

I do know without you in my life I would have sat here and become a bitter old man. Mad at the world, on the pity-pot and all that negative stuff. Anyway, sweetie pie, I am so glad & happy you are getting some recognition – you deserve it. However, I know you don't do it for the accolades, it's the goodness and kindness of your heart being manifested, your soul personified. You have seen and experienced hell in WW ll. I do believe that's maybe one reason you work so hard to make life on earth a better place for all people.

Whatever the reason, I just want you to know I admire you and love you from the bottom of my heart for letting me be a part of your life and for being my best good friend until the end. You have kept my hope alive.

Enclosed is a letter from David Hanson. I did meet yesterday with Ken Lee. He came up to introduce himself to me. He hasn't read my case yet so no new information – i.e. he couldn't tell me anything but he said he would write soon and let me know where I'm at in the legal process. Hell, I don't know if I'm in the 6th Circuit yet or not. I told him about you and I got his e-mail address for you. I told him to share all information good or bad with you and it's okay with me. He said you could contact him any time you wish but give him time to get familiar with my case.

No new news or new talk on moving death row to Youngstown. Good. I don't want that to happen.

Someday down the road I would like to read a book by Hunter S. Thompson: "Fear and Loathing in Las Vegas". Are you hip to him? I'll be back soon. Ciao.

Lots of love,

Rich

March 18, 2005

Dear Rich,

I am pretty much disturbed about your last letter of the scare about the supermax prison. Let's hope to God it won't happen. But keep in mind, people like to exaggerate – all those stories might not be true. But, of course, you are <u>relatively </u>in a good position – life is not a constant pain, there is rec outside, chess, ping-pong, etc. It would be bad, very bad…It's a terrible feeling that I can't do anything to prevent it.

It's OK wanting a drink …and a hug. I wish to give you both.

That's all I wanted to tell you today.

Love,

Agi

March 23, 2005

My Angel,

Goddamnshit! (Now that's a heck of a way to start a letter, eh?) oh man oh man what a drag it is the news today: we, all of death row, are moving to the supermax prison, in Youngstown, Ohio.

Can you believe this crap?! I hate it. I'm really going to miss DR 6, the library, the ping-pong, the chess games, the track outside, the grass (I bet I never touch grass again), and conversations and bible study.

Well anyway, I am not going into a tirade about this; acceptance is the key to serenity. And there's nothing I can do about it anyway. I'll just deal with it.

Agi, I got your letter of March 13th. Yeah, I would say your music student needs a "12-step meeting i.e. an AA (attitude adjustment) meeting. She's been holding resentments toward you going back to Kali which was years ago, of course. She's probably jealous too of your knowledge and talent. Her resentments were eating her up inside, so she used Lucky and Kali for an excuse to blow up at you – she's not a friend you need nor a student to put up with, I wouldn't. Who needs negative vibes, eh?

So, you are off to Texas next week, I see. Are you going alone? That I don't like, you traveling by yourself. Can't someone (Jan?) from your island group go with you? I hope so.

I heard on PBS Itzakh Perlman play a piece of music by Paganini. He called it Caprice(?) I think. Anyway, it was very fast 16th notes of scales and arpeggios like an exercise but melodic at the same time. It was very good.

I'm enclosing a letter I got from Kyle explaining where I'm at in the system. I figure I probably have at least a couple of years before my appeals are spent. What a drag I'll have to spend them at a supermax prison. I guess it's just part of my punishment. That's okay w/me it's not near as hard the punishment the Jews went through at Auschwitz and other concentration camps and they were innocent!! Sometimes you have to wonder where God was in 1940-45. I guess if we could figure out God he wouldn't be much of a god.

Ciao sweetheart. I love being your friend.

God bless you, Agi.

Lots of love,

Rich

P.S.   I don't know when we will be moving. On TV they said sometime in the summer.

April 5, 2005

My poor friend,

I wouldn't even say goddamshit – that's halfway joking. I feel awful – just got your letter of 3-23. I was hoping the rumor about Youngstown will die out.

What you say about it, it's great and wise.

But maybe it won't be that bad – maybe they also have a place for "elite" prisoners, like Dr 6. Rumors are more often than not exaggerating.

But it's bad, no denying it. I will write more often. I will… I don't know what I can do – damnit! Hell!

More later. Love

Agi

March 31, 2005

Dear Agi,

Hello Sweetheart. And how are you today? I hope you are feeling good and looking forward and excited about your trip to Texas this coming weekend. Do you think at your AI conference anyone will talk about Ohio's death row being made to move to a supermax prison in Youngstown? The case is on the TV news now here in Ohio. The US Supreme Court in Washington is looking into it. Jim Petro, Ohio's Attorney General, also, he's running for governor, argued his point for the move yesterday, Wed 30, in front of the Supreme Court in Wash. DC. Death Row inmates lawyer I can't remember his name – I think this lawyer may be from ACLU but I'm not sure – argued for our "Protected Liberty interest." Inmates do have some rights, not many, but some.

Here at DR 6 things have changed for us already. We used to get 5 ½ to 6 hours rec a day, but now we only get 1 ½ hour rec each day. We are locked in 22 ½ hours in our cells. We used to come out 18 guys at one time, the whole top tier, but now only 5 guys can come out at one time. We still don't get outside rec at all ☺ man, I miss that.

The people that work here, the guards, et al, are asking their union to fight this move. But, of course, it isn't for us inmates, they are concerned about their jobs, which I can understand.

Supermax is designed to break you down via complete isolation. For example, the cells have two doors so when you look out your cell door window, all you see is the other door. And when you look out your back wall window, all you see is a wall or I should say "another brick in the wall" (Pink Floyd).

I love your little letter of 3-8-05. It's your heart talking to me and I feel your beat – i.e.: someone wrote "when one has tears the other can taste salt." That's how close we are – we do have a oneness of some kind – kindred souls, my lady. Yes. It's not how many words you write that touches me; it's the few words in the right key that I feel. It's a hug on paper from you that brings me comfort. Thanks for the hug ☺ I do feel better. Have fun this weekend in Texas, Agi. I'll be thinking of you. Godspeed.

Lots of love,

Rich

PS I realize I owe God a death and I'm going to pay. But, I don't believe I owe Ohio a stay in supermax prison. Of course, that's my opinion. I could be wrong.

April 7, 2005

Dear Agi,

Welcome home sweetie-pie. How was your trip? Did you have some fun? Did you take some time to smell the roses, the yellow rose of Texas? Can you play that song on your fiddle? Ha-ha I bet you hate when people call a violin a fiddle.

I have gotten two letters from you since I have written but sadly the first one was destroyed before it got here. I don't know what happened but half of it is gone. The post office sent it anyway in one of their envelopes with an apology. Anyway, I thought I'd send it back to you and you can rewrite it because I can't make it out this way. I can see though you wrote a letter to the editor somewhere and that I want to read. Also, I see Lucky is doing well and that I'm happy to read. He's a good dog full of love for you and vice versa I know.

Manci showed us a good movie last night: "Sideways." I think you would enjoy it, I did. It's a good story, different. I'm sure you're hip to it; probably already rented it. If not, rent "Sideways", good acting, good writing – ie. the screenplay – and the scenery of N. Cal. Wine country is so beautiful.

Do you like wine? Are you knowledgeable about it? I'm not. I drank a lot of it though. Truth be told, wine, because usually I would drink too much, the next day I would have a terrible headache.

Here in DR 6 still no outside rec. The 1 ½ hour goes by pretty quick. I usually play ping-pong for an hour and then I rush into the library to look for new magazines, newspapers, and any books I might want to read. (Lately I've been reading Westerns.) Then I rush up and take my shower (in DR 6 we don't have showers in our cells) then I lock up back in my cell.

Even though this situation isn't as good as it used to be, I would rather stay here and put up with this than move to Youngstown. Now there's gossip we still have a small chance we might not go, so I'm keeping hope alive we don't move.

After you get settled, write and tell me about your Texas Convention, and if you want, rewrite that letter too. I'm glad you're home.

Ciao. Lots of love,
Rich

April 12, 2005
Dear Rich,

Yes, I had fun in Texas, although didn't smell any yellow roses. It was, like always, very well done, great speeches, good panels, discussions, etc. It was nice to see a few people I know from other meetings – one guy I like a lot, used to be the death penalty coordinator of Texas. I gave him a video of "Truth Be Told." I also sold things for the group: T-shirts, my necklaces, and my books, so we made some money to help with the expenses.

I even got in touch with two of my former colleagues there. One, a pianist, I used to play with and were quite good friends. She came to my hotel and we had dinner together. It was nice, but I found out she was a Bushie! But I managed not to get mad. I can't believe how stupid people are.

The traveling was a drag: you have to fly from here to Seattle, landing on a small airport, then they take you to the big airport. And there wasn't any direct flight to Austin, so I flew to Salt Lake City, waiting 2 ½ hours there before flying to Austin – it took a whole day.

I try to remember my letter which was damaged: I told you about the luncheon of the Soroptimists, and that I offered an opera-night for their fund-raising auction. So, four persons came and wanted to see "Don Giovanni" Mozart's great opera – a very good choice, it's one of my 2 or 3 top favorites. I have 3 different interpretations of it, but the best, which I wanted to put on for them, has deteriorated. But my guests were happy with the lesser one.

I also wrote down my letter to the editor, thinking you get a kick out of it. Here it is:

"On 23 of February a group of Republicans gathered outside of Sen. Rick Santorum's Social Security meeting, chanting: 'Hey hey, ho ho, Social Security has got to go.'

Great. But why stop halfway? Let's eliminate pensions and health care, too. Lower-and middle-class Americans should work until dropping dead, committing suicide, or go begging. Enormous amount of money could be saved this way, and could be used to attack Iran.

Since we go insane, let's do it thoroughly."

I had quite a success with this letter, people stopped me at the food-market, on the street to thank me for it.

No, I don't like wine very much. If it has to be, I tolerate white wine, but I rather stick to my gin and tonic or vodka. And I'm not knowledgeable about it. I know some kind, mostly Hungarian ones, like the famous Tokayer, or the "Bull's Blood." A good red one.

I had to get a new computer and I still can't handle it. I have close to 200 messages on my e-mail. Louisa is a computer wizard coming tomorrow to teach me and put our letters and my book into it.

OK, that's enough for today.

Love

Agi

April 17, 2005

Dear Agi,

Hi sweetheart. And how are you today? I hope all is well on your island.

Spring is here in Ohio; the weather is beautiful. I can't go out but can see it through my cell window.

There is a lot of talk, speculating and gossip going around about are we going or not going to Youngstown. No one knows really for sure. Last week on the TV news, it was reported that lawyers from the ACLU are taking the case to the Federal Courts to stop this move. That's good, huh? I don't know all the legal terms but two issues we have are "Protected Liberty Interest" and "lack of due process."

Technically speaking, to be sent to a supermax prison an inmate would have had to do a major infraction violation like escape attempt or attack a guard etc. etc. and found guilty by prison count, then that inmate can be sent to a supermax prison. "Lack of due process" means because we here in DR 6, and other pods too, where inmates have no write-ups i.e. no infractions, we shouldn't be sent to a supermax prison. I'm sure you get the picture even though I'm not drawing a very good one, sorry about that. I have to admit it, this situation has me down in a blue mood and I am a tad worried about it.

Like you wrote in your letter of 3-8, that now I am in relatively good position, life here in DR 6 is not a constant pain. Okay, enough of this subject.

Thank you Agi, I got the $40.00 m.o. w/your cute card w/the pictures of puppies & bear & eagle. I love the smell of puppies. Yes, the smell of puppies and horses I like. Have you ever rode a horse? Are there any horses on your island? Have you ever heard the song "Horse with No Name?" (ha-ha) I used to play that song back in the early '70s; it's a song by the folk-rock band America. I sure do miss playing music.

Oh well. Stay strong and keep the faith. I will too.

Ciao & lots of love,

Rich

April 24, 2005

Dear Agi,

Hello sweetheart. Well be with you. I got your letter of 4-12. I'm glad you're at home safe and that your trip to Texas was a success. Also, nice to read you had an opportunity to have lunch with an old colleague, even though she is a Bushie. I'm proud of you that you didn't get mad. It actually makes you bigger person when you have tolerance; in this case, sympathy for her beliefs.

Your letter to the editor was good. Tersely sarcastic. Sad but probably with some truth.

I'm hoping they bring down Tom Delay. He's a crook and a liar.

For the record: I do not like fundamentalism. I'm sure you don't either. I think fundamental religious groups today on earth are causing more problems than they are bringing peace and harmony into the world. When I hear fundamental Christians on TV speaking, I just get pissed off at that type of philosophy or interpretation. I think spirituality is a feeling in your heart and not just a mental interpretation of some book like the Bible or any religious book. I believe God speaks to everyone through their conscience and consciousness. It's an <u>experience</u> not a thesis. OK, I shall change the subject; thank God, Agi says, ha-ha.

Enclosed is a list of some books by Larry McMurtry. Since rec is only 1 ½ hour I have more time for reading. Put that list in your purse and the next time you go to the book store you can look for some of these. Just the ones that are highlighted. The other ones I have already read.

Winter is back here in Ohio. It's cold and today it's snowing.

I've heard that maybe in the near future we will be getting outside rec again but only 5 men at a time and for only 1 ½ hour. Better than nothing, huh? I do miss those long recs though. Being locked up 22 ½ hours in a cell everyday is lonesome. Oh well. Nothing we can do about that.

Ciao. Lots of love,

Rich

April 29, 2005

Dear Rich,

I got your letter of 4-24 today, and for the first time in almost six years I got a bit annoyed with you – pissed off, you would say? – for your lecture about tolerance, and feeling sympathy for a Bushie's beliefs.

My dear pal, you don't know what's going on here, and that's not your fault. You read only the corporation-controlled media.

You know my background – I smell Fascism here, you understand? Every day there's more abomination coming from the White House. They fuck up environment, Social Security – which is almost half of my income – civil liberties, healthcare, education, everything! It is the downfall of this country. If the Democrats can't do anything about the voting machines, we will get Jeb Bush in 2008, and that will be the complete ruin of this glorious country. Already the whole world is looking down on the U.S., and disgusted with it.

So, I have no tolerance, no! And no sympathy, hell, no!! Anybody being still "Bushie" is simply stupid!!

More next. I just had to get out some steam.

Ciao,

Agi

May 8, 2005

Dear Agi,

Hello sweetie pie. I do hope this letter doesn't annoy you like my letter of 4-24 did. Believe me, I didn't mean to get you riled up at me. Let me clarify, please.

I did not mean to have sympathy for Bush or Bush's beliefs or policies, or any right-winger's – I hate 'em all. I'm a liberal. Always have been.

What I meant to say was it was decent of you to have sympathy (and maybe that's the wrong word) for your friend's stupidity for being a Bushie. And I meant it as a compliment (and not a lecture) to you for not spoiling your lunch date w/an old colleague. But I do apologize and I do hope you're not still upset with me.

We are getting outside rec again. We can go out on Tues., Thur., Fri., and Sat., but only for 1 ½ hours. That's better than nothing. I sure do miss those long recs. With only an hour and a half, and you have to take your shower in that time, too, it goes by real fast, needless to say.

I don't know his name, but I heard an inmate over in DR – 2 (that's in another building) committed suicide over the weekend. I guess he paid heed to Roderigo's words: "It is silliness to live when to live is torment." (From

Othello.) I guess there's something to that, but not for me. I choose life, and I'm going to stay alive as long as I can.

The weather is nice now. It feels like spring. I went out yesterday and again early this morning and I walked (and jogged) five miles, 50 laps around the track.

They keep a guard out there with us now and there is one in a car watching us on the other side of the fence. He has a shotgun loaded with buckshot, which can put a hole in you the size of a basketball.

Man I'll tell ya', those two guys trying to escape sure did mess it up for everybody on death row.

Well, my lady, that's all for now.

Be happy – it's springtime – a life is anew.

Ciao. Lots of love,
Rich

May 13, 2005
Dear Rich,

I got your 5-8 letter. I feel bad about getting annoyed with you. I'm just so upset of what's going on here that I overreact. No, I'm not upset with you – you probably realized that when you got my birthday/anniversary check. So:

I am so glad you go outside now. Maybe it will be more time later. What about the gossip about Youngstown? I hope to God it won't happen. It seems to me that those guys overreact, too. Hell, the two who tried to escape had no chance whatsoever. I have seen those fences, 20 feet high with barbed wire, several courts. Those two were just stupid, and this terrible overreaction about it – it comes to my old saying: stupidity! all over. But you guys who didn't do anything, shouldn't suffer for it.

This Sunday I play with Andy in a fund-raising concert in a (splendid) private home. We play a quartet and some Bartok Duos (2 violins). The duets are based on folksongs and I like them.

Everything is okay here. Weather could be better, but not too bad. My rhododendrons are blooming, the farmer's market started. Lucky is well, so everything is fine.

Love,

Agi

May 15, 2005

Dear Agi,

Hello my lady. And how are you today? Feeling good, I hope.

Thank you Agi, so much, for my birthday card w/$60.00 m.o. You are so kind to me. Really, sometimes I get choked up to the point my eyes well up. I guess my negative "stinkin' thinkin'" side tells me I'm not worthy. For six years now, you have shown me unconditional love and friendship. I am eternally grateful Agi, for all you have done for me these past six years.

Man, six years we have been talking to each other, already. I feel as though our metronome is moving at top speed at 220 beats per minute. (Sorry I have forgotten the top speed of a metronome: 210? 220?)

Question: May is our anniversary, six years this year, but what day is it? We should have a day – pick one – and I'll write it down so I can remember next year.

I ordered two new pair of sweatpants, two sweat-shorts and one sweatshirt.

This past week a buddy of mine left death row to go to general population for life. Richard Frazier is his name. He'd been on the row for 14 years and his sentence was overturned from death to life in prison. There's some guys on the row that say they would rather be executed than go to general pop. for life. I say poppycock to that. I'd take life in prison rather than death, as long as I'm healthy.

I'm enjoying the book "Magic Hour" by Susan Isaacs you sent me. I am halfway through. Last week I took a break from it to read "The DaVinci Code" a fellow inmate lent me. It was good. Fast-paced story, a work of fiction, but I will say that some of the arguments it raises are very interesting and I did enjoy reading it.

How is Lucky doing? What have you been doing? Are you doing any walking? Exercising? Teaching? Playing music? Yardwork?

Know peace and serenity. Please be happy.

I love you. Ciao,

Rich

May 22, 2005

Dear Rich,

My first letter to you was written 5-4-99, so if you want a celebration date that would be it – or the date you received it? Whatever you want.

Glad you got yourself some new clothes.

So, Richard Frazier left the Death Row after 14 years, that's interesting. How was his sentence overturned? Did he have a lawyer or a Federal Judge decided it? Is there any way to try the same for you??

"The Da Vinci Code" is a best-seller and I started to read it but quit after 20-30 pages. I was outraged by the story. They find a corpse in the Louvre (!) naked – the guy got undressed after being shot and wrote the sign on his chest with blood. Come on! I hate this kind of shit and don't understand how come that so many people are not outraged.

Lucky is doing alright, except he has discharge of his eyes, the injured one is bloody – curse the bastard! I walk him just about every day on the beach, so we both get exercise...

Love,

Agi

May 22, 2005

Dear Agi,

Thank you for the birthday song. 😊 I got your letter of 5-13 and I am happy to see we are in harmony again, Even though, really, we do well with each other staying in tune. For six years, only a few times has one of us gone sharp or flat, and when we do we don't stay there for long. We have a great relationship, I think, with deep feelings and longevity. I know we will last until the end...

Love,

Rich

As of now — June 27, 2005 — it looks like Rich has about two years to go. We keep writing to each other, of course.

About the Author

Agnes Vadas is a musician and a human rights activist. She started to write when she was in her seventies, and that not even in her native language. Her autobiographical stories, "Tales from Hungary," were published in 2001. The continuation of that by the title of "Memoirs of a Stupid Woman," will be ready to publish very soon.

In her work for Amnesty International her personal focus is to fight against the death penalty, and so it happened that she started to correspond with a death row inmate, which became a wonderful friendship. Rich should not be on death row, but in this country money decides that matter. If you can't afford to pay a good lawyer you are easy victim of unscrupulous prosecutor whose "success" is to put the guy into the death chamber.

Printed in the United States
78373LV00004B/103-150